Race, Ethnicity, and Minority Housing in the United States

Recent Titles in
Contributions in Ethnic Studies
Series Editor: Leonard W. Doob

RACE, ETHNICITY, AND MINORITY HOUSING IN THE UNITED STATES

EDITED BY

Jamshid A. Momeni

FOREWORD BY

Joe T. Darden

CONTRIBUTIONS IN ETHNIC STUDIES, NUMBER 16

GREENWOOD PRESS

NEW YORK • WESTPORT, CONNECTICUT • LONDON

Library of Congress Cataloging-in-Publication Data

Race, ethnicity, and minority housing in the United
  States.

  (Contributions in ethnic studies, ISSN 0196–7088 ;
no. 16)
  Bibliography: p.
  Includes index.
  1. Minorities—Housing—United States.
2. Discrimination in housing—United States.
3. Minorities—housing—Government policy—United States.
I. Momeni, Jamshid A., 1938–   . II. Series.
HD7288.72.U5R33 1986   363.5′9   86–9971
ISBN 0–313–24848–6 (lib. bdg. : alk. paper)

Library of Congress Catalog Card Number: 86–9971
ISBN: 0–313–24848–6
ISSN: 0196–7088

First published in 1986

Greenwood Press, Inc.
88 Post Road West, Westport, Connecticut 06881

Printed in the United States of America

The paper used in this book complies with the
Permanent Paper Standard issued by the National
Information Standards Organization (Z39.48–1984).

10 9 8 7 6 5 4 3 2 1

To blacks and all other minorities
in the United States of America

Contents

Figure and Tables

Foreword

Joe T. Darden

One of the basic necessities of life is adequate housing. The degree to which a government ensures that all of its citizens are adequately housed can be considered a measure of that government's concern for the welfare of its citizens.

Since housing is an economic commodity, one would expect that in a nation as wealthy as the United States, adequate housing for all citizens would have long been a reality. For a sizable segment of America's population, however, adequate housing continues to be a dream deferred.

This book, edited by Jamshid Momeni, a leading population and housing scholar, focuses on the reasons why blacks, Hispanics, Asians, and American Indians continue to live in housing that is unequal in quality and quantity to that of their white counterparts. The authors of this book are housing scholars from diverse academic disciplines. All agree, however, that despite passage of the 1949 Federal Housing Act and the 1968 Fair Housing Act, racial minority households continue to experience housing deprivation. Compared to whites, racial minorities are more likely to have a lower rate of home ownership and to live in overcrowded, older, poor quality, segregated housing in central cities. In order to find homes comparable to those of whites, minorities must pay more and must overcome barriers of either subtle or direct forms of racial discrimination.

Access to adequate housing in the United States occurs along a color continuum. Asians, for example, have greater access to adequate housing than other minorities, followed by Hispanics and American Indians. Blacks, in general, have less access to adequate housing than other racial minorities, and black female-headed households have the least access of all groups.

The authors of this book agree that persistent discrimination against minorities is a more important barrier than minority poverty in perpetuating the deplorable housing conditions minorities face. Housing of Asian Americans, for example, is not comparable to that of whites, in spite of the fact that all Asian ethnic subgroups, with the exception of Vietnamese, exceed whites in income, education, and occupational status. In a color-blind society, one would expect Asians to be better housed than whites. Yet Japanese housing is inferior to that of whites, in spite of the fact that the median household income for Japanese Americans is 25 percent higher than the median household income for whites.

There is diversity of opinion on how to remedy the housing inequity problem. Traditional civil rights organizations view the federal government as crucial to any effective solution to the housing problem. They continue to lobby for more federal housing subsidies for minorities as well as for stronger fair housing laws. In recent years federal officials have taken the position, however, that the housing problem can best be solved in the private market, although there is little evidence that the private sector would be capable of or interested in removing discrimination and ensuring that racial minorities have access to adequate housing equal to that available to whites.

The private housing industry has accepted the myth that housing trickles down to the lower class after the middle class has left it for new housing. The authors of this book present evidence, however, that a host of factors, including location and cost, prevent this from occurring.

Because of the philosophical position that housing should be provided by the private sector, public housing has been funded at such minimal levels that only a small percentage of the eligible target populations have been served.

The solution to the housing problem is further complicated by the public's loss of enthusiasm for civil rights legislation and the apparent lack of an agreed-upon agenda by racial minority groups. These and other housing policy issues are addressed in detail in this volume.

This book provides comprehensive coverage on minority/majority inequality in the housing market. Housing conditions of each minority group are compared to those of whites. Each chapter provides empirical evidence regarding the nation's inability to ensure minorities equal access to quality housing. In view of only modest improvements and persistent problems that minorities face in the housing market, combined with a lack of strong federal involvement to remedy the situation, future access to adequate housing for minorities in the United States looks bleak.

As a contributor to and the editor of this scholarly work, Dr. Momeni has presented a challenge to us all: how to remove one of the last barriers to freedom—freedom of access to one of the basic necessities of life, adequate housing. The struggle for racial equality in America must continue.

Series Foreword

Leonard W. Doob

The Contributions in Ethnic Studies series focuses on the problems that arise when people with different cultures and goals come together and interact productively or tragically. The modes of adjustment and conflict are various, but usually one group dominates or attempts to dominate the other. Eventually some accommodation is reached: the process is likely to be long and, for the weaker group, painful. No one scholarly discipline monopolizes the research necessary to comprehend these intergroup relations. The emerging analysis, consequently, is of interest to historians, social scientists, psychologists, psychiatrists, and scholars in communication studies.

In the eleven contributions to this volume, edited by Professor Momeni, the control of access to adequate housing is viewed as one of the most significant indexes of relations between the American white majority and four ethnic groups: American Indians, Asians, Hispanics, and, above all, blacks. Within a family's home, living can be satisfactory or unsatisfactory, the potential for personal growth encouraging or discouraging. The authors have brought together and analyzed, in the best ecological and demographic traditions, available statistical information concerning the costs and distribution of rented and owned homes in the United States as well as the status of residential segregation in urban, suburban, and—for American Indians—rural or traditional areas. Here we learn about the relevant and prosaic but significant details that affect human beings, such as overcrowding, plumbing, costs in relation to income, and the American version of what we have now learned elsewhere to call apartheid.

Certainly "a net penalty associated within being black" and the "large inequities" imposed by ethnicity are incisively documented with data obtained from sources within the federal government and from scholarly research. Appropriately, the volume begins with a historical review of what the housing authorities in the federal government have and have not tried or accomplished during the last half century, and it ends with a survey of efforts by private and public civil rights agencies to remove some of the inequalities. By and large, improvements in the housing facilities for these ethnic groups are faintly visible, although, with almost no exceptions, the discrepancies between their homes and neighborhoods and those of the descendants of other ethnic groups, American whites, are both evident and deplorable.

When good people belonging to both the majority and the minorities seek to make this earthly existence more heavenly for all of us, they are wise to select the realistic issue of housing as a key part of their program. The present volume provides both a rationale and ample ammunition for their strivings.

Acknowledgments

I wish to express my gratitude to all those who have contributed to this volume. Foremost are the authors of various chapters, since without their efforts this book would not have been possible.

I am also indebted to Dr. Lawrence E. Gary, director of the Institute for Urban Affairs and Research, Howard University. In the fall of 1984, when I solicited his support for this project, he embraced the idea unhesitatingly. With the approval of Vice President Michael R. Winston, Dr. Gary appointed me as senior research associate at the Institute to enable me to use the Institute's resources. The support of other Institute staff, especially Dr. Diane R. Brown, director of the Housing and Community Development Studies Center, is highly appreciated.

I am grateful to my wife, Mahvash, for her cheerful patience and her taking care of various family chores while I was totally devoted to this and another forthcoming book. There is no way that I can repay them, but I am deeply indebted to my two sons, with whom I hardly had any time to spend while working on this project.

Introduction

Jamshid A. Momeni

Housing constitutes one of the most serious problems facing minority households, many of whom are poor or near poor. Much has been already said about the plight of this group—beseiged by the economic crisis facing them. Yet, it must be reiterated that today housing of the poor and low-income groups is in a dismal state.

Without well-paying jobs, it is highly unlikely that the poor and minorities will have sufficient income to afford adequate shelter. In addition to the lack of financial resources, they must spend an inordinate proportion of their income for housing. In 1980, 66.3 percent of all renters in the United States with income less than $5,000, spent 50 percent or more of their annual earnings for shelter, while no one with an income of $25,000 or more spent the same amount for gross rent (U.S. Bureau of the Census, 1972, 1984).

These figures clearly demonstrate the importance of housing in our lives. For the majority of households, the money spent on housing is the largest annual expenditure. The amount that a household can *afford* to spend on housing affects housing location and quality, which in turn affects the family's happiness, security, well-being, and housing satisfaction from both social and psychological points of views. As Bullard (chapter 4) emphasizes, for most minority households, home ownership and a decent shelter is a dream that has yet to be fulfilled.

In the 1940s and 1950s, the prevalence of substandard housing units had drawn significant public and governmental attention, resulting in the 1949 Housing Act proclaiming the national goal of providing "a decent home and suitable living environment for every American family." The 1960s were marked by urban ghetto riots that led President Johnson in 1967 to commission three blue-ribbon panels (Kaiser, Douglas, and Kerner Commissions) "to inquire into major social and housing problems threatening American Society" (Stegman, 1969: 422). These commissions' reports and some scholarly accounts of the events of the 1960s partly attributed the riots to poor and crowded housing conditions in the ghettos and black neighborhoods.

The Civil Rights Act of 1964 and the 1968 Fair Housing Act that paved the way for black access to public accommodations and provided leverage for attacks against discrimination, coupled with the landmark *Executive Orders* by Presidents Kennedy and Johnson relative to housing, jobs, and affirmative action greatly expanded the housing opportunities for blacks. These acts spurred the movement of nearly a million blacks into suburbia in the 1970s.

The seventies witnessed a significant change in the dynamics of metropolitan America, for the decade was dominated by the suburbanization phenomenon and the associated myth that suburbia meant improved living conditions for all, minorities included. In the 1970s, America became a suburban nation—the size of the population outside the major cities exceeded those living in them. In the 1960s the Kaiser, Douglas, and Kerner Commissions extensively examined ghettos and low income housing; but the 1970s were marked by extensive analyses of the suburbanization phenomenon.

Attention on the housing problem has resurfaced in the 1980s. Judged by scholarly analyses and media's coverage of the problem, the interest in housing seems high and increasing. Homelessness has captured the public's imagination. Activist Mitch Snyder went on hunger strike for more than fifty days to advance the cause of homeless people. Hollywood is currently making a movie of Snyder's story called "Race Against Winter."

No reliable statistics are available, but the estimates of the number of homeless in 1983 in the United States run from 350,000 to over 3,000,000 (HUD, 1984; Hombs and Snyder, 1982). Aside from the plight of the homeless, there is perhaps the larger problem of the shortage of decent, *affordable* housing for the low income groups. Carter (1985) writes, "When Alice Lowery first applied for public housing [in Washington, D.C.] she was homeless and pregnant with her youngest son. That son will be 13 in January [1986] and Lowery is still on the city's public housing waiting list.... The city's waiting list for public housing has grown to 13,000 families, mostly single mothers with children, and a large majority have been on the list for several years." The story goes on to indicate that ironically, Alice Lowery is currently renting one room at $100 per month "from a family that lives in a Northeast [Washington, D.C.] Public Housing Project." McQueen (1985) states: "Harry Hughes [Governor of Maryland], saying 'deplorable' housing conditions remain in some parts of this relatively affluent state, pledged today to make improvements in low-income housing a top-priority of the upcoming session of the [Maryland's] General Assembly." The *Washington Post* (March 1, 1986: F4) reported that based on a study, "19,000 Delaware families live in 'grossly substandard housing,' while more than 10,000 households are 'on a waiting list for affordable rental housing.' "

These are not isolated and anecdotal examples of the media coverage of housing problems. In addition to the ever increasing scholarly publications, a glance at the nation's major daily papers reveals that not a single day goes by without some major news event about the housing problem. This is despite the 1949 Housing Act, and despite the fact that since 1949 the U.S. government has annually pumped billions of dollars (the 1985 budget for the U.S. Department of Housing and Urban Development [HUD] was over $31 billion) into housing-related projects to encourage homeownership and improve the housing conditions for poor and low income groups.

The resurgence of the problem is partly due to the recent skyrocketing costs of housing, and partly due to the philosophical differences between the major political parties in dealing with the issue. While Democrats tend to increase HUD's budget, Republicans have been talking about the "privatization" of HUD. Studies have shown that black suburbanization in the 1970s did not provide a remedy. Rose (1976: xiv) studying the impact of suburbanization concluded that suburbanization was more akin to ghettoization of the suburbs. The coining of the terms such as the "ghettoization" and "urbanization" of the suburbs are indicative of the failure of black suburbanization to provide a solution on a large scale.

Brought together in this book are nine original and two previously published articles. Chapter 1 provides an historical review of changes in public housing policies and their impacts on minorities. Chapters 2–6 deal with various aspects of black housing. Chapter 7 examines residential segregation of blacks, Hispanics, American Indians, and Asian Americans in Michigan. Chapters 8, 9, and 10 analyze the housing conditions of Hispanics, American Indians, and Asian Americans, respectively. And, Chapter 11 examines the question of minority housing needs and civil rights enforcement. It is important to note that these independent authors have reached similar general conclusions: (1) that housing of an average American family has improved significantly since the 1950s; (2) that improvements have not been enough to ensure adequate housing for all Americans; (3) that there is much need for further improvements; (4) that improvements have been uneven, and a wide disparity between racial, ethnic, and minority groups persists; (5) that the upper- and upper-middle-class Americans have been as much the beneficiaries of governmental housing assistance (especially through tax deduction of interest paid for money borrowed for the purchase of homes) as the poor and the lower-income groups; (6) should the current trends continue, neither an end to housing problems nor the narrowing of the gap between the poor and the rich is in sight and; (7) invariably, the authors recommend that a plan be devised to provide more substantial help to the poor and the minorities.

Using ample empirical evidence, this collection shows that the 1949 stated goal of a decent home and living environment for all families has not been achieved. Why? To some, the simplest explanation is that not enough has been done to combat the problem. Another explanation may be that the theoretical arguments forming the basis for the past/current housing policies are not sound and need revisions. That is, the continued housing problem raises the fundamental question regarding the underlying theoretical perspectives and the adequacy of the mechanism devised to deal with it.

This book provides reliable data demonstrating the extent of disparity in housing among groups. Fresh data primarily drawn from recent census reports and the Annual Housing Surveys are utilized. The focus of this book is on the poor and the low income minorities. However, since the assessment of minority housing conditions requires a comparison with the dominant majority group, the housing of whites has also been necessarily discussed. The chapters are intended to provide a bridge between empirical data, theoretical perspectives, and policy. Also it may be noted that the authors of this collection are drawn from a variety of disciplines—demography, geography, urban planning, policy-making, sociology (in academics and applied settings), economics, and social work. Most of the authors are themselves members of minority groups. This may be regarded as a unique feature of this volume.

This book should be of value to housing researchers, academicians, urban policymakers, urban planners, realtors, developers, governmental officials at all levels, political leaders, private financiers, civil right groups, and the general public. In view of the fact that housing has become a basic component of city planning and urban development curricula at many colleges and universities, the present volume could also be used as a supplementary reading for courses in urban planning, urban sociology, housing, and related courses.

References

Carter, G. P. 1985. Waiting for District Public Housing: As Backlog Grows, So Does Despair for a Family on Hold for 13 Years. *Washington Post* (30 November): F1, F5.

Hombs, M. A., and M. Snyder. 1982. *Homelessness in America: A Forced March to Nowhere*. Washington, D.C.: Committee for Creative Non-Violence.

HUD (Department of Housing and Urban Development). 1984. *A Report to the Secretary on the Homeless and Emergency Shelters*. Washington, D.C.: HUD.

McQueen, Michel. 1985. Hughes Urges Housing Aid. *Washington Post* (7 December): D1, D6.

Rose, Harold M. 1976. *Black Suburbanization: Access to Improved Quality of Life or Maintenance of the Status Quo?* Cambridge, Mass.: Ballinger.

Stegman, Michael A. 1969. Kaiser, Douglas, and Kerner on Low-Income Housing Policy. *Journal of the American Institute of Planners* 35 (6): 422–27.

U.S. Bureau of the Census. 1972. *Metropolitan Housing Characteristics: United States and Regions.* 1970 Census of Housing, HC(2)–1. Washington, D.C.: GPO. Tables A–2, A–7, A–12, and A–17.

————. 1984. *Metropolitan Housing Characteristics. United States Summary.* 1980 Census of Housing, Subject Reports HC80–2–1. Washington, D.C.: GPO. Tables A–2, A–4, and A–26.

Race, Ethnicity, and Minority Housing in the United States

1

A Historical Review of Changes in Public Housing Policies and Their Impacts on Minorities

Peter Kivisto

Introduction

The federal government has played an important role in the provision of housing for racial minorities, particularly blacks, since the inception of the public housing program in 1937. Indeed, nearly a half century after the passage of the federal Housing Act of 1937, state-owned housing for the nonelderly has become, to a large extent, minority housing. A major reason for this is the fact that, unlike the experience of governments in housing markets in most of the advanced industrial societies of Western Europe, subsidized rental housing did not become a universal program, but was instead targeted to the poorest stratum of American society. The consequence has been a program beset by a lack of public support, resulting in a situation where the approximately 1.2 million units that have been constructed constitute less than 3 percent of the nation's total housing stock. This chapter examines changes in governmental policies regulating the public housing program over time, focusing on the effects of these policies on racial minorities.

One of the remarkable things about the program is that early supporters in the academic community and among social reformers frequently voiced second thoughts about the efficacy of government-owned housing, and within the span of three decades the overall assessments and perceptions of the program had changed dramatically. Once seen as not only part of the solution to the housing needs of the poor, but as a social locus wherein the pathologies generated by poverty would dissipate, public housing is now frequently seen as part of the problem. It is illustrative to contrast two sociologists whose views rather succinctly depict these changes. In 1940,

Chapin reported his conclusions of a study on the "effects of good housing." Not only was public housing seen as a provider of decent, safe, and affordable dwellings, but it helped to foster stable and positive social relations (Chapin, 1940: 87–90). Progressive social reformers and social scientists endorsed the idea of publically-owned, low-income housing as social engineering came increasingly under the domain of an expanding welfare state (cf., Straus and Wegg, 1938).

However, by the 1960s Rainwater's (1970) study of public housing in St. Louis treated housing developments as places of extensive and complex social pathologies. In his work, public housing was portrayed as both the inheritor and the generator of anomic conditions, necessitating adaptive lifestyles and survival strategies on the part of residents. Fractured social relations and pervasive fear of physical and emotional violence characterized daily life at the infamous (and later demolished) Pruitt-Igoe project. At best, housing was seen by lower-class residents as a haven from sources of fear, in contrast to the middle class, which treats housing as a mode of self-expression and enhancement. Suttles' (1968) study of the "social order of the slum" reinforced Rainwater's conclusions and adds another dimension to the critique. He argued that "the most important consequence of project living may be the way it restricts most opportunities to achieve a stake in the prospects of the local community and to develop the kind of leadership and social differentiation that is so critical in forming a stable moral community" (Suttles, 1968: 123).

Less than forty years after the passage of the enabling legislation, Ledbetter (1967) would describe public housing as a social experiment still seeking acceptance. Actually, this assessment is probably too sanguine. Rather, for many the "good housing" depicted by Chapin had become "vertical ghettos" (Moore, 1969), "Federal slums" (Rainwater, 1970), and "warehouses for the poor" (Savas, 1979: 13), while for supporters the program had been "condemned without trial" (Meehan, 1975). To understand the factors that contributed to the present dilemmas confronting public-sector housing, the following pages will examine four different, major stages in the history of public housing.

The New Deal and Beyond (1933–1948)

Prior to the advent of the depression, very little support existed for the direct intervention of the government in housing markets. Social reformers during the Progressive era were inclined to look to the private sector as the solely appropriate provider of housing for all sectors of American society. The problem of slum housing, according to Veiller (1910), would not find a remedy in municipal ownership. Not only was such housing viewed as too costly and inefficient, but there was a great deal of concern about the prospects for manipulation by local politicians in a situation lacking a well-established civil service. Furthermore, public ownership was deemed to be ideologically antithetical to American values, seen as both an assault on private enterprise and as fostering dependency, rather than self-reliance, on the part of the poor. However, reformers did argue for a "negative" or "restrictive" governmental role, regulating housing by the enforcement of codes that were designed to meet minimal standards insuring the health and safety of occupants. To the extent that charity was seen as appropriate, it was viewed as falling within the purview of private philanthropy (Bowly, 1978). Given the intense opposition to all challenges to an unrestricted market by the real estate, construction, and banking industries and the lack of a concerted movement to challenge them, it is not surprising that the government in the post-World War I period opted to disinvest itself of the approximately 30,000 units of housing it had been forced to construct to house workers in defense-related industries (Fisher, 1959; Friedman, 1978).

During the 1920s and early 1930s advocates of an expanded role for government in housing markets, many influenced by European developments (Aronovici, 1939; Bauer, 1934; Wood, 1934), began to form a housing movement that would press for a public sector role in providing and managing dwellings for the working class and the poor. Through such organizations as the Regional Planning Association, the Labor Housing Conference, and the National Association of Housing Officials, a movement emerged that united intellectuals, religious leaders, social workers, politicians, and organized labor officials. Housing consumers, the ill-housed, played only a minor role; as Marcuse (1980: 48) has observed, they "never constituted a major force in U.S. housing policy."

It was, of course, the economic devastation wrought by the depression that made possible the entry of the federal government into the rental housing field. The creation of the Emergency Public Works Administration (PWA) occurred with the passage of the National Industrial Recovery Act in 1933 (see Nenno and Brophy, 1982 for a chronology of housing legislation). The Housing Division of the PWA was authorized to produce and manage low-rent housing. The most important function of this program, according to PWA administrator Harold Ickes, was the provision of jobs for workers in the hard-hit construction industry (Friedman, 1978: 101). Two corollary functions were the construction of decent and affordable housing for the economically disadvantaged and the elimination of slum housing. Between 1933 and 1937, the PWA razed over 10,000 units of slum housing and built nearly 22,000 dwellings nationwide. However, when a series of court decisions deprived the PWA of the right to eminent domain, while granting the right to local authorities, new legislation was proposed that stipulated a major role for localities in the provision of public housing.

With the passage of the Wagner–Steagall bill, the Housing Act of 1937 established the essential basis for the public housing program (Bredemeier, 1955: 85; McDonnell, 1957). The emergency program which had begun

four years earlier, became a permanent one. For this to be possible in the
face of intense opposition from the private sector, the housing problems of
the poor were divorced from the housing concerns of the rest of the populace
(Rowlands, 1937: 88). There was a concerted effort, in the words of legislative sponsor Senator Robert Wagner, directed at "avoiding competition"
between the private and public sectors (Bredemeier, 1955: 86). To insure
that this did not occur, the law required a 20 percent gap between the upper
income limits for admission to public housing projects and the lowest limits
at which the private sector provided decent housing. As a consequence, the
program was designed at its inception as housing for the poor.

The federal Housing Authority was authorized to both lend money and
to provide annual contributions and capital grants to Local Housing Authorities (LHAs), who were responsible for the actual construction and
operation of housing developments. Federal outlays, in effect, had the result
of paying for the capital costs associated with housing construction, with
the rents charged to tenants being utilized to pay for current operating
expenses (Ashley, 1941: 239–241). The system of annual contributions
required relatively small outlays of funds each year, thereby making the
program politically acceptable, while committing the federal government to
long-term financial obligations.

Though clearly designated for the poor, public housing advocates sought
to make the program ideologically palatable. Responding to a variety of
opponents who condemned it as socialistic and essentially un-American,
they depicted it as temporary housing for the submerged middle class; in
other words, it was intended for the deserving poor rather than the disre-
putable underclass. Portrayed as "slums of hope," public housing projects
were seen as temporary way stations. However, within the framework of
the enabling legislation, the seeds of the future transformation of the program into housing of last resort for the poorest segments of the population
were present.

The class segregation inherent in the program had clear consequences for
blacks, given their overrepresentation in the ranks of the very poor. Between
1933 and 1937, the PWA set aside fully half of its units for blacks. However,
the agency also agreed to follow the practices of the real estate industry in
enforcing segregated housing (Wright, 1981: 225). With the passage of the
federal Housing Act, localities obtained a greater role in the implementation
of racial policies, and overt discrimination was made easier. Civil rights
groups tended to take a pragmatic approach to this situation. Despite the
creation of segregated projects and evidence of discrimination, they seemed
cognizant of the fact that blacks were "represented in subsidized housing
projects to a much greater extent than in the general population," and saw
this as compensating "in some measure for the fact that (blacks) have not
received a proportionate share of other governmental housing activities"
(Sterner et al., 1943: 317). As a consequence, no campaign materialized to

challenge the policy of creating black-only and white-only projects, even in localities where residential segregation in the private sector market was not the norm (Friedman, 1978: 123).

During the first eleven years, high quality housing, often aesthetically successful and architecturally integrated into surrounding neighborhoods, was constructed and this stage was characterized by high demand and financial stability. While some states passed legislation during the 1940s that was intended to remedy racial discrimination, Jahoda and West (1951: 133) reported that housing officials overwhelmingly maintained policies fostering segregation.

Postwar Prosperity and the Other America (1949–1968)

During the next stage, significant changes occurred, in large part because of the provisions of the Housing Act of 1949 and major subsequent housing legislation amendments (Phares, 1977). At first glance, the 1949 act appeared to indicate a significant victory for supporters of public housing. First, the objective of the legislation was unambiguously and boldly proclaimed, seeking to realize nothing less than "the goal of a decent home and a suitable living environment for every American family." Second, Local Housing Authorities were authorized to produce 810,000 units of public housing during the following six years, a sizeable expansion of the program, which had built only 135,000 dwellings since 1933.

However, the ultimate results of the program were seriously disappointing. Hirsch (1983: 212) is quite right to characterize legislation enacted during this period as instrumental in "making the second ghetto," since patterns of urban residential segregation were actually exacerbated by policies that encouraged white flight to the suburbs and minority concentration in inner cities. A major effort to encourage homeownership was vigorously pushed by the construction and banking industries, and it culminated in the expanded availability of low-interest Federal Housing Administration (FHA) and Veterans Administration (VA) mortgages. When linked with federal funding for urban expressways, it became not only feasible, but economically advantageous to purchase newly-constructed homes in suburbs where the construction industry was actively purchasing large tracts of land and mass-producing detached, single family dwellings. Blacks were largely excluded from homeownership options, not only because a majority did not qualify financially for preferential mortgages, but those that could were often denied access to suburbs since the government persisted in adopting the real estate industries' racist policies of establishing and maintaining segregated residential neighborhoods.

A second feature of the 1949 Act had a profound impact on the racial and economic character of public housing tenants. Linked to the provision providing for new construction was a policy of equivalent elimination of slum housing and a related requirement to grant priority treatment on LHA waiting lists for displaced families whose homes had been scheduled for demolition by the federal bulldozer. Since minority housing was overrepresented in those areas targeted for slum clearance efforts, this stipulation resulted in the rapid increase of blacks in public housing. Since the pace of new construction lagged behind the level of housing demolition, blacks, out of necessity, began to enter previously segregated white housing projects. While in some localities the transition to integration proceeded rather smoothly, in others racial tensions were evident (Hirsch, 1983: 171–211).

In 1948 blacks comprised 37 percent of the public housing population. Nine years later, that figure had risen to 48 percent (Fisher, 1959: 165). Their representation steadily increased, and by 1965 blacks came to constitute for the first time an absolute majority of the occupants of public housing (Freedman, 1969: 140). Correlated with this trend was an increase in the percentage of tenants who were unemployed or underemployed. The rise in the portion of tenants receiving various forms of public or private assistance was paralleled by a rise in broken homes or households that were female-headed. Indeed, it was in public housing that the phenomenon currently referred to as the "feminization of poverty" first revealed itself. As a consequence, the overall tenancy pattern began to point to strains on the fiscal integrity of the system, as a poorer tenant population proved to be increasingly incapable of paying rents in amounts that would insure covering the operation expenses of the program.

The opponents of public housing mounted a sustained attack on the program during the early years of postwar prosperity, and the Eisenhower administration dramatically scaled back the budget allocations for funding new subsidized units. However, it did not attempt to terminate the program. Indeed, during the eight years of Republican rule, the number of units under management grew slowly, but steadily, so that by the Democratic electoral victory in 1960, there were slightly less than one-half million units (Aaron, 1972: 110). However, ideologically the Eisenhower administration consistently suggested that government ought not to have a role in either the production or ownership of housing, and public support for the program waned.

This was reflected both in policies related to site selection and in terms of architectural design. Regarding the former, although changing urban land values played a part in site determination, Fisher (1959: 257) observed that frequently noneconomic criteria were an even more significant factor, with race considerations being of singular importance. Site selection was made at the local level, and urban politicians feared for their political lives if they dared to situate new projects, destined to be largely black since the new residents would be the displacees of urban renewal, in essentially white residential neighborhoods. Socioeconomic segregation served to determine what choices were made. Friedman (1978: 123) accurately captures the problem clearly evident by the late 1950s when he wrote, "The siting of public housing has become, in some cities, one major mode of segregation."

In contrast to the earlier period, when projects tended to be low-rise apartments and townhouses located on relatively spacious and open settings, new construction was frequently high-rise and high-density. Furthermore, the bleak homogeneity of architectural design was accentuated by a Spartan-like attitude concerning amenities.

Design features that prevented neighborhood surveillance and destroyed a "human scale" environment conspired to isolate public housing developments from surrounding neighborhoods (Cooper, 1975). This would prompt ameliorist social scientists such as Kriesberg (1969: 276, 287) to argue for the need to locate projects in middle-class neighborhoods in order to provide the underprivileged residents with "new (role) models, new opportunities for action" that were not available in lower-income environments. However, he was acutely aware that racial factors could be an impediment to realizing this in terms of policy initiatives.

The belief that public housing had entered into a state of drift and had evolved in a manner quite different from the original intentions of its early proponents was most cogently and pessimistically expressed in a well-known article by Bauer (1957), writing from the vantage point of someone who had played an important role in the formulation of the 1937 Housing Act. In "The Dreary Deadlock of Public Housing" (1957: 140), Bauer observed that "public housing, after more than two decades, still drags along in a kind of limbo, continuously controversial; not dead but never more than half alive.... If the dreary deadlock is to be broken, it is first necessary to figure what really ails the program."

Though the 1960s signalled some changes in the housing program, the fundamental assessment called for by Bauer was never forthcoming. The number of units under Local Housing Authority management throughout the country increased significantly during the Kennedy and Johnson administrations. However, this did not result in a stock adequate to meet the demand of poor minority families. Due to increased antipathy towards subsidized housing, Congress reoriented production to favor smaller communities, with generally smaller minority populations. They also targeted production to meet the needs of the elderly, at the expense of family units. Housing for the elderly proved to be popular with the public. Administrators generally did not confront the siting problems that inevitably emerged in building family developments. Neighborhood residents neither feared an increased crime level nor a reduction in property values, and local merchants were often anxious to cultivate the elderly as patrons. As a consequence, within a five year period beginning in 1953, the portion of the public housing stock devoted to the elderly (with a majority of the resident population being white) rose from 15 percent to 36 percent (Stafford, 1976: 70).

The problems afflicting public housing by the late 1960s can be divided into three major, though interrelated areas: physical, social, and financial. Regarding the first, the architectural styles favored during the preceding decade, with an emphasis on high-rise buildings, conspired with construction practices that undermined over time the integrity and quality of the structures. In terms of family developments, the emphasis had clearly shifted from producing new units to preserving the existing stock (Leigh and Mitchell, 1980: 58; Hirshen and LeGates, 1975: 7). From 1967 one begins to see the beginning of sustained efforts to focus funding on modernizing and upgrading developments.

Related to the physical problems were design flaws that drastically reduced the amount of "defensible space" (Newman, 1973; Merry, 1981) and undermined the chances of establishing a sense of community. From the point of view of management, this meant that issues of social control related to the prevention of crime became problematic, and solutions had to include costly architectural innovations. From the perspective of tenants, the evidence of a number of studies suggests a pervasive fear of crime and violence (Rouse and Rubenstein, 1978). And, indeed, that fear was justified. Case studies of selected cities revealed levels of property crimes in public housing exceeding national averages by 3 to 19 times (Brill, 1976) while assaults occurred twice as often as the national average (Brill, 1977).

This fact led to an increased preoccupation with the "problem tenant" (Scobie, 1975). Numerous attempts were made to devise techniques that could identify such families prior to admission. While race per se was not a criterion in the selection of tenants, the "gatekeepers" tended to treat certain categories of applicants in which blacks were overrepresented with particular suspicion—singling out, for example, welfare dependency, female-headed households, and large families (Deutscher, 1968). Without recourse to adequate legal representation, applicants and existing tenants faced managerial decisions that were often arbitrary and discriminatory. This led to management-tenant tensions that changed insofar as tenants began to obtain the representation of Office of Economic Opportunity (OEO)-funded legal assistance attorneys.

Conflict between the two parties intensified, particularly involving management officials located in the projects and dealing face-to-face with residents, those that Lipsky (1972) has termed "street level bureaucrats." There was, at least in part, a racial dimension to the conflict. Hartman and Levi (1973: 134) report that in the late 1960s, 80 percent of managers were white, while a majority of tenants in family projects were black. Further, they indicate that these public housing officials had "a fairly negative attitude toward the tenant population." For their part, tenants began to question their long-standing exclusion from the decision-making process and became increasingly critical of the performance of the administrators of the program.

These increasingly troubled relations were exacerbated by the changing financial character of the Public Housing Authorities (PHA) (during this period, "PHA" began to be used in place of "LHA"). The costs of the program rose dramatically due to increased maintenance outlays, modernization programs, inflation, and the expanded provision of social services to the program clientele. To offset these costs, PHAs were forced to institute a series of substantial rent increases, resulting in an unbearable burden for a tenant population that was becoming progressively poorer. Whereas the median income of residents was 63.5 percent of the national family median income in 1950, by 1968 it had dropped to 41 percent (White et al., 1979: 24). As a consequence, rental delinquencies became endemic and in some cases, with St. Louis's Pruitt-Igoe and Boston's Columbia Point being perhaps the most noteworthy, bitter and protracted rent strikes ensued. Such actions mobilized tenants for the first time in the history of the program, and the National Tenant Organization became an increasingly influential lobbying group. Their demands went beyond merely reducing the financial burden placed on tenants and challenging what were perceived to be unfair policies; they included growing demands for community control, a demand in part encouraged by various sectors of the federal government as it directly intervened in local affairs during the War on Poverty (Miller and Rein, 1969).

Disillusion and Dissent (1969–1979)

The third phase in the history of the public housing program is marked by a growing disenchantment that precluded any attempts aimed at far-reaching revisions (Prescott, 1974). As a consequence, two major developments occurred during this time. First, a variety of incremental policies were introduced to stem the tide of decline and numerous experiments or demonstrations were undertaken. Second, alternative means of housing delivery to low-income families, relying on an increased role by the private sector were explored (Solomon, 1974).

This period began with a significant attempt to remedy both the financial crisis confronting many PHAs while simultaneously seeking to reduce the rental burden to tenants. Action came in the form of a series of amendments to the Housing Act of 1937 sponsored by Senator Edward Brooke (R. Mass.). The first of these "Brooke Amendments" was passed in 1969. It called for two forms of financial assistance to local Authorities: a one-time bail-out subsidy to PHAs that were in serious financial condition and universal operating subsidies to assist with expenses for maintenance, management, tenant services, and so forth. These subsidies were intended to meet, in part, the losses that would result from the provision of the amendment directed at rental charges. Fixed rents would be replaced by rental assessments predicated on the tenants' ability to pay, with rents not to exceed 25 percent of the occupant's net adjusted income. This proved to be a major boon to tenants, who in general found their housing costs reduced appreciably, thus placing them in a favorable financial position vis à vis their counterparts in the private sector.

Unfortunately, PHAs did not fare as well. Initially, the Department of Housing and Urban Development (HUD) delayed implementing the operating subsidies provision and later sought to predicate such outlays on proof of improved management performance on the part of Authorities. Such actions led Hirshen and LeGates (1975: 17) to accurately conclude that, "For political reasons, the federal bureaucracy thus perverted tenant-oriented legislation in the name of efficiency, control of local bureaucracy by the federal bureaucracy, and federal budget control." By 1975 an econometric formula, known as the Performance Funding System (PFS), had been designed and was mandated to provide operating subsidies that would be distributed equitably and would meet the real financial needs of PHAs. However, design flaws that tended to penalize the largest PHAs (which had the heaviest concentrations of black residents) resulted in a growing disparity between expenses and receipts during the decade.

A nadir in the program's history was marked in 1973 as the Nixon administration imposed a moratorium on new construction. Although public housing served less than 4 percent of the eligible population, with the completion of projects already in the pipeline, the expansion of the program ceased. Various studies were undertaken to assess the multitude of problems afflicting the existing stock as well as residents' assessments of them (Francescato et al., 1979). In one study it was estimated that about 180,000 units could be seen as seriously troubled, mainly all-black, inner-city projects (Jones et al., 1979).

A series of programs were initiated during the 1970s that were designed to remedy the most serious problems. None of them, as a result, were implemented across the board. In fact, given the limited amounts of money allocated, the funding was provided to PHAs on a competitive basis. The three most important were the Housing Management Improvement Program (HMIP), the Target Projects Program (TPP), and the Public Housing Urban Initiatives Program (UIP). Despite their differences, they were similar insofar as they offered a mix of hard and soft money, or, in other words, monies intended for physical improvements and for various tenant services.

Of relevance to tenant demands for a greater say in the management of public housing was the National Tenant Management Demonstration. Conducted between 1977 and 1982, it was based on a model established in St. Louis in the wake of its long rent strike, when tenants were accorded significant managerial responsibilities (Baron, 1974). The results were somewhat ambiguous, and the experiment was politically controversial. While advocates portrayed it as a mode of empowering the poor, critics perceived it to be a form of cooptation. Lending credence to the critics' charges, many tenant managers viewed themselves over time as having become the bureaucrats they had sought to challenge, and they frequently described the emergence of an antagonistic relationship with other tenants (Kivisto, 1984). The demonstration was never expanded and, in fact, a subsequent policy related to tenant participation in general recommended only a minimal advisory role.

More significant signs of the political climate were efforts directed at creating alternatives to conventional public housing (Weicher, 1980). The Section 23 Leased Housing Program and its successor, the Section 8 Program (both generally administered by PHAs), relied on private-sector housing. Administrative agencies were allocated a specific number of certificates, which were then passed on to eligible applicants. The applicants were required to find housing within a rental range known as the local Fair Market Rent. They were expected, as in public housing, to pay only 25 percent of their adjusted incomes, with federal funds administered by local agencies providing the balance of the difference between the market rent and the tenant assessment. In the more elaborate Section 8 Program (first authorized in 1974), provisions were made to not only utilize the existing housing stock, but to offer various financial incentives to developers to rehabilitate older units and to undertake new construction efforts.

Related to these policy initiatives was one of the most expensive social science experiments in the nation's history: the Experimental Housing Allowance Program (EHAP). In twelve selected cities, low-income families were provided with outright payments in the form of vouchers that, unlike Section 23 or Section 8, provided the recipients with considerable discretion in terms of the kinds of use they made of the money. For instance, they were permitted to upgrade the quality of their housing by spending more than 25 percent of their incomes on rent. The experiment has been hailed by advocates who contend that it managed to reduce the rental burdens of low-income participants while opening up expanded locational opportunities for them (Frieden, 1980; Welfeld, 1982). Critics, concerned about a shortage of an adequate housing supply for low-income families, argued that a major fault of a voucher plan is that it does not contain any mechanism that would stimulate housing production (Hartman, 1983). Furthermore, though somewhat ambiguous, the results of the experiment suggested that blacks did not fare as well as their white counterparts, confirming the view of some that for minorities "shortages of standard housing and discrimination would offset the value of cash payments to the hard-to-house" (Frieden, 1980: 31).

In these alternative approaches the dispersal of program beneficiaries was construed by policymakers as a positive alternative to the high concentration of low-income households in inner-city developments. Indeed, middle-class neighborhoods and suburbs that had adamantly opposed conventional public housing tended to be more amenable to subsidized housing that remained privately owned. Program recipients frequently found that the stigma attached to public housing was avoided. Though blacks were overrepresented in the Section 8 Program, which by 1979 was equivalent in size to the conventional program, they competed with whites to a greater extent than in public housing for the limited number of available slots (Burke, 1982: 6–7).

The quandary confronting blacks regarding the future of conventional public housing and its various alternatives is, perhaps, no better illustrated than in the *Gautreaux v. The Housing Authority of Chicago* case and its aftermath. In 1966 a class action suit was filed by the American Civil Liberties Union on behalf of Dorothy Gautreaux and other tenants as well as applicants for public housing in Chicago. The suit claimed that both the Chicago Housing Authority (CHA) and HUD had violated the plaintiffs' constitutional rights by engaging in racially discriminatory practices in the administration of the public housing program. Specifically, it charged that since 1950 all new construction sites were "in Negro neighborhoods and within areas known as the Negro Ghetto because the Authority had deliberately chosen sites for such projects which would avoid the placement of Negro families in white neighborhoods" (Bowly, 1978: 189). As a consequence, a pattern of residential segregation was created and sustained over time. Three years later a U.S. District Court found that the CHA had violated the constitutional rights of the plaintiffs, and two years later HUD was also found to have violated the rights of tenants and applicants.

To remedy this situation, the Court divided the city into two areas, the "Limited Public Housing Area" (with census tracts containing a nonwhite population of 30 percent or more) and the "General Public Housing Area." The Court's decree required that the next 700 units of housing be built in the General Public Housing Area, relying on low-density, low-rise buildings (Peroff et al., 1979: 23). When the CHA did not build new projects, the plaintiffs returned to court to seek an alternative remedy. Finally, by June, 1976, "HUD agreed to voluntarily undertake a demonstration program designed to assist Gautreaux class families to find housing in suburban or other non-minority impacted areas of the Chicago SMSA" (Peroff et al., 1979: 28). Although there were 43,000 eligible participants in the city, the demonstration provided housing certificates that could be used in the Section 8 Program for only 870 applicants. Less than 400 applicants actually took part in the demonstration, and although 90 percent of them found Section 8 housing in the General Public Housing Area, by the end of the demonstration the fact remained that 80 percent of all families in Section 8 housing still resided in the Limited Public Housing Area (Peroff et al., 1979: 57).

One other feature of the decree was intended to prevent "racial tipping." It stipulated that assignments to new sites would insure 50 percent of the residents were from the neighborhood, in effect insuring that projects would remain at least half white, a situation that would not result if the CHA relied on its primarily black waiting list. Related to this, in four existing white projects, it was stipulated that blacks would be limited to 15 percent of the units, with all minorities limited to 25 percent. These features of the decision amply reflect the dilemmas of social reform. As Bowly (1978: 191) aptly concluded: "It is ironic that a suit filed by black CHA tenants and applicants,... actually had the effect of making public housing in Chicago more attractive to whites, and thus providing less public housing to black families than would have otherwise been the case."

The Privatization Debate (1980–1985)

It is not surprising that this ambiguous legacy, where many former supporters of public housing pushed for an expansion of alternative means of housing delivery (and this despite the fact that public housing per unit costs were lower than programs relying on the private sector), would be severely challenged by the Reagan administration. In this most conservative administration since the New Deal, where ideological discourse tends to supercede critical social analysis, a frontal assault was launched on public housing.

The Report of the President's Commission on Housing, issued in 1982, included options favoring the "deprogramming" (i.e., the sale, conversion, planned deterioration, or demolishment of projects) of sections of the public housing stock and the outright sale of units to tenants as a means of providing homeownership opportunities for low-income families. At the same time, the administration essentially stopped all new construction activities, in not only public housing, but with Section 8, as well. These efforts aimed at shrinking the small quantity of housing in the public sector even further were part of an overall strategy designed to roll back the welfare state, predicated on a fetishized conception of the "free market." HUD contended that the major problem confronting poor families was affordability, and not the supply of decent housing. Thus, the Department developed plans to divest itself of 8 percent of its current stock. This claim, however, has been challenged by a report issued by the Urban Institute that views substandard housing to be a persistent and unresolved problem for the poor (Struyk et al., 1983: 71). At the same time, in the interest of pursuing a fiscal austerity program regarding domestic spending, the Reagan administration has drastically reduced the funding levels for operating subsidies and for modernization. The likely result will be the further deterioration of the existing stock.

Arguing that recipients of government housing programs for low-income families have benefited by the Brooke amendments in a way those living in the private sector have not, the administration sought successfully to raise the tenant portion of the rental payment to 30 percent of the net adjusted income. In addition, they have proposed to include the monetary value of food stamps as income. It is estimated that this would result on average an additional 3 percent increase in the tenant contribution. The consequence of these changes, according to the Urban Institute, is that "beneficiaries will be increasingly impoverished" (Struyk et al., 1983: 67).

In attempting to focus resources only on the poorest of the poor, benefits have been reduced for those in the upper ranks of the lower class. For example, HUD has limited families with incomes between 50 percent and 80 percent of area medians to only 10 percent of housing that becomes available for occupancy. Linked with the HUD forecast that fully 80 percent of the over 100,000 tenants who are expected to leave public housing during the next several years will be from this category (where one finds the largest proportion of both stable families and employed tenants), public housing will become further confined to only the most impoverished. Thus, the Reagan administration will further accelerate the trend that has been evident since 1950.

The EHAP experiment from the preceding decade serves as a model for the direction that this administration would like to move housing policy. Though they have not to date been legislatively successful in implementing a voucher program, this is the course they want to pursue. However, as critics stress, there are weaknesses in the approach that can have a particularly negative impact on racial minorities. First, adequate mechanisms are lacking to redress private landlord discrimination. Second, it is argued that there is not an adequate supply of housing in the private sector to house certain hard-to-place cases, such as large families (Boyd, 1984).

By relying on the existing stock, there is an implicit assumption that housing trickles down to the lower class after the middle class has left it for new housing. However, a host of factors, including location and cost, serve to suggest that this does not occur. By seeking to disengage government from either the construction or management of housing, there is an equally unsupported assumption that, standing outside the market, such housing will be more expensive than it otherwise would be. This is not the case. Despite its manifold problems, public housing has proven to be the least costly form of subsidized housing. Nonetheless, these and similar assumptions underpin policy initiatives of the 1980s.

Conclusion

As this historical review indicates, the public housing program during the past fifty years has been an extremely important provider of affordable housing for low-income black citizens. At the same time, it is a program that has been incapable of eliciting widespread public support. This lack of support has been due largely to the power of the ideology of the unfettered market combined with the enduring problem of race prejudice and discrimination. Though the private sector has provided no evidence that, if left to its own devices, it would be capable or interested in providing decent and affordable housing for the poor, it traditionally has been unresponsive to the efforts of the public sector to take an active role in the delivery of housing to the general populace.

The consequence of this is a segmented housing market in which the state has been permitted to play an overt role in the provision of housing for specifically targeted groups. In contrast to the British experience (Merrett, 1979; Dunleavy, 1981), housing in the United States did not become a universal entitlement program. In fact, public housing and related programs have been funded at such minimal levels that only a small percentage of the eligible target populations have been served. The past five years have witnessed a further attempt to constrict the definitions of those who would qualify for governmental assistance, but in some respects this is a quantitative and not a qualitative change from preceding administrations. At this particular historical juncture, the call for an entitlement program (Hartman, 1983: 51–53), especially if seen as a prelude for moving towards a social welfare program that would entail the "decommodification of housing" (Achtenberg and Marcuse, 1983: 202–31) has very little political support. Indeed, the immediate future would seem to signal an increasingly leaner and meaner welfare state. Because of this, the goal of the Housing Act of 1949 will remain, for a sizable portion of the lower-class minority community, unrealized.

References

Aaron, Henry. 1972. *Shelter and Subsidies: Who Benefits from Federal Housing Policies?* Washington, D.C.: The Brookings Institution.

Achtenberg, Emily, and Peter Marcuse. 1983. Toward a Decommodification of Housing. In *America's Housing Crisis*, edited by Chester Hartman, 202–31. Boston: Routledge and Kegan Paul.

Aronovici, Carol. 1939. *Housing the Masses*. New York: John Wiley and Sons.

Ashley, E. Everett. 1941. Government Housing Activities. *Harvard Business Review* 19 (2): 230–42.

Baron, Richard. 1974. St. Louis Restoring its Public Housing Image by Moving into Tenant Management. In *Public Housing Management in the Seventies*, edited by Frederic Vogelsang. Washington, D.C.: NAHRO.

Bauer, Catherine. 1934. Housing: Paper Plans or a Workers' Movement? In *America Can't Have Housing*, edited by Carol Aronovici. New York: Museum of Modern Art.

———. 1957. The Dreary Deadlock of Public Housing. *Architectural Forum* (May): 138–48.

Bowly, Devereaux. 1978. *The Poorhouse: Subsidized Housing in Chicago, 1895–1976*. Carbondale: Southern Illinois University Press.

Boyd, Gerald. 1984. Vouchers—Key to Housing the Poor? *New York Times* (19 February): 4E.

Bredemeier, Harry. 1955. "The Federal Public Housing Movement: A Case Study of Social Change." Ph.D. dissertation. New York: Columbia University.

Brill, William. 1976. *Comprehensive Security Planning*. Washington, D.C.: GPO.

————. 1977. *Victimization, Fear of Crime, and Altered Behavior.* Washington, D.C.: GPO.

Burke, Paul. 1982. Trends in Subsidized Housing: 1976–1981. Washington, D.C.: HUD, Office of Policy Development and Research.

Chapin, F. Stuart. 1940. An Experiment on the Social Effects of Good Housing. *American Sociological Review* 4 (6): 868–79.

Cooper, Clare. 1975. *Easter Hill Village.* New York: The Free Press.

Deutscher, Irwin. 1968. The Gatekeeper in Public Housing. In *Among the People: Encounters with the Poor,* edited by Irwin Deutscher and Elizabeth Thompson, 38–52. New York: Basic Books.

Dunleavy, Patrick. 1981. *The Politics of Mass Housing in Britain, 1945–1975.* Oxford: Clarendon Press.

Fisher, Robert. 1959. *Twenty Years of Public Housing.* New York: Harper and Brothers.

Francescato, Guido, et al. 1979. *Residents' Satisfaction in HUD-Assisted Housing.* Washington, D.C.: GPO.

Freedman, Leonard. 1969. *Public Housing: The Politics of Poverty.* New York: Holt, Rinehart, and Winston.

Frieden, Bernard. 1980. Housing Allowances: An Experiment that Worked. *The Public Interest* (59): 15–35.

Friedman, Lawrence. 1978. *Government and Slum Housing.* New York: Arno Press.

Hartman, Chester. 1975. *Housing and Social Policy.* Englewood Cliffs, N.J.: Prentice-Hall.

————. 1983. Introduction. In *America's Housing Crisis,* edited by Chester Hartman, 1–28. Boston: Routledge and Kegan Paul.

Hartman, Chester, and Margaret Levi. 1973. Public Housing Managers: An Appraisal. *American Institute of Planners Journal* 34 (2): 125–37.

Hirsch, Arnold. 1983. *Making the Second Ghetto.* Cambridge: Cambridge University Press.

Hirshen, Al, and Richard LeGates. 1975. Neglected Dimensions in Low-Income Housing and Development Programs. *Urban Law Annual* 9 (3): 3–32.

Jahoda, Marie, and Patricia West. 1951. Race Relations in Public Housing. *Social Policy and Social Research in Housing* 1 (2): 132–39.

Jones, Ronald, et al. 1979. *Problems Affecting Low-Rent Public Housing Projects.* Washington, D.C.: GPO.

Kivisto, Peter. 1984. From Tenant Advocates to "Street-Level Bureaucrats." Paper presented at the annual Conference on Ethnic and Minority Studies, Kansas City, Mo. March 1.

Kriesberg, Louis. 1969. Neighborhood Setting and the Isolation of Public Housing Tenants. In *Urbanism, Urbanization, and Change,* edited by Paul Meadows and Ephraim Mizruchi, 276–91. Reading, Mass.: Addison-Wesley.

Ledbetter, William. 1967. Public Housing—A Social Experiment Seeks Acceptance. *Law and Contemporary Problems* 32: 490–527.

Leigh, Wilhelmina, and Mildred Mitchell. 1980. Public Housing and the Black Community. *The Review of Black Political Economy* 11 (1): 53–75.

Lipsky, Michael. 1972. Toward a Theory of Street-Level Bureaucracy. In *Politics, Public Administration, and Neighborhood Control,* edited by H. G. Frederickson, 103–15. San Francisco: Chandler.

McDonnell, Timothy. 1957. *The Wagner Housing Act*. Chicago: Loyola University Press.

Marcuse, Peter. 1980. Housing Policy and City Planning. In *Shaping an Urban World*, edited by Gordon Cherry, 23–58. New York: St. Martin's Press.

Meehan, Eugene. 1975. *Public Housing Policy: Convention Versus Reality*. New Brunswick, N.J.: Center for Urban Policy Research.

Merrett, Stephen. 1979. *State Housing in Britain*. London: Routledge and Kegan Paul.

Merry, Sally. 1981. Defensible Space Undefended: Social Factors in Crime Control through Environmental Design. *Urban Affairs Quarterly* 16 (4): 397–422.

Miller, S. M., and Martin Rein. 1969. Participation, Poverty, and Administration. *Public Administration Review* 29: 15–24.

Moore, William. 1969. *The Vertical Ghetto*. New York: Random House.

Nenno, Mary, and Paul Brophy. 1982. *Housing and Local Government*. Washington, D.C.: International City Management Association.

Newman, Oscar. 1973. *Defensible Space*. New York: Collier Books.

Peroff, Kathleen, et al. 1979. *Gautreaux Housing Demonstration*. Washington, D.C.: GPO.

Phares, Donald. 1977. *A Decent Home and Environment: Housing Urban America*. Cambridge, Mass.: Ballinger.

Prescott, James. 1974. *Economic Aspects of Public Housing*. Beverly Hills: Sage Publishers.

Rainwater, Lee. 1970. *Behind Ghetto Walls: Black Family Life in a Federal Slum*. Chicago: Aldine.

Rouse, W. Victor, and Herb Rubenstein. 1978. *Crime in Public Housing*, vol. 1. Washington, D.C.: GPO.

Rowlands, David T. 1937. Urban Housing Activities of the Federal Government. *Annals of the American Academy of Political and Social Science* 285 (March): 83–93.

Savas, Emanuel. 1979. Federal Housing Policy: An Agenda. An unpublished manuscript.

Scobie, Richard. 1975. *Problem Tenants in Public Housing*. New York: Praeger.

Solomon, Arthur. 1974. *Housing the Urban Poor*. Cambridge, Mass.: MIT Press.

Stafford, Walter. 1976. Dilemmas of Civil Rights Groups in Developing Urban Strategies and Changes in American Federalism, 1933–1970. *Phylon* 37 (1): 59–72.

Sterner, Richard, et al. 1943. *The Negro's Share*. New York: Harper and Brothers.

Straus, Michael, and Talbot Wegg. 1938. *Housing Comes of Age*. New York: Oxford University Press.

Struyk, Raymond. 1980. *A New System for Public Housing*. Washington, D.C.: The Urban Institute Press.

Struyk, Raymond, et al. 1983. *Federal Housing Policy at President Reagan's Midterm*. Washington, D.C.: The Urban Institute Press.

Suttles, Gerald. 1968. *The Social Order of the Slum*. Chicago: University of Chicago Press.

Veiller, Lawrence. 1910. *Housing Reform*. New York: Charities Publication Committee.

Weicher, John. 1980. *Housing: Federal Policies and Programs.* Washington, D.C.:
      American Enterprise Institute.
Welfeld, Irving. 1982. Improving Housing Allowances. *The Public Interest* 66: 110–
      18.
White, Edward, et al. 1979. *The History and Overview of the Performance Funding
      System.* Cambridge, Mass.: Abt Associates.
Wood, Edith Elmer. 1934. The Housing Situation in the United States. In *America
      Can't Have Housing,* edited by Carol Aronovici, 24–27. New York: Museum
      of Modern Art.
Wright, Gwendolyn. 1981. *Building the Dream: A Social History of Housing in
      America.* New York: Pantheon Books.

2

Racial Inequalities in Housing: An Examination of Recent Trends

Suzanne M. Bianchi, Reynolds Farley, and Daphne Spain

Introduction

A major objective of housing legislation since 1949 has been to insure adequate housing for all Americans, regardless of race. The slow progress toward that goal was reflected in the passage of another Fair Housing Act in 1968. More than a decade has passed since then, and there is still evidence that blacks and whites do not have equal access to good housing.

Two types of racial differentiation in the housing market can be identified. First, there is a high level of racial residential segregation in metropolitan areas (Simkus, 1978; Van Valey, et al., 1977). Blacks are concentrated in central cities while the suburbs remain predominantly white. In 1977, 24 percent of black metropolitan households were in the suburbs, compared with 59 percent of white metropolitan households (U.S. Bureau of the Census, 1979b).

A second kind of racial differentiation involves the type and quality of housing occupied by blacks and whites. Blacks typically live in lower quality housing than whites, occupy older housing, and are less likely to own their own homes (Jackman and Jackman, 1980). Not only is initial housing equity difficult for blacks to acquire; it is also more difficult for blacks than whites to recover accumulated equity. Controlling for type of unit, neighborhood, and buyers' characteristics, Lake (1981) found that houses sold by blacks command an average of 10 percent less than comparable houses sold by whites.

Reprinted, with changes, from *Demography* 19(1): 37–51 (February 1982), by permission of the authors and publisher. Copyright 1982 by *Demography*.

The purpose of this research is to examine the degree to which racial differences in housing have narrowed over time. We have chosen 1960 and 1977 as two time points at which to assess racial differences. The 1960 Census provides baseline data prior to 1968 Fair Housing legislation, and the 1977 Annual Housing Survey is the most recent for which comparable national data on housing are available. The research focuses on three questions:

1. Have racial differences in housing quality and rates of homeownership diminished since 1960?
2. What portion of the racial differential in homeownership and housing quality remains after an adjustment is made for socioeconomic, family composition and location differences among households?
3. Among those who have recently engaged in housing search (i.e., households which moved on or after January 1, 1976), have racial differentials in housing quality and homeownership disappeared altogether?

Competing Theories of Racial Differentiation

Neoclassical or "free market" economic theory suggests that, whereas housing markets may be in temporary disequilibrium when large numbers of blacks move into a city, in the long run there should be no difference in the quality of housing obtained by blacks and whites who have similar resources. If there is active discrimination against blacks, white prejudice should result in lower housing prices for blacks as whites must pay a premium for their "taste" for discrimination. Homeowners and real estate agents who refuse to do business with a minority group are restricting themselves to a fraction of the market and hence should incur financial losses which are not experienced by their competitors who deal with all prospective clients (Becker, 1957; Muth, 1969, pp. 106–112; Muth, 1974, pp. 110–113).

"Free market" explanations are at odds, however, with empirical studies which find that blacks are frequently restricted to "segments" of the housing market in which they must pay more than whites for comparable housing (Kain and Quigley, 1975; King and Mieszkowski, 1973). In the past, real estate practices have operated to restrict the housing choices of blacks, and there is evidence that these practices have not yet been totally eliminated (Pearce, 1976; Saltman, 1975; Wienk et al., 1979). Perhaps the most interesting theoretical formulation linking the existence of "segmented" housing markets to racial inequality in housing costs and quality is Courant's (1978) housing search model. Courant argues that if only a few whites discriminate against blacks, a long-run stable equilibrium can exist in which blacks pay more for comparable housing than whites. That is, in the presence of discrimination, housing search costs will be greater for blacks than whites.

because a certain number of white landlords/homeowners will not rent/sell to blacks. Hence, it becomes economically rational for blacks to look for housing in black neighborhoods, since search costs are lower than in white neighborhoods. However, this has the adverse effect of driving up housing prices in black neighborhoods and limiting the housing quality available to blacks, particularly higher income blacks who could afford housing elsewhere.

That blacks typically live in lower quality housing, occupy older housing, and are less likely than whites to own their own houses has been documented (Lake, 1979; U.S. Bureau of the Census, 1979b). What remains open to dispute is whether blacks obtain lower quality housing and have lower rates of homeownership because they are poorer, on average, than whites, or because they are discriminated against in the housing market. Not only are there opposing theoretical predictions; there are also conflicting empirical investigations. Muth (1969; 1974), for example, studied the housing of blacks and whites in Chicago and concluded that blacks "typically have lower incomes than whites and live in poorer quality housing on the average for this reason, not because of race as such" (1969, p. 303). Daniels (1975, pp. 120–121), in an analysis of 1960 census tract data for Oakland, concluded that "white renters paid a premium to live in the relatively segregated white submarket" and that "competition, rather than collusion and discrimination, prevailed in the rental housing market." On the other hand, Kain and Quigley (1975, Table 7–1), who studied St. Louis in the late 1960s, reported that blacks obtained lower quality housing in less desirable neighborhoods than whites who paid similar prices. Likewise, King and Mieszkowski (1973), who analyzed the cost of rental units in New Haven in the late 1960s, found that blacks paid 6 to 13 percent more than whites for comparable units. Analysis of recent national data by Jackman and Jackman (1980) and Wilson (1979) showed that a sizeable racial difference in the probability of homeownership remained even after socioeconomic differences between the races were taken into account.

Empirical investigations of racial differences in housing have typically made use of data from individual case studies, conducted in different cities and at quite different points in time. As Berry (1976) illustrates, even when studies are conducted in the same location but at different points in time, results can be quite divergent. Blacks in Chicago, for example, fared much better vis-a-vis whites during the 1960s and early 1970s, when the housing stock was expanding rapidly, than they did during the 1940s and 1950s, when housing was tight and there was a great influx of blacks to the city (Berry, 1976; Duncan and Duncan, 1957; Duncan and Hauser, 1960). This research supplements the myriad case studies of urban housing markets by providing an assessment of changes in the housing conditions of U.S. blacks and whites on the national level.[1]

Data and Indicators of Housing Quality

The one-in-one thousand Public Use File from the 1960 Census is used in conjunction with the 1977 Public Use File from the Annual Housing Survey (AHS). The unit of analysis is the household: groups of persons, related or unrelated, who live in the same physical housing unit. The AHS was created, in part, to monitor the progress of legislation in improving housing quality for minorities. The survey is funded by the Department of Housing and Urban Development and has been conducted annually by the U.S. Bureau of the Census since 1973. The survey consists of interviews with household heads of approximately 63,000 housing units, and the sample is updated yearly to compensate for lost units and new construction. In this analysis, data from the 1977 AHS are compared with those from the 1960 Census in order to assess change over time. The availability of comparable data allows a comparison of four objective housing indicators for 1960 and 1977.

Structural Inadequacy

Both the 1960 Census and the 1977 AHS contain questions on whether a house or apartment is minimally adequate. That is, does the unit have complete kitchen facilities, piped in water, and complete plumbing? The proportion of black and white households living in units lacking one or more of these facilities provides a measure of structural inadequacy.

Crowded Units

Both data files contain a measure of "within unit crowding," the number of persons per room. The proportion of households with more than one person per room is used as an indicator of crowding. The detrimental effects of crowding in the home have been reviewed by Baldassare (1978) and Gove et al. (1979).

"Old" Units

It can be determined from the 1960 file whether a housing unit was built in 1929 or earlier, that is, whether the unit is more than 30 years old.[2] Due to the code categories used in 1977, an exactly comparable indicator cannot be constructed. However, whether a unit was built prior to 1950 (that is, whether it is 28 or more years old) is ascertainable. The proportion of households living in units built before 1930 (in 1960) and before 1950 (in 1977) is used as a measure of the percentage of households living in "old" housing. This measure is recognizably imperfect, since there are many older buildings which are structurally more sound than newer ones. A further drawback to its use is the higher demand (and thus higher prices) for older housing in cities undergoing extensive renovation (Black, 1980). However, older housing has traditionally been relegated to those unable to afford newer housing.

Owner Occupancy

Homeownership is an important form of asset accumulation for many families. Investment in real estate provides both a hedge against inflation and a modicum of security, independence, and privacy for a family. Since tenure status is available in both 1960 and 1977, the proportion of households living in owned units is also investigated.

Factors Related to Housing Quality Differentials: 1960 and 1977

Since families with high incomes are able to buy better housing than those with low incomes, much of the difference in housing quality and tenure may result from economic differences. Many analysts who describe racial differences in housing contend that these occur largely because of differences in economic status (Straszheim, 1974). Figure 2.1 shows the relationship between characteristics of housing units and family income. Income is reported in constant 1977 dollars and refers to money income received during the previous year by all family members. For households comprised of one or more unrelated individuals, the data refer to income of the household head. In both 1960 and 1977, there was a strong link between economic resources and the quality of housing: the larger a family's income, the less likely that the unit in which they lived was old, structurally inadequate or crowded, and the more likely that it was owned. There is convincing evidence that improvements in housing quality between 1960 and 1977 involved households at almost all income levels. Within incomes categories, the decreases in the proportion of units which were crowded or structurally deficient are striking.

Differences in income do not totally account for the racial differences in housing quality or tenure. Within most income categories and on all indicators of quality, blacks remain "behind" whites. For instance, in 1977, if households with incomes exceeding $35,000 are considered, about 12 percent of the blacks but only 2 percent of the whites lived in units which contained more persons than rooms. Racial differences in the age of housing were also substantial, since high income blacks were much more likely than high income whites to live in units classified as old.

Two problems with this simple bivariate look at family income and housing quality can be noted, however. (a) Families with capital assets can better afford quality housing, and some of the racial differential may result because black families have fewer assets than do white. This economic difference is

Figure 2.1
Characteristics of Housing Units by Family Income
for Blacks and Whites, 1960 and 1977

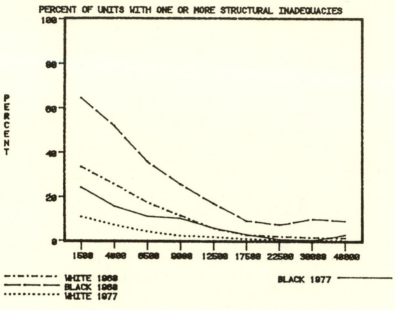

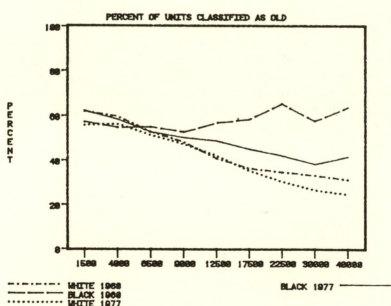

Figure 2.1 (*continued*)

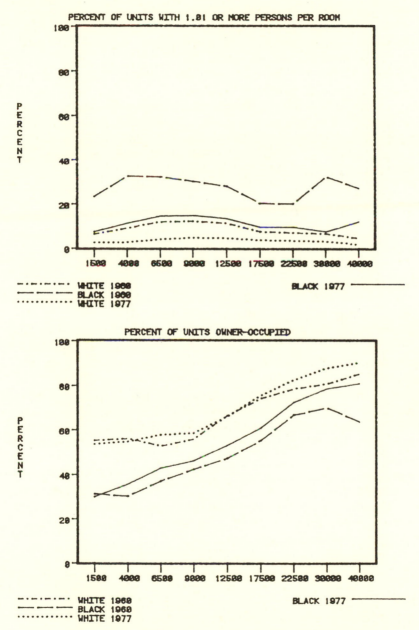

Sources: U. S. Bureau of the Census, *Census of Population, 1960,* Public Use
Sample; *Annual Housing Survey—1977,* National Public Use Sample

25

not indexed by current money income, but unfortunately no measurement of wealth is afforded by either the 1960 Census or the 1977 AHS. (b) A second problem is that racial differences which remain after controlling for income may be due not to discrimination but to differences between blacks and whites in family composition—and hence differences in housing needs or desires—or to differences in regional-metropolitan location—and hence differences in the available housing stock.

In order to circumvent these problems to the extent possible, we move to a multivariate context in which the dependent variables investigated include the three dichotomous indicators of housing quality (coded 1 if a unit is crowded, old or structurally inadequate; 0 otherwise) and tenure (coded 1 if a unit is owner occupied; 0 otherwise). Independent variables fall into four categories: socioeconomic indicators, family compositional factors, residential location variables, and race.

Socioeconomic Indicators

Family income (in 1977 dollars) is the primary socioeconomic indicator we use, but to obviate problems with this measure, we restrict the analysis to households in which the heads are 25 to 59 years old. That is, we exclude retired persons and young household heads—two groups for which current income may not adequately index economic well-being. (The assumption is that the elderly may derive a substantial portion of income from sources not measured in the census or AHS, e.g., savings. Young household heads may still be dependent on parental transfers from outside the household—another source of income not measured in the census or AHS. A similar age restriction has been used by Roistacher and Goodman (1976), who argue that current money income provides a fairly accurate gauge of permanent income for persons within the age range of 25 to 59.)

Educational attainment of head is included, since this may index social class differences, beyond those captured by family income, which affect housing consumption.

Tenure is entered as an independent variable in the analysis of the three quality indicators of crowding, structural inadequacy and old housing. Owner-occupied units are typically in better condition and less crowded than those of renters. Owning a home also reflects a financial investment; indeed for almost all families it is their chief asset.

Family Compositional Factors

Differences in economic status between blacks and whites are not the only factors affecting differences in housing conditions. Several characteristics of housing, such as age of the unit and tenure, are linked to the *age of the household head* occupying the unit, so this variable is included.

There have been demographic changes in household composition which also have had an impact on racial differences in housing. A decreasing proportion of all households include a husband, wife, and their dependent children living together. In 1978, only 32 percent of all households, compared with 44 percent in 1960, included a husband-wife family with children (U.S. Bureau of the Census, 1979a, Table A). Trends have been parallel for whites and blacks, but changes are more accentuated among blacks; in 1978, 45 percent of black compared with 14 percent of white households with children were maintained by a woman (U.S. Bureau of the Census, 1979a, Table 20).

The economic importance of this shift is beginning to emerge. Per capita income is much lower in female-headed households and improvements over time have been less substantial than in husband-wife households. Home-ownership is an indicator of economic well-being; the ability to afford a home often represents the ability to buy space and privacy and provide financial security and stability for dependent family members. Between 1960 and 1977, an increasing proportion of white couples with children lived in owned units (from 68.5% to 79.1%). Among black couples with children, the improvement was even more striking (from 41.0% to 63.3%). In contrast, there was no increase in the probability of owning a home among female-headed families of either race. Only a quarter of black and about half of white female-headed families with children lived in owned units in 1977.

Because tenure varies by type of household (and the other quality indicators may vary as well, due to the differential needs of various type households), we include a family-type variable in the analysis. Households are divided into husband-wife, female- and male-headed households. Husband-wife families are further separated into those with and without dependent children; female-headed households are separated into those with dependent children, women who live alone and a residual "other" category. Male-headed households are separated into men living alone and all others.

Residential Location Variables

Ideally, in assessing black-white differences in housing, one would like to control for metropolitan housing market differences. The census and AHS allow for a rough control; particular SMSAs are not identified on the public use tapes, but the regional location of a household (i.e., Northeast, North Central, South and West) can be identified. Hence, *region* is included in the model.

Metropolitan vs. nonmetropolitan residence is also specified, though there is some suppression on this variable for confidentiality reasons. In 1960, we can identify most central city and suburban households; a residual number of households that are metropolitan but in which we do not know whether residence is in the central city or in the suburbs; nonmetropolitan households; and a residual category in which we are unable to ascertain whether the household is located in a metropolitan or a nonmetropolitan area. In 1977, we can ascertain whether all households are located in metropolitan or in nonmetropolitan areas. For most metropolitan residences, we can ascertain whether location is in the central city or the suburbs, although there are a small number of metropolitan households that cannot be so allocated.

Race

The final variable entered in the model is race. The goal is to ascertain whether the effect of race—net of factors known to influence a household's ability to buy a home and obtain quality housing, factors such as socioeconomic status, household composition and residential location—diminished in importance over the 17-year time span which is the focus of this analysis.

Multiple classification analysis (MCA) is the statistical procedure selected. A logistic or log linear estimation procedure is technically more appropriate when the dependent variable is a dichotomy than is multiple classification analysis. However, in analyses of homeownership by Jackman and Jackman (1980) and Roistacher and Goodman (1976), results from ordinary least squares regression procedures are quite similar to those obtained using a maximum likelihood logistic estimation procedure. Knoke (1975) argues that different methods yield similar results when the range in proportions of the dependent dichotomy are between .25 and .75. Outside the .25–.75 range, different methods may lead to different conclusions about which effects are statistically significant, but substantive differences remain small. It should be noted that our findings for tenure and age of housing may be more reliable than those for structural defects and crowding because the range of proportions is more extreme for the latter two measures than for the former two indicators.

MCA treats each category of every independent variable as a dichotomous or dummy variable which assumes the value 1 if a household falls within the category and 0 if it does not. Four categories for age of head are used, six for educational attainment, nine for income, seven for household type, two for tenure, four for region, and five (in 1960, four in 1977) for metropolitan location. MCA models produce gross and net coefficients for each category of an independent variable. The net coefficient measures the effect of membership in a given category independent of the effects of the other variables, and thus it is analogous to a partial regression coefficient. These net coefficients are expressed as deviations from the overall mean of the dependent variable and are shown in Table 2.1.[3]

Focusing first on factors other than race and on units with one or more structural inadequacies, age of head did not have a very strong effect.

Table 2.1

Multiple Classification Analysis of Housing Quality Indicators and Tenure, 1960 and 1977[a]

Independent Variables	Sample Sizes		Structurally Inadequate		Crowded		Old		Owner Occupied	
	1960	1977	1960	1977	1960	1977	1960	1977	1960	1977
Age of Head										
25-29	4,305	6,491	- 1.0%	- 0.2%	1.2%	- 1.4%	-10.5%	- 1.4%	-22.7%	-19.9%
30-39	11,224	11,585	0.2	- 0.3	3.4	0.5	- 4.8	- 2.8	- 4.4	- 4.0
40-49	11,361	9,497	1.0	0.2	- 1.1	1.2	1.9	- 0.6	3.4	4.7
50-59	9,880	9,638	- 1.0	0.2	- 3.1	- 0.8	7.8	4.8	11.1	13.7
Education of Head										
0- 7 years	6,562	2,328	12.1	5.4	8.6	11.9	4.2	11.7	- 5.0	- 9.8
8 years	5,633	2,205	2.5	2.9	4.0	6.9	5.5	8.2	- 0.8	- 1.7
9-11 years	7,664	5,320	- 2.0	0.5	0.5	3.5	0.9	4.4	0.8	- 2.4
12 years	9,198	13,599	- 4.1	- 0.7	- 3.4	- 0.9	- 1.7	0.0	3.0	2.2
13-15 years	3,690	6,177	- 4.7	- 0.7	- 4.9	- 2.8	- 5.6	- 3.9	1.6	1.3
16 years	4,023	7,642	- 5.9	- 0.7	- 8.3	- 3.3	- 7.3	- 4.8	- 0.7	0.0
Family Income (1977$)										
< 3,000	3,008	1,947	21.6	6.3	3.0	- 0.3	6.1	10.0	-11.8	-14.2
3,000- 4,999	2,367	1,776	15.1	4.8	4.4	2.1	8.0	9.2	-14.2	-21.4
5,000- 7,999	4,663	3,243	4.2	1.5	2.9	2.6	4.2	7.3	-11.0	-16.0
8,000- 9,999	4,143	2,512	- 1.4	- 0.3	1.0	2.2	2.5	5.7	- 5.9	-13.2
10,000-14,999	10,850	7,440	- 5.0	- 0.7	- 0.8	0.9	- 1.0	2.9	2.3	- 3.9
15,000-19,999	6,027	6,819	- 5.8	- 1.1	- 3.3	- 1.0	- 3.6	- 1.2	8.0	3.6
20,000-24,999	2,457	5,175	- 5.0	- 1.0	- 1.6	- 1.2	- 5.7	- 4.1	11.0	8.5
25,000-34,999	2,017	5,056	- 4.4	- 0.8	- 1.2	- 1.0	- 6.4	- 6.5	12.1	11.6
> 35,000	1,238	2,082	- 3.6	- 0.4	- 1.7	- 1.3	- 6.1	- 8.2	16.1	12.4

Table 2.1 (*continued*)

Independent Variables	Sample Sizes		Structurally Inadequate		Crowded		Old		Owner Occupied	
	1960	1977	1960	1977	1960	1977	1960	1977	1960	1977
Family Type										
H-W with child	21,867	18,551	0.3%	0.0%	7.6%	4.6%	- 0.9%	0.5%	5.5%	9.5%
H-W no child	8,085	8,581	- 1.6	-0.6	-11.2	-3.9	- 0.7	- 0.9	- 2.3	0.9
Male with others	938	1,409	2.8	0.5	- 7.6	-3.2	9.4	3.8	- 6.6	-14.1
Male alone	1,324	2,408	21.2	0.6	-19.4	-7.9	5.8	3.4	-30.0	-29.5
Female with child	1,834	2,924	- 6.6	-2.3	0.8	0.0	- 1.9	- 4.3	- 8.3	- 8.8
Female with others	981	1,256	- 3.9	-0.7	-13.8	-5.2	8.2	2.3	- 8.1	- 7.4
Female alone	1,741	2,082	- 5.3	-0.8	-17.5	-8.0	3.0	- 2.7	-18.4	-21.6
Region										
Northeast	9,523	7,805	- 2.4	-0.3	- 2.4	-0.9	15.5	15.9	- 6.7	- 4.4
North central	10,438	9,996	0.8	-0.2	- 0.5	-1.0	10.4	8.1	3.0	2.5
South	10,935	12,914	4.3	0.7	1.6	0.4	-16.5	-12.8	3.8	1.7
West	5,874	6,496	- 5.4	-0.6	1.9	1.7	-13.0	- 8.1	- 1.5	1.2
Metro Status										
Central city	11,457	6,443	- 6.2	-1.4	- 0.1	-0.2	5.5	9.7	-12.7	-11.2
Suburb	10,085	9,981	- 1.7	-0.4	- 0.9	0.1	-12.1	- 7.5	8.8	0.7
Metro, N.A.[b]	1,000	6,468	- 5.3	-0.6	- 1.2	-0.4	1.6	- 4.5	1.6	3.3
Nonmetro	9,292	14,319	5.0	1.9	0.2	0.3	3.6	3.9	3.9	5.4
N.A.[b]	4,936		9.5		1.8		4.8		4.0	
Tenure										
Renter	13,768	11,250	4.1	1.2	4.8	3.1	12.2	8.9		
Owner	23,002	25,961	- 2.5	-0.6	- 2.9	-1.4	- 7.3	- 4.1		
Race										
White	33,231	33,513	- 1.3	-0.3	- 1.2	-0.6	- 0.4	- 0.5	1.2	1.0
Black	3,539	3,698	11.9	2.7	11.4	5.3	3.4	4.1	-11.7	- 8.5
Overall mean			12.8%	2.1%	14.2%	5.8%	41.1%	33.7%	62.6%	68.4%
Total N	36,770	37,211								
Adjusted R²			.280	.081	.155	.098	.203	.159	.192	.296

Sources: 1960 Census of Population and Housing; 1977 Annual Housing Survey

[a] Net deviations from the overall mean are shown in the body of the table.

[b] Not available; data suppressed due to confidentiality reasons.

Educational attainment of the head and household income were inversely related to the likelihood that a unit lacked complete kitchen and plumbing facilities. Net deviations were larger in 1960 than in 1977; there was greater differentiation among education and income levels in 1960 than in 1977. Male household heads were most likely to live in structurally inadequate units in 1960, but only slightly more likely than other types of households to live in such units in 1977. Not surprisingly, renters were more likely to live in structurally inadequate units than owners, although by 1977 these differences were greatly diminished. In 1960, households in the South, as well as nonmetropolitan areas, were more likely to be in structurally inadequate units than were households in other residential locations. This was still true in 1977, but the differences by location were quite small. In general, the picture—whether by educational level, income, tenure, age, family type, region or metropolitan status—is one of greatly diminishing differentials between 1960 and 1977. This parallels the decrease in the overall mean from 13 percent of units structurally inadequate in 1960 to only 2 percent in 1977.

As far as crowding, overall means again show a decline from 14 to 6 percent of all units between 1960 and 1977. Households most likely to live in crowded units (i.e., units with 1.01 or more persons per room) were those headed by persons aged 30 to 39—the ages when families most frequently include young children. At both points in time, the higher the income and educational attainment of the head, the lower the probability that a household lived in a crowded unit. As suggested by the relationship of age of head to crowding, husband-wife couples with children were most likely to live in crowded units followed by female heads with children. Owner-occupied units were less often crowded than renter-occupied units. Units located in the South and West and in nonmetropolitan areas were slightly more likely to be crowded than units in other areas, but differences were very small both in 1960 and 1977.

Between 1960 and 1977, the overall proportion of households in units more than 30 years old declined slightly from 41 to 33.7 percent. There was a strong relationship between age of head and age of housing, with older household heads most likely to live in older units. Household income and educational attainment of head were negatively related to age of unit at both points in time. Housing was oldest for male-headed households and female-headed households without children in 1960. The same was true in 1977 with the exception of females living alone (who were likely to be in new housing in 1977). The newest units, at both points in time, were found in the suburbs and in the South and West.

As Table 2.1 shows, the probability of homeownership increased from 63 to 68 percent between 1960 and 1977. The proportion of homeowners rises steadily with age; in 1977, persons in their fifties were almost twice as likely as those in their twenties to own a home. As anticipated, the higher

Table 2.2
Racial Differences in Housing Quality and Home Ownership, 1960 and 1977
(Total Sample)

Recent Movers[a]	Structurally Inadequate	Crowded	Old	Owner Occupied
Unadjusted means				
Whites	2.1%	5.0%	31.7%	49.7%
Blacks	6.0	11.4	47.8	25.0
Unadjusted mean racial difference	3.9	6.4	16.1	24.7
Adjusted means[b]				
Whites	2.2	5.2	32.9	47.8
Blacks	4.8	9.1	37.4	41.1
Adjusted mean racial difference	2.6	3.9	4.5	6.7

Source: 1977 Annual Housing Survey
[a]Moved in on or after January 1, 1976.
[b]Adjusted for effects of age, educational attainment, family income, family
   composition, tenure, region, and metropolitan location.

a family's income, the higher the rate of homeownership. However, the net relationship of education to tenure was quite weak and curvilinear, with high school graduates showing the highest rates of homeownership. There was a fairly strong relationship of household type to tenure, with husband-wife households owning their homes more often than other type households. Finally, homeownership was highest in the South and North Central, lowest in the Northeast, and intermediate in the West. In both 1960 and 1977, homeownership was lowest in central cities. In 1960, it was highest in the suburbs, whereas in 1977 it was highest in nonmetropolitan areas.

Racial Differences in Housing: 1960 and 1977

For answering questions about racial change and possible discrimination in the housing market, the most important coefficients in Table 2.1 are those for race. Table 2.2, which extracts from the full MCA results, presents both unadjusted and adjusted means and mean differences between blacks and whites for each of the four housing indicators. The adjusted mean differences between blacks and whites are *net* of age, income, education, family type, tenure, region and metropolitan location differences.

Several observations can be made. First, housing conditions of blacks were extremely poor in 1960 and racial differentials were quite large. Over one-third of black households were in units that were not minimally adequate, that is, that lacked piped-in water, plumbing or a complete kitchen.

The comparable figure for whites was one-tenth, and only about half of the racial difference could be attributed to socioeconomic, compositional and locational differences between blacks and whites. In addition, almost one-third of black households were crowded, compared to 12 percent of white households, and only one-third of this differential could be eliminated by adjusting for other variables in the model. Over half of black households were in older units compared to 40 percent of white households. Here, though, a large portion of the differential (i.e., 72 percent) could be attributed to socioeconomic, family, compositional and locational factors. Finally, whereas a full 65 percent of white households were owner-occupied, only 36 percent of black households owned the unit in which they resided. About 57 percent of this differential could be attributed to factors other than race per se.

The second thing to note (see Table 2.3) is the large decrease in crowded and structurally inadequate units among both races, but particularly among blacks, between 1960 and 1977. Because housing improvements were greater among blacks, adjusted mean racial differences declined from 13 to 3 percentage points for the structural inadequacy indicator and from 13 to 6 percentage points for the crowding indicator. Increases in homeownership occurred for both races but were also somewhat larger for blacks than for whites. Hence, whereas the adjusted percentage point difference had been a full 13 points in 1960, it declined to 10 percentage points in 1977. The one indicator which showed no diminishing of either the unadjusted or adjusted mean racial differential was the percentage in older housing.

Finally, although racial differences narrowed between 1960 and 1977, they had not disappeared by 1977. If one focuses on the adjusted means, only 2 percent of white but 5 percent of black units were structurally inadequate in 1977. Whereas 5 percent of white units were crowded, 11 percent of black units had more than one person per room. Forty percent of black compared to 35 percent of white households resided in older units. And whereas 69 percent of white units were owner occupied, only 60 percent of black units were owned. The adjusted racial difference was smallest for the structural inadequacy variable and largest for the homeownership indicator. Also, a very similar portion of the remaining racial gap could not be explained by other factors in 1977 as in 1960. That is, taking the adjusted mean difference as a percent of the unadjusted mean difference, 55 percent of the structural inadequacy, 66 percent of the crowding, 30 percent of the old housing, and 35 percent of the owner-occupied racial differential remained after socioeconomic, compositional and locational factors were controlled.

Note on Racial Differences among Recent Movers

The analysis of data from 1960 and 1977 suggests an improvement over time in the position of blacks in the housing market. If this is occurring,

Table 2.3
Racial Differences in Housing Quality and Home Ownership among Recent Movers

Black/White Differences	Structurally Inadequate			Crowded			Old			Owner Occupied		
	1960	1977	Δ 1960-77	1960	1977	Δ 1960-77	1960	1977	Δ 1960-77	1960	1977	Δ 1960-77
Unadjusted means												
Whites	10.1%	1.6%	- 8.5%	12.3%	4.9%	- 7.4%	39.8	34.1%	-5.7%	65.4%	71.4%	+6.0%
Blacks	37.5	6.5	-31.0	31.9	13.8	-18.1	53.6	49.4	-4.2	35.7	44.0	+8.3
Unadjusted mean racial difference	27.4	4.9		19.6	8.9		13.8	15.3		29.7	27.4	
Adjusted means[a]												
Whites	11.5	1.8	- 9.7	13.0	5.2	- 7.8	40.7	35.2	-5.5	63.8	69.4	+5.6
Blacks	24.7	4.5	-20.2	25.6	11.1	-14.5	44.5	39.8	-4.7	51.0	59.9	+9.9
Adjusted mean racial difference	13.2	2.7		12.6	5.9		3.8	4.6		12.8	9.5	

Sources: 1960 Census of Population and Housing; 1977 Annual Housing Survey

[a] Adjusted for effects of age, educational attainment, family income, family composition, tenure, region and metropolitan status.

we would expect that when the investigation of racial differences is restricted to people who have recently sought housing, we might find even fewer or no penalties associated with being black. If fair housing legislation was effective in the first half of the 1970s, recent movers should show less racial difference in tenure and housing quality than all households in 1977, because recent movers engaged in housing searches after discriminatory practices were made illegal.

How much the Fair Housing Act has contributed to improvement remains an empirical question. Kain and Quigley (1975) found a large racial differential in homeownership rates in 1967, before passage of the Act. Roistacher and Goodman (1976) found that the race differential had disappeared among recent movers by 1971. More recent work by Ladenson (1978), however, indicates that racial differences in homeownership reappeared in 1974. He attributed this reversal to Nixon's 1973 cancellation of HUD's Section 235 homeownership subsidy program, which had also been initiated in 1968. Ladenson concluded that the racial difference in the probability of home purchase fell in the years after passage of the Fair Housing Act and Section 235, but rose again after the suspension of Section 235.

Using 1977 AHS data, MCA models identical to those reported in Table 2.1 were run for a restricted sample of recent movers, i.e., those who had moved into their present house on or after January 1, 1976. Unadjusted and adjusted mean racial differences are reported in Table 2.3.

On each indicator, racial differences were evident among recent movers. In general, adjusted racial differences among recent movers were similar to those for the total sample, although adjusted mean differences in crowding and owner occupancy were somewhat smaller for the recent mover subsample. There is therefore a suggestion of gradual, continued movement toward racial equality in the latter half of the 1970s. But there is no evidence that racial differences have disappeared altogether.

Summary and Conclusions

This analysis has focused on the change between 1960 and 1977 in the housing quality of blacks compared with whites. Among both races, there were substantial improvements during the period. Although blacks remain more likely to live in crowded, structurally inadequate and old units, and less likely to live in owner-occupied units than whites, racial differences in most of these indicators narrowed between 1960 and 1977.

Adjustment for socioeconomic, compositional and locational differences among households accounted for over 70 percent of the racial differential in older housing, a little over half of the racial differential in owner-occupied and structurally inadequate housing, and only one-third of the racial differential in within-unit crowding. Conversely, depending on the housing indicator, anywhere from 30 to 70 percent of racial differentials in housing could not be attributed to other factors such as socioeconomic, family compositional or residential location differences between blacks and whites.

In sum, we have demonstrated that racial differences in housing quality and tenure are not entirely the result of racial differences in economic resources, household composition or residential location. Rather, there is a net penalty associated with being black. The data do suggest that the significance of race declined between 1960 and 1977, as Wilson (1978) proposed, but that race remains a salient factor in the housing market. To the extent that the net effect of race represents racial discrimination in the housing market, we have evidence that discrimination has decreased over time but has not been eliminated. However, we have not directly studied racial discrimination, so we must draw conclusions cautiously. Nevertheless, a variety of recent local and national studies of the housing market show that if similar blacks and whites seek housing, they are often treated differently. Whites are typically provided with more information about the housing market than blacks, while blacks are steered to all-black or largely-black areas (Pearce, 1976; Saltman, 1975). In a 1977 national study of racial discrimination, sponsored by the Department of Housing and Urban Development and conducted in each of 40 metropolitan areas, approximately 300 whites and 300 blacks in matched pairs shopped for advertised housing (Wienk et al., 1979). If a black visited four rental agents, he or she could expect to encounter at least one instance of racial discrimination 72 percent of the time. If a black visited four sales agents, he or she would expect to encounter at least one instance of discrimination 48 percent of the time. These practices of discrimination, we believe, help to account for the persistence of racial differences in housing quality and tenure described in this paper.

Notes

1. One study that has recently provided a very thorough analysis of racial differences in home purchase, value of home and housing quality at the national level, is Franklin Wilson's *Residential Consumption, Economic Opportunity and Race* (1979). In Chapter 7, Wilson uses the 1975 Annual Housing Survey to assess the net effect of race in the housing market. The present study is complementary to Wilson's in that our focus is on change over time in the net effect of race.

2. The exact year in which a structure was built is not coded nor is any age of structure detail beyond "built in 1929 or earlier" available.

3. Data for 1960 are from a self-weighting one-in-one thousand sample of the nation's households. The 1977 data are weighted to correct for differential probabilities of selection in the sample.

Acknowledgments

This is a revision of a paper presented at the annual meeting of the Population Association of America, in Denver, Colorado, April 10–12, 1980. We wish to thank

Donald Dahmann and Jack Goodman for their helpful comments on an earlier version. Authors' names are listed in alphabetical order.

References

Baldassare, Mark. 1978. Residential Crowding in Urban America. Berkeley: University of California Press.

Becker, G. 1957. The Economics of Discrimination. Chicago: University of Chicago Press.

Berry, B. J. L. 1976. Ghetto Expansion and Single-Family Housing: 1968–1972. Journal of Urban Economics 3:397–423.

Black, J. Thomas. 1980. Private-Market Housing Renovation in Central Cities: An Urban Land Institute Survey. In: Shirley Laska and Daphne Spain (eds.), Back to the City: Issues in Neighborhood Renovation. Elmsford, N.Y.: Pergamon Press.

Courant, P. N. 1978. Racial Prejudice in a Search Model of the Urban Housing Market. Journal of Urban Economics 5:329–345.

Daniels, C. B. 1975. The Influence of Racial Segregation on Housing Prices. Journal of Urban Economics 2:105–122.

Duncan, B. and P. Hauser. 1960. Housing and Metropolis. Glencoe, Ill.: The Free Press.

Duncan, O. 1969. Inheritance of Poverty or Inheritance of Race? In: Daniel Moynihan (ed.), On Understanding Poverty. New York: Basic Books.

Duncan, O. D. and Beverly Duncan. 1957. The Negro Population of Chicago. Chicago: University of Chicago Press.

Gove, W., M. Hughes, and O. Galle. 1979. Overcrowding in the Home: An Empirical Investigation of Its Possible Pathological Consequences. American Sociological Review 44:59–80.

Jackman, M. and R. Jackman. 1980. Racial Inequalities in Homeownership. Social Forces 58:1221–1234.

Kain, J. F. and J. M. Quigley. 1975. Housing Markets and Racial Discrimination: A Microeconomic Analysis. New York: National Bureau of Economic Research.

King, T. and P. Mieszkowski. 1973. Racial Discrimination, Segregation and the Price of Housing. Journal of Political Economy (May/June):590–606.

Knoke, D. 1975. A Comparison of Log-Linear and Regression Models for Systems of Dichotomous Variables. Sociological Methods and Research 3:416–422.

Ladenson, M. I. 1978. Race and Sex Discrimination in Housing: The Evidence from Probabilities of Homeownership. Southern Economic Journal 45:559–575.

Lake, Robert W. 1979. Racial Transition and Black Homeownership in American Suburbs. Annals of the American Academy of Political and Social Science 441:142–156.

———. 1981. The Fair Housing Act in a Discriminatory Market: The Persisting Dilemma. Journal of the American Planning Association 47:48–58.

Muth, R. F. 1969. Cities and Housing. Chicago: University of Chicago Press.

———. 1974. Residential Segregation and Discrimination. In: G. M. von Furstenberg, B. Harrison, and A. H. Horowitz (eds.), Patterns of Racial Discrimination, Vol. I: Housing. Lexington, Mass.: Lexington Books.

Pearce, D. 1976. Black, White and Many Shades of Gray: Real Estate Brokers and Their Racial Practices. Unpublished Ph.D. dissertation. Ann Arbor: University of Michigan.

Roistacher, E. A. and J. L. Goodman. 1976. Race and Homeownership: Is Discrimination Disappearing? Economic Inquiry 14:59–70.

Saltman, J. 1975. Implementing Open Housing Laws through Social Action. Journal of Applied Behavioral Science, II(1):39–61.

Simkus, Albert A. 1978. Residential Segregation by Occupation and Race in Ten Urbanized Areas, 1950–1970. American Sociological Review 43:81–93.

Straszheim, M. R. 1974. Racial Discrimination in the Urban Housing Market and Its Effects on Black Housing Consumption. In: G. M. von Furstenberg, B. Harrison and A. H. Horowitz (eds.), Patterns of Racial Discrimination, Vol. I: Housing. Lexington, Mass.: Lexington Books.

U.S. Bureau of the Census, 1979a. Current Population Reports, Series P–20 No. 340. Household and Family Characteristics: March 1978. Washington, D.C.: U.S. Government Printing Office.

———. 1979b. Current Housing Reports, Series H–150–77. Annual Housing Survey: 1977, Part A. General Housing Characteristics for the United States and Regions. Washington, D.C.: U.S. Government Printing Office.

Van Valey, T. L., W. C. Roof and J. E. Wilcox. 1977. Trends in Residential Segregation: 1960–1970. American Journal of Sociology 82:826–844.

Wienk, R. E., C. E. Reid, J. C. Simonson, and F. J. Eggers, 1979. Measuring Racial Discrimination in American Housing Markets: The Housing Market Practices Survey. Washington, D.C.: U.S. Department of Housing and Urban Development.

Wilson, Franklin. 1979. Residential Consumption, Economic Opportunity, and Race. New York: Academic Press.

Wilson, William Julius. 1978. The Declining Significance of Race: Blacks and Changing American Institutions. Chicago: University of Chicago Press.

3

Racial Inequalities in Home Ownership

Mary R. Jackman and Robert W. Jackman

Home ownership is an intrinsic part of the American dream. The purchase of a home has a special significance in the establishment of a family: it is, in fact, the single most important purchase that most families face. Apart from its importance as a symbol of status and security, home ownership also bestows considerable financial benefits. Since housing absorbs a bigger fraction of their budget, these financial benefits are particularly significant for people of low to middle income, who have fewer opportunities for alternative investment. In fact, home ownership is generally regarded as a primary method of capital accumulation, especially for low to middle income families (e.g., Kain and Quigley, b). Besides the wealth that accrues from housing equity itself, the well-known tax savings from home ownership also contribute to capital formation. While these tax savings increase with income (Aaron), they are more significant for families of low to middle income because there are fewer other tax shelters available for them. Finally, of course, home ownership is an important hedge against inflation, especially for those who must devote a larger portion of their income to housing (e.g., the calculations in Kain and Quigley, b, Appendix C).

In this chapter, we examine patterns of home ownership among white and black Americans. Major inequalities between blacks and whites have been shown in the distributions of educational attainment, occupational

This chapter is in every sense a joint effort. The research was supported by grants from the National Institute for Mental Health (MH–26433) and the National Science Foundation (SOC75–00495). We would like to thank Mary Scheuer Senter for her assistance, and both her and Anne Adams for their comments.

status, and income (e.g., B. Duncan; O. D. Duncan, a; Farley; Hauser and Featherman, a; Johnson and Sell; Siegel). However, we know relatively little about the extent to which these inequalities are perpetuated or exacerbated in consumption and investment patterns. For the majority of families, especially low to middle income families where blacks are disproportionately represented, housing constitutes the most conspicuous item of consumption and the clearest opportunity for investment. To what extent do both blacks and whites achieve this part of the American dream?

Surprisingly, most previous studies of racial inequalities in patterns of home ownership have relied on relatively aggregated data and have not gone much beyond simple tabular presentations of the probability of home ownership by race and earned income (e.g., Levitan et al.), despite the fact that a series of other factors are known to affect the demand for housing. A notable exception is a study by Kain and Quigley (b), which presents extensive analyses of these issues. However, their analyses are based on data from a single city (St. Louis, Missouri), which were gathered in 1967. Kain and Quigley's results indicate (b, 175) that even for households of otherwise comparable composition and socioeconomic status (SES) in St. Louis, nonwhites are less likely to be homeowners than whites. They also find (b, chap. 7) that among St. Louis homeowners, nonwhites own homes of lower value than do whites, and that the size of this racial difference increases with family earnings.

Kain and Quigley's results have important implications. In the following analysis, we draw on fresh national survey data to assess whether the racial inequalities in housing that they found in St. Louis are more generally present in the United States as a whole in the mid 1970s.

Analysis

Our data come from a national probability sample of the 48 contiguous United States surveyed in the Fall of 1975 by the Survey Research Center of the Institute for Social Research in Ann Arbor, Michigan. In all, 1,914 individuals aged 18 and over were personally interviewed, of whom 1,648 are whites, 195 are blacks, and the remaining 71 are other nonwhites. A total of 1,752 (91.5 percent) provided useable responses to an item asking whether they owned their home (the remainder are divided almost equally between those for whom no information was obtained on this item, and those living in housing provided free by a relative).[1] A total of 1,164 respondents (two-thirds of those providing useable responses) reported that they are homeowners. Whites are considerably more likely to be owners than blacks: 71.3 percent of the whites and 41.2 percent of the blacks indicated that they own their home. In the following analyses, we focus exclusively on black-white differences: other nonwhites are not included.

Racial Differences in the Probability of Home Ownership

A variety of factors are known to affect the demand for and supply of housing (e.g., Kain and Quigley, b; Lee; Orcutt et al.). To avoid spurious inferences, our analysis therefore includes three sets of explanatory variables in addition to race: the socioeconomic characteristics of the household, its composition, and its location. We briefly introduce these in turn.

The two household socioeconomic characteristics of interest are annual earned family income and socioeconomic status. Earned income is perhaps the most obvious determinant of home ownership, and we need not dwell on that relationship here. In addition, since housing is a visible form of consumption, we expect the probability of home ownership to increase with SES, more broadly conceived. SES is included not only for its intrinsic interest but also because it identifies permanent status more directly than do annual earnings (which have a substantial transitory component).[2]

Three features of household composition are also relevant. First, one would expect the age of the head of household to have a positive effect on the probability of home ownership, since younger families have had less time to accumulate sufficient capital for a down payment. Specifically, we expect age to have a nonlinear effect that places primary emphasis on the distinction between young and other families. Second, households consisting of single persons should be less likely to be homeowners than households consisting of married couples, since home ownership (like marriage) is traditionally associated with getting settled. Third, families with children are more likely to buy their own homes, partly because rental housing tends to be smaller, and partly because much rental housing excludes families with children.

Finally, we distinguish households according to two features of their location. First, we classify them according to whether they are in large cities, suburbs and towns, or rural areas. We anticipate that the supply of rental housing varies with size of place, such that it is most available in large cities, and least available in rural areas. All other things equal, this should directly affect the probability of home ownership. Second, we separate southern households from others, given the distinctive history of race relations in the South, and because blacks in the non-South are located disproportionately in central-city areas.

Family earnings should refer to all income received during the previous year, and can come from a variety of sources besides the main earner's job. Our measure therefore includes all income received from any or all of seven possible sources: respondent's main job, spouse's main job, other jobs, retirement benefits, unemployment compensation, welfare payments, and a small miscellaneous category comprising such sources as alimony and veteran's benefits. Note that apart from the first two, these sources of income refer to income received by respondents *or* spouses. Note also that the last three categories were used by a relatively small proportion of respondents.

Our measure of SES is Duncan's Socioeconomic Index or SEI (O. D. Duncan, a), as updated by Hauser and Featherman. Specifically, we focus on the head of household's SEI. To locate the head of household, all respondents (apart from those living alone, who we assume are heads) were asked to identify the head of household. Approximately 85 percent of these respondents named themselves or another individual,[3] while most of the rest claimed joint headship. For these latter respondents, we take head of household's SEI to be either the higher of the two SEI scores (where both heads were currently in the labor force), or the SEI score for the individual currently in the labor force (where one head was not currently in the labor force).

The question identifying the head of household is also used in the construction of our measure of the age of the head of household. For most cases, we follow the procedure just described for SES, so that the age of the head of household is the age of the individual identified as head. However, where joint headship was claimed, we take the age of the older of the two individuals. Since we expect the effect of age of head of household to follow the nonlinear form discussed earlier, this variable is also transformed logarithmically. The other two measures of household composition are more straightforward. Marital status is defined as a dummy variable that equals 1 if the respondent is currently married, and zero otherwise. An additional dummy variable equals 1 if any children are currently living in the household, and zero otherwise.[4]

We classify households' location on two dimensions. First, we distinguish between large cities (population $\geq 350,000$), suburbs and towns (2,500–349,999), and rural areas (population <2,500). Second, southern households are identified by a dummy variable that equals 1 if the household is located in one of the eleven former Confederate states, and zero otherwise.

The estimated effects of race and these other three sets of explanatory variables on the probability of home ownership are reported in Table 3.1. Note that we specify this probability as being an additive function of race, the socioeconomic characteristics of the household, its composition, and its location, in order to evaluate the net effects of race. The first column of Table 3.1 contains ordinary least-squares estimates, while the second column presents maximum likelihood estimates from a logit model. We report the latter because the dependent variable is dichotomous, a condition that often results in inefficient parameter estimates with ordinary least squares.[5] However, it is clear from a comparison of the two columns in Table 3.1 that in this case, the two estimating procedures produce the same results both in the signs and the statistical significance (*t*-ratios) of the parameter estimates.

The figures in Table 3.1 indicate that the three sets of variables other than race have the expected effects: the probability of home ownership

Table 3.1
Ordinary Least Squares (OLS) and Maximum Likelihood Logit (MLL) Estimates
of the Probability of Home Ownership ($N=1,500$)*

Variables	OLS	MLL
Earned family income	.005** (4.78)	.051 (5.11)
Head of household's SEI	.001 (2.44)	.007 (2.05)
Age of head of household	.330 (12.48)	2.069 (11.03)
Married?	.285 (11.57)	1.468 (9.17)
Children?	.133 (5.03)	.669 (4.15)
Large cities	-.232 (6.72)	-.719*** (6.27)
Suburbs and towns	-.088 (3.76)	
South	.029 (1.20)	.148 (0.92)
Black	-.102 (2.85)	-.503 (2.23)
Constant	-.888 (8.58)	-7.908 (10.30)
R^2	.319 (F = 77.41)	.333 (χ^2 = 525.74)

*Observations with missing data on any of the variables in the table are excluded from the analysis.

**Main table entries are parameter estimates, and numbers below them in parentheses are their t-ratios.

***In the OLS estimates, the effects of city size are represented by two dummy variables (the excluded category being "rural"); in the logit model, the effects of city size are represented by a single trichotomous qualitative variable.

increases with the socioeconomic characteristics of the household—both annual family earnings and the more permanent component of SES that is measured by the head of household's SEI. Likewise, the estimates for household composition are all positive and statistically significant, indicating that younger households are less likely to be homeowners, while the probability of ownership is higher for both married households and families with children, respectively. Of the household location parameter estimates, those representing size of place show that the probability of ownership, as expected, is highest in rural areas and lowest in large cities. However, the figures in Table 3.1 suggest that there are no meaningful regional differences, since both estimates for the southern dummy variable are small and statistically insignificant (the logit estimate in the second column is smaller than its standard error).

More importantly, the estimates in Table 3.1 show that the net effect of race is pronounced and statistically significant. This means that even for otherwise comparable households, blacks are considerably less likely to live in owner-occupied housing, which is consistent with Kain and Quigley's results for St. Louis.

An important assumption underlying the model in Table 3.1 is that the effect of race on the probability of home ownership is additive. Some, however, have argued that such an additivity constraint is unreasonable. Instead, it has been suggested that blacks and whites have different investment patterns such that, for example, the effect of annual earnings on the probability of home ownership varies by race. Race differences may also be present in some of the other coefficients (Birnbaum and Weston).

To pursue these possibilities, we reestimated the maximum likelihood logit model in the second column of Table 3.1 for blacks and whites separately. This procedure indicated that with one possible exception (head of household's SEI) there are no pronounced differences by race in the parameter estimates. In order to determine how much the coefficient for head of household's SEI differs by race, we then reestimated the pooled model of the second column in Table 3.1, adding an interaction term (Race * SEI) which allows the coefficient for head of household's SEI to vary by race. The estimates for this second modified model show that such an interaction term is unnecessary: its parameter estimate is smaller than the corresponding standard error. We therefore conclude that, Birnbaum and Weston to the contrary, there are no meaningful race differences in the coefficients, and that the additive model of Table 3.1 is the most reasonable specification.[6]

What then is the meaning of the additive effect of race? Without the model, we observe that 71.3 percent of the whites are homeowners, compared to 41.2 percent of the blacks. Thus, in gross terms, the probability of ownership is .301 lower for blacks than it is for whites. The ordinary least-squares estimates in Table 3.1 indicate that the conditional (or net) probability of ownership is .102 lower for blacks (which is also the same as the maximum likelihood logit estimate of $-.105$).[7] This means that two-thirds of the overall race differences can be attributed to the effects of the other variables in Table 3.1. However, the probability of ownership for blacks remains 10 percent lower than it is for whites, regardless of their socioeconomic characteristics, family composition, or location. That this net effect is pronounced becomes clear when we compare it with the effects of other variables. For example, the logit estimates imply that to raise the probability of home ownership by 10 percent, earned family income would have to be raised by approximately $10,000. In other words, the size of the net race effect is equivalent to a net earned income effect of $10,000.

Racial Differences in the Value of Owner-Occupied Housing

We now turn to the second question: Restricting our attention to home-owners, to what extent does race influence the value of the home? Again, this issue must be examined within the context of other factors that might be expected to influence the value of people's homes, in order to minimize the possibility of observing spurious race effects.

As with the probability of home ownership, the socioeconomic charac-teristics of the household should affect the value of the home. In fact, these variables should be more important in accounting for the *value* of homes than they are in accounting for the simple probability of ownership. We therefore include earned family income and head of household's SEI as explanatory factors. We also include type of location in the model since it reflects different housing markets. (As in the last section, we distinguish among large cities, suburbs and towns, and rural areas, as well as between the South and the non-South.) However, we do not expect the value of the home to be sensitive to household composition. While the latter is important in the prior decision to purchase, there is no reason to expect it to influence the value of the home, net of the other explanatory factors. Thus, age of household head, marital status, and presence of children in the household are not included in the model.[8]

Our measure of the value of owner-occupied housing comes from re-spondents' estimates of the value of their home. These estimates were ob-tained from homeowners only, as part of a series of questions on family income and assets. To maximize their sense of privacy, respondents an-swered interviewers' questions by filling out an "income sheet," rather than responding orally. Homeowners were asked, "Would you please write down the letter that comes closest to the estimated value of your home in Box 12, labelled 'House'." In a series of seventeen categories ranging from less than $500 to $60,000 or more, the median reported home value is $27,000 for blacks and whites together. The median value for whites only is $27,500 (mean: $29,300), while the median value for blacks of $16,000 (mean: $19,600) is substantially lower. In the analysis below, home value is coded in thousand-dollar units.

How accurate and reliable are these owner estimates? While we have no evidence from our own data, two other studies are helpful in assessing these issues. Kish and Lansing compared owner-occupant estimates of housing value for a national sample of homes with estimates prepared by professional appraisers, while Kain and Quigley (a) have made a similar comparison with their sample from St. Louis. Both of these studies conclude that despite individual discrepancies, errors in owner estimates are largely offsetting for reasonably sized samples. In fact, Kain and Quigley (a, 804) report a simple correlation of .84 between owners' and appraisers' evaluations, which is an acceptable reliability figure. They also report that while there was a slight tendency for undervaluing to increase with SES in St. Louis, knowledge of SES can be used to improve this minor source of inaccuracy in owner estimates. Such knowledge is incorporated in our own model by way of earned family income and head of household's SEI.[9] Taken together, then, these two studies imply that the accuracy and reliability of owner estimates of home value are more than adequate for our present purposes.

Finally, it is important to note that we focus on the total estimated value of the home rather than on the owner's equity in it, because the former most closely represents the home's value as an item of visible consumption. Total value is also the more relevant quantity to the extent that housing is one central manifestation of life style, either aspired or real. In addition, estimates of total value are more reliable than estimates of equity, since the latter require the respondent to recall four pieces of information: the sum of (1) the down payment, (2) the amortized portion of the mortgage, and (3) the current total value of the home minus (4) its purchase price.

The first column of Table 3.2 reports the basic estimates for our model of home value. In general, each of the independent variables has the expected effect. As anticipated, the household's socioeconomic characteristics have strong, positive effects on home value: the *t*-ratio for family earnings is larger than 14, while that for head of household's SEI is greater than 8. The dummy variables for size of place indicate that people in large cities own homes of the same value as do people in rural areas, once the other independent variables are taken into account. People living in suburbs or towns own homes of slightly higher value (the adjustment is less than $1,800), although this effect should be interpreted with some caution since the *t*-ratio for this estimate is 1.82, indicating statistical significance at the .07 level. The figures also show that in the South, people own homes of lower value (by $3,500) than do people elsewhere.

Most important to our analysis is the parameter estimate for race in the first column of Table 3.2. While this estimate is negative, as expected, it is less than twice its standard error with a significance level of .09. This suggests that once we take the socioeconomic characteristics and location of the household into account, race differences in the value of homes are marginal. Apparently, the significant negative effect of being black on the probability of ownership is not repeated so dramatically in the case of home value.

This conclusion, however, is based on a model of additive race effects. Kain and Quigley (b) concluded that for St. Louis, at least, such a model is unjustified. Instead, they found evidence of a race-income interaction, such that the income coefficients for whites were at least twice the size of those for blacks. To check for any such race differences in our national

Table 3.2
Ordinary Least Squares Estimates of the Value of Owner-Occupied Housing
(*N*= 1,018)*

Variables	Additive Model	Non-Additive Model
Earned family income	.563** (14.12)	.561 (14.13)
Head of household's SEI	.171 (8.30)	.173 (8.38)
Large cities	.056 (0.03)	.283 (0.17)
Suburbs and towns	1.772 (1.82)	1.740 (1.78)
South	-3.549 (3.35)	-3.994 (3.72)
Black	-3.232 (1.69)	-6.286 (2.45)
Black * south		6.640 (1.79)
Constant	13.047 (11.52)	13.143 (11.60)
R^2	.328	.331
F	82.41	71.24

*Observations with missing data on any of the variables in the table are excluded from the analysis, as are non-homeowners.

**Main table entries are parameter estimates, and numbers below them in parentheses are their t-ratios.

sample, we reestimated the model in the first column of Table 3.2 for blacks and whites separately. This procedure provided little evidence of a race-income interaction: the coefficient for earned family income was .56 for whites, which was quite similar to the corresponding estimate for blacks of .48. Indeed, the separate estimates by race indicated that, with one important exception, pooling black and white respondents in the context of an additive model is justified. The exception occurred with the estimated effects of region: for whites, the coefficient for the South was negative, but for blacks the corresponding estimate was *positive.*[10]

In light of this, the second column of Table 3.2 reports estimates for a model that allows the effect of race to vary by region. While the t-ratio for the black-South interaction term is only 1.8 (indicating statistical significance at the .07 level), excluding this parameter from the model suppresses the effect of race. Despite the fact that they are based on only 31 and 37 respondents, respectively, the estimates for southern and nonsouthern blacks in the second column both have higher t-ratios than does the additive coefficient for race in the first column (which is based on all 68 black home-owners in the sample).

These estimates modify and extend Kain and Quigley's results for St. Louis. First, our national data indicate that there is no racial inequality in home value within the old Confederate states: southerners own homes that are worth $4,000 less than those of nonsouthern whites, regardless of race ($-6.286 + 6.640 \approx 0$). However, outside the South, there is a pronounced effect of race. On the average, black homeowners in the non-South have homes worth approximately $6,300 less than otherwise comparable non-southern whites. Second, we find no evidence of a race-income interaction, even outside the South. Instead, the racial gap in home values in the non-South is constant at all levels of socioeconomic achievement. The size of this gap remains substantial. Compare it with the estimate for family income, which shows that a jump of more than $11,000 in family income ($6.286/.561 = 11.2$) would be required to increase the value of one's home by $6,300.

Conclusions

The analyses in this chapter indicate that there are substantial racial in-equalities in patterns of home ownership in the United States. These in-equalities are apparent at two steps. First, blacks are considerably less likely than whites to own the home they live in. Whatever their characteristics on other variables that influence the probability of home ownership, blacks remain 10 percent less likely than comparable whites to be homeowners. To set this in perspective, the effect of race on the probability of home ownership is equivalent to a difference in earned income of approximately $10,000. Second, outside the South, blacks who are homeowners live in homes that are worth, on the average, about $6,300 less than the homes of comparable whites. This effect of race on the value of owner-occupied homes outside the South is equivalent to a difference of about $11,000 in earned family income.

In evaluating these results, the critical issue is the extent to which they reflect racial discrimination. This question should be assessed against the familiar backdrop of pervasive residential segregation by race in the United States (e.g., Taeuber and Taeuber; Van Valey et al.). However, before we can attribute racial inequalities in housing to discrimination, two other explanations must be assessed: first, that blacks have different housing tastes than whites; and second, that blacks get better bargains on the housing market than do whites.

The fact of segregation makes it difficult to separate taste from discrim-ination, since segregation produces a dual housing market. This provides the context within which blacks frame their preferences and realistic ex-pectations. Despite the dual market, data reported by Pettigrew and Farley et al. indicate that blacks are nearly unanimous in their preference for integrated neighborhoods. However, more detailed data from Detroit (Farley et al.), also show that a majority of blacks perceive specific white suburbs as hostile environments for blacks, and almost no blacks would choose to be the *first* black family moving into a white neighborhood. Thus, there is little evidence to suggest that blacks freely choose to participate in a separate housing market or to live in segregated neighborhoods. On the other hand, there is evidence that many whites seek to minimize black participation in the white housing market. Data from Detroit (Farley et al.) show that anything more than token residential integration is unattractive to a majority of whites. This suggests that racial inequalities in housing are more plausibly seen as a reflection of *white*, rather than black, tastes.

Do blacks get better bargains on the housing market? It might be tempting to reason that because blacks tend to live in areas that are unattractive to whites, the price of black homes should be lower than white homes of comparable quality. However, this reasoning is inconsistent with the fact that southern blacks who do manage to purchase a home do not encounter the same "bargains" as nonsouthern blacks, despite similar patterns of residential segregation in both areas (Van Valey et al.). What seems more plausible is that the dual housing market works to restrict the supply of housing available to blacks, which should force the price of black housing up. The available evidence, though scattered, suggests that blacks pay at least as much, and probably more, than do whites for comparable housing (e.g., Kain and Quigley, b; Phares).[11]

In short, while the evidence is indirect, it seems most reasonable to attribute racial inequalities in home ownership to the inability of the dual market to meet black demand, that is, to racial discrimination. Thus, residential segregation is not the only form of discrimination that blacks face on the housing market. Further, the racial inequalities in home ownership outlined in this chapter cannot be seen as a simple corollary of segregation. While the South does not appear to have a distinctive pattern of residential segregation, the southern pattern of racial inequality in home ownership is distinctive. There, it lowers blacks' likelihood of home ownership, while in the non-South it operates in two cumulative steps to lower both their probability of ownership *and* the value of the home that is purchased. Further research with richer data is needed to examine regional differences more closely, as well as to isolate the exact market mechanisms that generate different forms of housing discrimination.

It is important to remember that these inequalities in home ownership compound prior racial inequalities. The rate of return to occupational attainment that blacks receive from education is lower than it is for whites (e.g., Featherman and Hauser). Further, the rate of return to earned income received by blacks from occupational attainment is also lower than it is for whites (e.g., Farley; Johnson and Sell). These constitute two well-known barriers to black achievement in the United States. Beyond these barriers, our results indicate that black families who do experience any hard earned socioeconomic gains face further hurdles in trying to incorporate these gains into their standard of living. For most families, housing is the most conspicuous form of consumption and the clearest opportunity for investment. The cumulative constraints facing blacks in the housing market therefore constitute a serious impediment to their participation in the mainstream of American society.

Notes

1. Those living in housing provided free by a relative are young single persons, almost all between the ages of 18 and 25 years, living with their parents. We exclude these individuals from the analysis.
2. Kain and Quigley (b) attempt to avoid this difficulty with annual earnings by introducing a measure of "permanent" income, which they construct by averaging the annual income of the head of household, within levels of education. Thus defined, permanent income becomes a crude approximation of socioeconomic status. Our use of a direct indicator of the latter identifies the permanent component of status more satisfactorily than does Kain and Quigley's empirical formulation of permanent income.
3. Those reporting one or both parents as head(s) of household are already excluded from the analysis for the reason given in note 1.
4. We chose these measures of household composition after experimenting with a variety of alternatives, on the grounds that (a) they are simplest to interpret, and (b) they provide the most precise estimates. For example, we found no evidence to warrant further distinctions according to marital status (widowed, divorced, etc.), or the exact number of children. Our three measures of household composition reflect the essence of Kain and Quigley's eleven "life cycle" variables (b, 212–26) while avoiding the unnecessary complexity and redundancy that these variables introduce (e.g., between the number of persons and the number of children in the household).
5. For a comparison of ordinary least squares and maximum likelihood logit estimates, see, e.g., Hanushek and Jackson (chap. 7).
6. Birnbaum and Weston have also questioned Kain and Quigley's results on the grounds that measures of assets should be included as explanatory variables. Their estimates indicate that if assets are included in the model, then the effect of race on home ownership is considerably weakened. However, the introduction of assets variables into a single equation model that seeks to account for the probability of home ownership creates a severe simultaneity problem (since "wealth" appears on both sides of the equation). As Birnbaum and Weston themselves partially acknowledge, this undermines their results substantially (see also, Kain and Quigley, b).
7. The logit model takes the following form:

$$1n\ P(Y=1)/(Y=2) = \beta_0 X_0 + \beta_1 X_1 + \ldots + \beta_7 X_7 + \beta_8 X_8 \qquad (1)$$

where X_8 equals 1 if the respondent is black, and 0 if the respondent is white, and the remaining seven independent variables are those identified in Table 3.1. To estimate black-white differences in the probability of ownership, equation (1) can be expressed as

$$P(Y=1) = 1/(\underline{e}^{-\beta_0 X_0 - \beta_1 \overline{X}_1 - \ldots - \beta_7 \overline{X}_7 - \beta_8 X_8})$$ (2)

Note that we have inserted mean values for the variables other than race in equation (2), in order to gauge black-white difference for otherwise "average" households. For whites, equation (2) is then evaluated with β_8 set equal to zero to give a net probability of ownership for whites of .750. For blacks, equation (2) is evaluated with β_8 set equal to 1, which gives a net probability of ownership for blacks of .645.

8. This contrasts with Kain and Quigley's (b) retention of the household composition variables in their "full models" of housing expenditures. However, these variables have no statistically significant effects on home value in their analyses. Similarly, if our own models of home value below are expanded to include family composition, none of the composition measures has any effect on the dependent variable.

9. To the extent that there is a tendency for undervaluing to increase with socioeconomic status, the estimated effects of earned family income and head of household's SEI will be biased downward. The exact size of any such bias is not particularly important for our analysis, given that we are concerned primarily with race differences, but Kain and Quigley's evidence suggests that the bias would be marginal.

10. In view of the race-region interaction and the fact that St. Louis is a non-southern city, we performed an additional test, to check if the race-income interaction found in St. Louis holds throughout the non-South. We added a race-income interaction term to the basic model in the first column of Table 3.2, and estimated this revised model separately for the South and the non-South. The estimates provided no evidence for any region-specific race-income interactions.

11. Kain and Quigley (b, 299) calculate that in St. Louis, comparable owner-occupied dwellings cost 5 to 6 percent more in ghetto than in non-ghetto neighborhoods. They also demonstrate that St. Louis blacks have lower quality housing than comparable whites. Further research is needed to examine directly the relationship between home value and quality of home for blacks and whites.

References

Aaron, H. 1970. "Income Taxes and Housing." *American Economic Review* 60:789–806.

Birnbaum, H., and R. Weston. 1974. "Home Ownership and the Wealth Position of Black and White Americans." *Review of Income and Wealth* 20:103–18.

Duncan, B. 1968. "Trends in Output and Distribution of Schooling." In E. Sheldon and W. Moore (eds.), *Indicators of Social Change*. New York: Russell Sage.

Duncan, O. D. a:1961. "A Socioeconomic Index for all Occupations," and "Properties and Characteristics of the Socioeconomic Index." In A. J. Reiss (ed.), *Occupations and Social Status*. New York: Free Press.

——. b:1969. "Inheritance of Poverty or Inheritance of Race?" In D. Moynihan (ed.), *On Understanding Poverty*. New York: Basic Books.

Farley, R. 1977. "Trends in Racial Inequalities: Have the Gains of the 1960s Disappeared in the 1970s?" *American Sociological Review* 42:189–208.

Farley, R., H. Schuman, S. Bianchi, D. Colasanto, and S. Hatchett. 1978. "Chocolate City, Vanilla Suburbs: Will the Trend Toward Racially Separate Communities Continue?" *Social Science Research* 7:319–44.

Featherman, D. L., and R. M. Hauser. 1976. "Changes in the Socioeconomic Stratification of the Races, 1962–73." *American Journal of Sociology* 82:621–51.

Hanushek, E. A., and J. E. Jackson. 1977. *Statistical Methods for Social Scientists.* New York: Academic Press.

Hauser, R. M., and D. L. Featherman. a:1976. "Equality of Schooling: Trends and Prospects." *Sociology of Education* 49:99–120.

———. b:1977. *The Process of Stratification: Trends and Analyses.* New York: Academic Press.

Johnson, M. P., and R. R. Sell. "The Cost of Being Black: A 1970 Update." *American Journal of Sociology* 82:183–90.

Kain, J. F., and J. M. Quigley. a:1972. "Note on Owner's Estimate of Housing Value." *Journal of the American Statistical Association* 67:803–6.

———. b:1975. *Housing Markets and Racial Discrimination: A Microeconomic Analysis.* New York: National Bureau for Economic Research.

Kish, L., and J. B. Lansing. 1954. "Response Errors in Estimating the Value of Homes." *Journal of the American Statistical Association* 49:520–38.

Lee, T. H. 1963. "Demand for Housing: A Cross-Section Analysis." *Review of Economics and Statistics* 45:190–6.

Levitan, S. A., W. B. Johnson, and R. Taggart. 1975. *Still a Dream: The Changing Status of Blacks Since 1960.* Cambridge: Harvard University Press.

Orcutt, G. H., M. Greenberger, J. Korbel, and A. M. Rivlin. 1961. *Microanalysis of Socioeconomic Systems: A Simulation Study.* New York: Harper & Row.

Pettigrew, T. F. 1973. "Attitudes on Race and Housing: A Social-Psychological View." In A. H. Hawley and V. P. Rock (eds.), *Segregation in Residential Areas.* Washington: National Academy of Sciences.

Phares, D. 1971. "Racial Change and Housing Values: Transition in an Inner Suburb." *Social Science Quarterly* 52:560–73.

Siegel, P. M. 1965. "On the Cost of Being a Negro." *Sociological Inquiry* 35:41–57.

Taeuber, K. E., and A. E. Taeuber. 1965. *Negroes in Cities: Residential Segregation and Neighborhood Change.* Chicago: Aldine.

Van Valey, T. L., W. C. Roof, and J. E. Wilcox. 1977. "Trends in Residential Segregation: 1960–1970." *American Journal of Sociology* 82:826–44.

4

Blacks and the American Dream of Housing

Robert D. Bullard

The goal of a "decent home for all Americans" became a slogan and model in 1949 from which a general housing policy was to have emerged. The postdepression and post–World War II strategies of the federal government exerted a great deal of influence over the private housing industry through mortgage loan guarantees, tax incentives, and construction financing, to mention a few. Moreover, federal policy shifts over the past thirty-five years have affected housing markets and have contributed to shaping residential areas and the quality of life in the nation's urban centers.

Government intervention into the housing industry has not affected all segments of the population equally. The nation's blacks, for example, have not benefited to the same degree as their white counterparts by the changing opportunity structure. The housing options and opportunities that are available to blacks have been shaped largely by a number of factors which include: (1) federal housing policies, (2) institutional and individual discrimination in housing markets, (3) geographic location and housing construction priorities, and (4) demographic changes that have taken place in the nation's urban areas.

Compared to whites today, the end result of these factors on black households has meant reduced housing choices and limited mobility for a significant segment of the American population.

Federal Housing Policy

Federal housing policies were the chief sponsor of suburban development in the 1950s and 1960s. Much of the current residential housing patterns and problems of segregation can be traced directly to the government's role during this period (Houseman, 1981). Morris (1981), for example, summarized the failures of the federal government's first "attack" on the nation's urban housing problems through urban renewal. Morris (1981: 6–7) writes:

It was 1949 that the government began its first "attack" on the slum through the infamous "Urban Renewal" program. Unlike public housing programs, the rehousing of displaced residents was subordinated to the primary goal of clearance and redevelopment. Of all the federal programs, none has had a more devastating effect on housing for blacks than urban renewal which was soon dubbed "Negro Removal." Blacks did not benefit from slum clearance; rather they became victims. The housing which they occupied prior to demolition was, for the most part, never replaced.

Another case in point is the Federal Housing Administration (FHA) which as late as the 1960s operated from the position that racial homogeneity was essential to a neighborhood's financial stability. Many of the early FHA housing developments included restrictive covenants which discriminated against blacks. The FHA insured millions of dollars in mortgages which placed higher values on properties that were located in white areas than on those that were located in racially integrated areas (Tabb, 1970; North and Miller, 1973). In 1965 alone, the FHA and the Veterans Administration (VA) insured or guaranteed over $150 billion in mortgage loans for over 15 million units of housing (Schiller, 1980: 212).

Middle-class whites were the primary benefactors of government-insured loans; quite often middle-class families got loans while blacks and the poor were confined to overpriced and inadequate housing. In a sense, the federal housing policy at the time contributed to the white exodus from the central city to the suburbs. Conversely, the residential choices of black households were constrained by these same federal housing policies (Kushner, 1980: 130; Marshall, 1981; Fairchild and Tucker, 1982).

Federal policies have played a central role in the development of a spatially differentiated metropolis in which blacks and other visible ethnic minorities are separate from whites; and the poor from the more affluent (Taeuber and Taeuber, 1965; Taeuber, 1975, 1983; Danielson, 1976). Kushner (1980: 130) asserts that "government action is the proximate and essential cause of urban apartheid" in this country. America's cities remain racially segregated in the 1980s as illustrated in Table 4.1.

The nation's apartheid-type housing policies contributed to the development and growth of black ghettos. Ford and Griffin (1979) described five major types of black ghettos that emerged in the United States: (1) the "early southern" ghetto—dispersed pockets of blacks who lived in "alley dwellings" and worked primarily as servants and laborers, (2) the "early northern" ghetto—distinct geographic boundaries of high density dwellings, (3)

Table 4.1
U.S. Cities with Black Population of More than 100,000 in 1980

City	Population (in 1000s)		% Black	Segregation Index* (Dissimilarity)	
	Total	Black		1980	1970
New York, NY	7,071	1,784	25	75	77
Chicago, IL	3,003	1,197	40	92	93
Detroit, MI	1,203	759	63	73	82
Philadelphia, PA	1,688	639	38	88	84
Los Angeles, CA	2,967	505	17	81	90
Washington, DC	638	448	70	79	79
Houston, TX	1,594	440	28	81	93
Baltimore, MD	787	431	55	86	89
New Orleans, LA	557	308	55	76	84
Memphis, TN	646	308	48	85	92
Atlanta, GA	425	283	67	86	92
Dallas, TX	904	266	29	83	96
Cleveland, OH	574	251	44	91	90
St. Louis, MO	453	206	46	90	90
Newark, NJ	392	192	58	76	76
Oakland, CA	339	159	47	59	70
Birmingham, AL	284	158	56	85	92
Indianapolis, IN	701	153	22	83	90
Milwaukee, WI	636	147	23	80	88
Jacksonville, FL	541	137	25	82	94
Cincinnati, OH	385	130	34	79	84
Boston, MA	565	125	22	75	86
Kansas City, MO	448	123	27	86	90
Richmond, VA	219	112	51	79	91
Gary, IN	152	106	71	68	84
Nashville, TN	456	106	23	80	90
Pittsburgh, PA	424	102	24	83	86

* Segregation measures are based upon the census count of black and nonblack persons in each city block.

Source: Taeuber (1983: Table 1).

the "classic southern" ghetto—resulting from legalized housing segregation of areas "reserved" for blacks, (4) the "classic northern" ghetto—arising from white flight, and (5) the "ghetto of the fifth kind"—including middle- to upper-middle class neighborhoods which have "suburban-like" qualities.

The federal government has initiated a number of housing subsidy programs over the years to assist both owners and renters. For example, the Section 235 housing program was initiated as a subsidy program under the national Housing Act of 1968. This program was designed to assist low and moderate income households to become home owners. It has had provisions for assisting in the construction and rehabilitation of single-family and multi-family housing for these households. Under the Section 235 housing program, a family would pay 20 percent of its income for principal, interest, taxes, and insurance.

The U.S. Commission on Civil Rights (1970) in its evaluation of the Section 235 program found that the traditional pattern of "separate" and "unequal" housing markets for white and black families was being perpetuated by this federal housing. New 235 housing was usually found in suburban areas and all was being purchased by white families. On the other hand, black families who purchased 235 homes were located in subdivisions "reserved" for blacks. In addition, most of the existing 235 housing was located in transitional areas of the inner-city and nearly all were being purchased by black and other minority families.

The Section 235 program also experienced a number of problems with real estate speculation and loan defaults. While taking into consideration the many problems that plagued this subsidy program, it did provide opportunities for a segment of society to become home owners (see chapter 5 by Silver in this book). The program provided another vehicle for moderate-income black households to own properties in traditionally black neighborhoods. It also accelerated the "trickle down" process for black owners.

Recent trends in federal housing subsidy programs have been geared toward the renter market. In an attempt to allow low and moderate income households to compete for decent, uncrowded, and safe housing, the federal government initiated the Section 8 rental assistance program. This subsidy program was created under the Housing and Community Development Act of 1974. The Section 8 program in 1980 was the second largest housing program in a country providing over 800,000 units of existing housing.

The strategy for providing housing under the Section 8 program met some difficulty that was not anticipated by its framers, namely: (1) the program ignored the shortage of decent housing that may exist in response to increased demand, (2) it did not take into consideration possible discrimination based on race, sex, number of children, and welfare status, and (3) landlords objected to the "fair market rent" ceilings that were determined by the U.S. Department of Housing and Urban Development (HUD) (Hartman, 1975; Bullard, 1978). The rent ceiling issue became especially critical in those areas where demand for market apartments was high and vacancy rates were low—e.g., in areas experiencing housing shortages.

The historical patterns of racial and economic segregation are often perpetuated by the Section 8 housing program. Black program participants generally secure housing in predominantly black neighorhoods, while white program participants secure housing in neighborhoods where their race predominates. A large share of black Section 8 tenants secure housing in high density lower-income areas where housing is often deteriorating, deficient, and abandoned. Overall, the Section 8 program has had a minimal impact in reversing residential housing segregation (Bullard, 1978, 1984).

Other governmental efforts to expand the housing opportunities for lower and moderate income blacks have achieved mixed results. For instance,

HUD's Regional Housing Mobility Program, Area Housing Opportunity Program, and similar efforts to promote "spatial deconcentration"—limiting the number of subsidized housing units in neighborhoods that have high concentrations of minority and low-income households—have met resistance from both central city blacks and suburban whites. HUD's policy of limiting the number of new subsidized family developments constructed in "impacted" neighborhoods appears to be subsidizing market apartments in urban areas for residents of the suburbs. Barriers to free choice often exist for many central city families who need subsidized housing but must relocate to the suburbs. The problems of informal residency preferences, inadequate transportation, selective marketing techniques, and the lack of an adequate number of large-size apartments (e.g., two to three bedroom units) have restricted the number of families in federally subsidized family developments. As few subsidized family developments are being built in inner-city black neighborhoods, the choice of these residents is limited largely to an *aging* and shrinking housing stock (Bullard and Tryman, 1980b).

Housing Quality

The goal of a "decent home" for every American family has not been realized as a sizable portion of the population continues to be ill-housed. However, the proportion of inadequate housing has declined in the postwar era. Housing analysts often use the availability of complete plumbing systems to measure housing deficiencies. Blackwell (1975: 142) delineated a number of key elements which comprise "decent" housing:

Although standards of decency vary from region to region and from class to class, an acceptable dwelling has certain attributes in common: (1) good physical condition—that is, the dwelling is not dilapidated; (2) the presence of hot running water and a private bath; and (3) adequate space—that is, there is not overcrowding. A dwelling that does not meet these minimum conditions becomes suspect.

Housing quality among blacks improved dramatically between 1940 and 1960. For example, over three out of four units occupied by blacks in 1940 lacked some or all plumbing facilities. The percentage had dropped to one out of every four in 1960 (U.S. Bureau of the Census, 1979: 136). There were over one million black-occupied housing units in 1970 which lacked complete plumbing—hot and cold water, a flush toilet, and a bath or shower for exclusive use of the household. The number dropped to 459,000 in 1980, or a 59 percent decrease. Despite the improvement in housing quality, over 5 percent of black households and 1 percent of white households lived in units which lacked complete plumbing facilities in 1980 (Matney and Johnson, 1983: 23).

The most dramatic improvement in the housing conditions of central city blacks occurred in the 1960s and 1970s, when nearly 20 percent of central city units had been built since 1965. The South was the only region which showed marked differences between black and white housing quality. As late as 1975, over 15 percent of black households and 3 percent of white households in the South had incomplete plumbing facilities. By contrast, only 2 percent of the black and white housing units in the North and West had incomplete plumbing (U.S. Bureau of the Census, 1979: 140; Leigh, 1980: 153; Marshall, 1981: 29).

Inadequate housing is disproportionately clustered in central city neighborhoods where over one-half of all poor black families live. Nearly one-third of all metropolitan housing units are located in central cities, but approximately one-half of all inadequate metropolitan housing units are located there. Housing inadequacy has been increasing in the nation's large urban areas. Nearly 25 percent of all rental units and 20 percent of all owner-occupied units suffer from one or more significant deficiencies. The problem is even more revealing when one compares "high needs" (e.g., many of the snowbelt cities) and "low needs" areas, such as many of the Sunbelt cities. Between one-fourth and one-third of the housing stock in the "high needs" cities are deficient, while less than one-fourth of the occupied housing units in "low needs" cities are deficient (HUD, 1980).

Home Ownership Trend

Home ownership continues to be an integral part of the American dream. The United States has made tremendous strides in the area of promoting home ownership. Prior to World War II, the United States was primarily a nation of renters: only 45 percent of all housing units in the nation at that time were owner-occupied housing. At present, over two-thirds of the nation's households own their homes. The shift from a nation of renters to that of home owners has not been equally distributed across all population subgroups, however. This is particularly true for blacks. Specifically, blacks as a group have not fully shared in the benefits that accrue to the home ownership. Black home ownership rates have continued to lag behind that of whites.

Black home ownership rates have increased over the past four decades. Only 23 percent of black households owned their homes in 1940 as compared to 46 percent of whites. The 1960 home ownership rates increased to 38 percent for blacks and to 64 percent for whites. The two decades following 1960 witnessed the increase in black home ownership to 42 percent in 1970 and to 44 percent in 1980; the corresponding increase for whites were 65 and 68 percent, respectively (U.S. Bureau of the Census, 1983: 20–23). The major factors which contributed to boosting home ownership include rising incomes, high rates of marriage and household for-

Table 4.2
Home Ownership Rates by Census Region, 1980

```
                   Home Ownership Rate (Percent)
                   -------------------------------
                      All
Census Region      Households    Whites    Blacks
-------------      ----------    ------    ------

United States        64.4         67.8      44.4
Northeast            59.0         63.3      31.1
North Central        68.8         71.6      44.1
South                67.0         70.7      50.5
West                 60.3         72.4      39.9
```

Source: U.S. Bureau of the Census (1982)

mation, and federal government programs designed to facilitate home ownership.

Black home ownership is growing at a faster rate than for whites. Black home owners numbered around 2.6 million in 1970 and 3.7 million in 1980, or a 45 percent increase. In contrast, the number of white home owners rose from 37 million in 1970 to 46.7 million in 1980, only 26 percent increase (Matney and Johnson, 1983: 20). Black home ownership rates also vary by region. The rate is highest in the southern United States. The regional differences have existed for some time. The variation in black home ownership by region (North, North Central, South, and West) has actually widened in the past four decades as a result of greater gains made in home ownership by southern blacks. Over 24 percent of blacks in the South owned their homes in 1940 as compared to 19 percent in the North and West. The rates in 1960 showed that 42 percent of Southern blacks and 35 percent of the blacks in the North and West owned their homes. Comparable figures for 1970 reveal that 47 percent of Southern blacks and 36 percent of blacks in the North and West were home owners (U.S. Bureau of the Census, 1979: 136). The 1980 black home ownership rates also varied by region with over one-half of Southern blacks owning their homes; this compares with the black home ownership rate of 44 percent in the North Central Region, 40 percent in the West, and 31 percent in the Northeast region (Table 4.2).

Home ownership rates increased substantially as families moved up the economic ladder. For those blacks who have incomes greater than $20,000, nearly three-fourths own their own homes as compared to the 85 percent home ownership rate for all households with comparable incomes (HUD, 1980: 523). The median income for America's families more than doubled between 1967 and 1979, while the price of homes more than tripled over the same period. The changing housing market has far-reaching impacts on families who would like to realize the dream of home ownership. The nature of housing demand has been altered in recent years as home ownership has become less financially possible for a large segment of the nation's young "nesters" or the "baby boom" generation (Newitt, 1980; Jones, 1980).

Black home ownership in America is inextricably linked to both race and economic conditions. Blacks as a group continue to pay a higher proportion of their income for housing, they are more likely to live in older and/or inadequate residences, and they are less likely to be home owners (Blackwell, 1975: 143; Harris, 1979). The problem of housing affordability is not limited to black households. However, blacks are differentially affected because of their large "underclass" population which is locked in poverty. One-third of the nation's black families and one-half of all white families could afford the average price of a house in 1975 which sold for $36,750. The figures for 1979 show that less than one-fourth of the country's black families and less than one-half of the nation's white families could afford the average house which sold for $57,000. An even smaller percentage of the nation's families could afford the price of a new home in 1979. Only 10 percent of the blacks and 15 percent of whites could afford the average price of a new house in 1979 which sold for more than $70,000 (Clay, 1981: 93).

Much of the new housing constructed in the 1970s occurred in the suburbs with little building taking place in the central cities. Many lower-income and minority neighborhoods were passed over by the housing "boom" of the 1970s. The end result of these market factors have left many black and lower-income areas in a state of incipient decline (Bullard, 1984; Bullard and Pierce, 1979). The demand for one-family homes has resulted in suburban areas obtaining a larger share of new housing construction. Houses constructed in central cities, for example, accounted for 36 percent of new constructions in 1970, but only 29 percent in 1978. This is not a small point since over 60 percent of the nation's blacks lived in central cities in 1980, an increase of 13 percent over 1970 (Matney and Johnson, 1983). Restricting black households to older inner-city neighborhoods reduces their prospects of home ownership; only 36 percent of central city blacks are home owners, while over 50 percent of suburban blacks own their homes.

Black home ownership rates and growth in housing for selected metropolitan areas (e.g., SMSAs with large concentration of blacks) are presented in Table 4.3. Variations are also found in black home ownership rates in

Table 4.3
Home Ownership Rates and Housing Gains in Selected Metropolitan Areas
(SMSAs), 1980

| SMSA | 1980 Home Ownership | | Housing Units | | |
	Total SMSA	Blacks	1980	1970	% Change
New York	31.0	18.4	3,676	3,584	2.6
Chicago	57.3	33.5	2,630	2,294	14.7
Detroit	71.2	52.8	1,590	1,401	13.5
Philadelphia	67.8	53.6	1,757	1,539	14.2
Los Angeles	48.5	39.2	2,854	2,542	12.3
Washington, D.C.	54.3	37.1	1,181	952	24.1
Houston	58.8	47.2	1,160	673	72.4
Baltimore	60.0	36.4	799	657	21.6
New Orleans	53.8	35.2	455	346	31.6
Memphis	60.3	47.3	332	256	29.8
Atlanta	61.4	41.8	769	515	49.2
Dallas-Ft. Worth	62.3	46.6	1,174	810	45.0
Cleveland	64.5	42.7	733	677	8.3
St. Louis	68.2	47.7	895	801	11.7
Newark	56.3	28.3	708	661	7.0
San Francisco-Oakland	53.1	37.6	1,337	1,130	18.3
Birmingham	67.6	52.9	320	254	26.2
Indianapolis	65.2	47.7	451	370	21.9
Milwaukee	60.1	34.5	520	449	15.9
Jacksonville	65.4	54.0	290	174	66.6
Cincinnatti	62.7	35.3	529	454	16.6
Boston	53.2	23.0	1,043	936	11.4
Columbus, OH	60.2	43.3	424	330	28.5
Kansas City	66.4	52.4	530	443	19.5
Richmond	63.6	49.5	241	140	41.7
Gary-Hammond	69.2	52.9	227	193	17.6
Nashville-Davidson	65.1	45.4	319	231	38.4
Pittsburgh	69.0	40.0	874	790	10.7

Source: U.S. Bureau of the Census (1982).

the large metropolitan areas. The highest black home ownership rates were found in the Jacksonville, Philadelphia, Kansas City, Gary, Birmingham and Detroit metropolitan areas. Blacks were least likely to own their homes in the New York, Boston, and Newark metropolitan areas.

The nation's fifty largest metropolitan areas gained over 7.6 million housing units in the 1970s, compared to a population gain of only 6.7 million. The growth of housing units by census region reveals that the South added 2.9 million housing units, the West added 2.5 million units, the North Central region added 1.3 million units, and the Northeast added 859,000 units in the 1970s. While most of the country's metropolitan areas experienced growth in their housing stock in the 1970s, the greatest increase occurred in the South and West. The southern "Sunbelt" is a classic example of this housing boom. Housing construction in many growing cities barely kept pace with the demand for housing. The Houston SMSA, for example, added over 487,000 new housing units in the seventies—a 72 percent increase.

High demand contributed to the spiraling housing costs. The value of owner-occupied housing rose most rapidly in metropolitan areas where demand for home ownership was strongest, namely the South and West. The days of cheap land and cheap mortgages appear to be long gone. Much of the past growth in housing was due primarily to low interest rates, low down payments, and tax incentives for home ownership. The tax incentives have proven to be especially important in the housing market. The federal income tax structure provides a housing subsidy for mainly middle-income owners. This subsidy amounted to over $25 billion in tax credits in 1979; this was more than ten times the $2.5 billion budget for all federal housing subsidy programs (Clay, 1981: 107).

The bulk of the single-family homes which were built in suburbia opened up housing opportunities primarily for whites, higher income households, and former home owners who had accumulated equity capital to finance down payments (Wilson, 1979; Lake, 1979; Bullard, 1983). Recent sub-urbanization data show that some 19 percent of the U.S. blacks live in the suburbs as compared to 43 percent of whites. While blacks have been moving into the suburbs in larger numbers, they comprise only 6 percent of the suburban population in the United States. Blacks who make the move to the suburbs do fare better than their central city counterparts in terms of living in newer and better quality housing, and in upgrading their general housing condition. However, suburban residence by blacks does not au-tomatically translate into home ownership.

The black suburbanization trends reveal the following: (1) black-owned homes are more likely than white-owned homes to shift to renter occupancy, (2) white home buyers are more likely than black home buyers of suburban homes to have equity capital from a previous home sale; and, (3) black-owned suburban homes are more likely than white-owned homes to yield lower equity returns upon transfer to another household (Lake, 1979). Recent trends also show that lower and moderate income blacks are being resegregated in the suburbs. Black suburbanization, in a sense, has often meant successive spillover from black neighborhoods or the extension of the segregated housing pattern which typified the central city (Grier and Grier, 1977; Clay, 1979; Nelson, 1979; Long and DeAre, 1981; HUD, 1981). Many of the problems which have been associated with life in the central city (e.g., crime, crowding, and physical decline of the housing stock) have become problems that more and more suburban residents face in their daily lives (Joint Center for Political Studies, 1982: 62).

Persisting Barriers

While many barriers to decent and affordable housing for black Ameri-cans have been overcome, they still do not enjoy complete freedom in the housing market. Over forty years of federal housing policies, programs, and legislation have not eliminated housing discrimination. Title VI of the Civil Rights Act of 1964 and Title VIII of the Civil Rights Act of 1968 (Fair Housing Act) are two major pieces of federal legislation designed to remove the barriers to free choice in the housing market.

It has been over a decade and a half since the federal Fair Housing Act banned racial discrimination in housing. However, the problems of individual and institutional discrimination remain as major obstacles for many blacks seeking decent housing (HUD, 1979; U.S. Commission on Civil Rights, 1979; Wilson, 1979; Kain, 1979, 1980; Pearce, 1979; Lake, 1981; Taggart and Smith, 1981; Krivo, 1982; Pol and Guy, 1982; Feins and Bratt, 1983; James et al., 1984). Discriminatory practices complicate the housing search for millions of black families. The various forms of discrimination have contributed to the decline of many inner-city neighborhoods and continue to deny a substantial segment of the American society a basic form of wealth accumulation and investment through home ownership.

The practices of refusing to sell or lease housing to blacks, coding records and applications to indicate racial preferences of landlords, selective marketing and advertising, racial steering, redlining, and threats or acts of intimidation are still problems that confront black households in their housing search (HUD, 1979: 69). Fair housing laws have not been enforced by the same means used to obtain compliance with other laws (Taeuber, 1975; Saltman, 1979). Recent efforts to strengthen the Fair Housing Act of 1968 have fallen short. As decent and affordable housing becomes scarce, and as housing markets constrict, discrimination is likely to increase.

Families with children are also encountering problems obtaining decent housing. If a family is black, female-headed, or a large household with children, the chances of being poorly housed increase substantially. This problem is especially acute in the rental market. Over one in four rental units in the United States did not allow children in 1980 compared to one in six units built prior to 1975 (Marans et al., 1980: 71). Exclusionary and restrictive policies against families with children are greatest in recently-constructed housing developments and in high-quality residential areas. The "no children" practices tend to place undue restrictions and limitations on the choices that were available to black and other minority families which tend to be larger than the average family (Greene and Blake, 1980: 34). These exclusionary practices reinforce segregated housing by race, age, and sex (Ashford and Eston, 1979).

Black home seekers generally must expend more time, effort, and resources than whites for the same end (Lake, 1981: 173; Feins and Bratt, 1983: 344). Realtors and lending institutions often serve as "gatekeepers" in distributing residential packages (Pearce, 1979). The number of black home owners would probably be higher in the absence of discrimination by lending institutions. The U.S. Department of Housing and Urban Development (HUD, 1978) documented that affluent blacks—households with

income of $25,000 or higher—were more than twice as likely to be denied
mortgage loans when compared to their white counterparts with similar
assets and economic background. Logan and Schneider (1984) suggest that
discriminatory practices in the housing industry may be declining for blacks
who can afford to move into the suburbs. However, these changes have
little impact on the vast majority of blacks who lived in the nation's central
cities.

Finally, the federal commitment to enforcement of fair housing laws appears to have weakened in recent years. Financial and personnel support to
"rigorously pursue fair housing efforts have been inadequate" (U.S. Commission on Civil Rights, 1979: 230). There is a growing sentiment at the
federal level that special efforts are no longer needed to assure equal opportunity in housing for low-income and minority households. Civil rights
violations in the area of fair housing continue to go uncorrected which
signal a low priority accorded to enforcement of the current laws (U.S.
Commission on Civil Rights, 1979: 6). It is recognized that the federal
government working alone can not eliminate housing discrimination. Efforts
to strengthen federal fair housing laws must include state and local fair
housing agencies and incorporate strong enforcement measures and provisions (James et al., 1984: 142).

Conclusion

The goal of a "decent" home for all Americans has not been achieved.
Federal housing policies have improved the quality of housing and have
stimulated home ownership for millions of Americans. However, many of
the federal policies and programs that were implemented after World War
II had a differential impact on the housing markets for black and white
families. White families have been the primary benefactors of federal efforts
to promote home ownership. Many of the federal housing policies have
subsidized the growth and development of the suburbs which remain largely
white. These policies, at the same time, have accelerated the decline of
America's central cities, which are becoming increasingly black.

The housing conditions for many Americans have been complicated as a
result of spiraling rents and utility costs, high interest rates, and rising
construction costs. Black families must contend with these problems as well
as with individual and institutional housing barriers. Housing discrimination
has not disappeared. However, it is practiced with greater sophistication.
Housing discrimination continues to deny blacks a basic form of investment
(home ownership) and has contributed to the decline of many inner-city
neighborhoods.

Black families can expect less from the government in terms of housing
and home ownership. Blacks in "neartown" inner-city neighborhoods can
expect an intensification in the competition with more affluent "urban pi-

oneers" for a dwindling supply of decent and affordable housing. Sagging housing construction, scarce mortgage money, high interest rates, spiraling energy costs, and soaring utility rates and transportation costs make housing in close-in black neighborhoods even more attractive. The question that remains in the 1980s is plain and simple: Will blacks be able to *preserve* and *reclaim* their neighborhoods?

References

Ashford, D., and P. Eston. 1979. *The Extent and Effects of Discrimination Against Children in Rental Housing*. Santa Monica, Calif.: Fair Housing for Children Coalition.

Blackwell, James E. 1975. *The Black Community: Diversity and Unity*. New York: Harper and Row.

Bullard, Robert D. 1978. Does Section 8 Promote an Ethnic and Economic Mix? *Journal of Housing* 35 (July): 364–65.

———. 1979. Housing and the Quality of Life in the Urban Community: A Focus on Dynamic Factors Affecting Blacks in the Housing Market. *Journal of Social and Behavioral Sciences* 25 (Spring): 46–52.

———. 1980. Black Housing in the Golden Buckle of the Sunbelt. *Free Inquiry* 8 (November): 169–72.

———. 1983. Persistent Barriers in Housing Black Americans. *Journal of Applied Social Sciences* 7 (Fall/Winter): 19–31.

———. 1984. The Black Family: Housing Alternatives in the 80s. *Journal of Black Studies* 14 (March): 341–51.

Bullard, R. D., and Odessa L. Pierce. 1979. Black Housing in a Southern Metropolis: Competition for Housing in a Shrinking Market. *The Black Scholar* 11 (November/December): 60–67.

Bullard, R. D., and Donald L. Tryman. 1980a. Competition for Decent Housing: A Focus on Housing Discrimination in a Sunbelt City. *The Journal of Ethnic Studies* 7 (Winter): 51–63.

———. 1980b. *Housing Mobility in the Houston Metropolitan Area: A Survey of HUD Assisted Family Developments*. A Report Prepared for the HUD. Houston, Texas: Demographic Environs Research Inc.

Clay, Phillip L. 1979. The Process of Black Suburbanization. *Urban Affairs Quarterly* 14 (June): 405–23.

———. 1981. Housing and Neighborhoods. In *The State of Black America, 1981*, edited by National Urban League, 87–118. New York: National Urban League.

Danielson, Michael N. 1976. *The Politics of Exclusion*. New York: Columbia University Press.

Fairchild, Halford, and M. Belinda Tucker. 1982. Black Residential Mobility: Trends and Characteristics. *Journal of Social Issues* 38: 51–74.

Feins, Judith D., and Rachel G. Bratt. 1983. Barred in Boston: Racial Discrimination in Housing. *Journal of the American Planning Association* 49 (Summer): 344–55.

Ford, L., and E. Griffin. 1979. The Ghettoization of Paradise. *Geographical Review* 69: 140–58.

Greene, Jane E., and G. P. Blake. 1980. *A Study of How Restrictive Rental Practices Affect Families with Children.* A Report Prepared for HUD. Washington, D.C.: GPO.

Grier, Eunice, and George Grier. 1977. *Black Suburbanization at the Mid–1970s.* Washington, D.C.: Washington Center for Metropolitan Studies.

Harris, R. A., Jr. 1979. The Applicability of Parson's Theory of Social System to Blacks in Urban Places. *The Journal of Negro Education* 48: 139–48.

Hartman, Chester. 1975. *Housing and Social Policy.* Englewood Cliffs, N.J.: Prentice-Hall.

Houseman, G. L. 1981. Access of Minorities to Suburbs. *The Urban and Social Change Review* 14: 11–20.

HUD (U.S. Department of Housing and Urban Development). 1978. *A New Partnership to Conserve America's Communities: A National Urban Policy.* The President's Urban and Regional Policy Group Report. Washington, D.C.: GPO.

———. 1979. *The Tenth Annual Report of the National Housing Goal.* Washington, D.C.: HUD, Office of Policy Development and Research.

———. 1980. *The President's National Urban Policy Report: 1980.* Washington, D.C.: HUD.

———. 1981. *Annual Housing Survey: 1979: Current Housing Report.* Washington, D.C.: GPO.

James, Franklin J., et al. 1984. *Minorities in the Sunbelt.* New Brunswick, N.J.: Center for Policy Research.

Joint Center for Political Studies. 1982. *Blacks on the Move: A Decade of Demographic Change.* Washington, D.C.: Joint Center for Political Studies.

Jones, Landon Y. 1980. *Great Expectations: America and the Baby Boom Generation.* New York: Ballantine Books.

Kain, John. 1979. Racial Discrimination in Urban Housing Markets and Goals for Public Policy. A paper prepared for the Conference on Blacks, Presidential Politics, and Public Policy. (October). Washington, D.C.: Howard University.

———. 1980. National Urban Policy Paper on the Impact of Housing Market Discrimination and Segregation on the Welfare of Minorities. A paper prepared for the Office of Community Planning and Development, Department of Housing and Urban Development. Cambridge, Mass.: Harvard University.

Krivo, Lauren J. 1982. Housing Price Discrimination: A Comparison of Anglos, Blacks, and Spanish-Origin Populations. *Urban Affairs Quarterly* 17 (June): 445–62.

Kushner, J. A. 1980. *Apartheid in America: An Historical and Legal Analysis of Contemporary Racial Segregation in the United States.* Arlington, Va.: Carrolton Press.

Lake, Robert W. 1979. Racial Transition and Black Home Ownership in American Suburbs. *Annals of the American Academy of Political and Social Sciences* 441 (January): 142–56.

———. 1981. *The New Suburbanites: Race and Housing in the Suburbs.* New Brunswick, N.J.: Center for Policy Research.

Leigh, Wilhelmina A. 1980. Changing Trends in Housing. In *The State of Blacks,*

1980, edited by National Urban League, 149–97. New York: National Urban League.

Logan, John R., and Mark Schneider. 1984. Racial Segregation and Racial Change in American Suburbs, 1970–1980. *American Journal of Sociology* 89: 874–88.

Long, Larry, and Diana DeAre. 1981. The Suburbanization of Blacks. *American Demographics* 3 (8): 16–21, 44.

Marans, Robert W., et al. 1980. *Measuring Restrictive Rental Practices Affecting Families with Children: A National Survey*. A report prepared for the U.S. Department of Housing and Urban Development. Ann Arbor, Michigan: University of Michigan, Survey Research Center.

Marshall, Sue A. 1981. The Community Development Block Grant Program and Unmet Urban Housing Needs. *The Urban League Review* 5 (Summer): 27–34.

Matney, William C., and D. L. Johnson. 1983. *America's Black Population: 1970 to 1982*. Washington, D.C.: GPO.

Morris, William R. 1981. The Black Struggle for Fair Housing: 1900–1980. *The Urban League Review* 5 (Summer): 4–8.

Nelson, Kathryn P. 1979. Recent Suburbanization of Blacks: How Much, Who, and Where? Washington, D.C.: HUD.

Newitt, Jane. 1980. The Future of Home Sweet Home. *American Demographics* 2 (November/December): 17–19.

North, Douglas C., and R. L. Miller. 1973. The Economics of Slum Housing. In *The Economics of Public Issues*, edited by R. L. Miller, and D. North, 138–42. New York: Harper and Row.

Pearce, Diane. 1979. Gatekeepers and Homeseekers: Institutional Factors in Racial Steering. *Social Problems* 26 (February): 325–42.

Pol, Lui, and Rebecca F. Guy. 1982. Discrimination in the Home Lending Market: A Macro Perspective. *Social Science Quarterly* 63 (December): 716–26.

Saltman, Juliet. 1979. Housing Discrimination: Policy Research, Methods and Results. *Annals of the American Academy of Political and Social Sciences* 441 (January): 186–96.

Schiller, Bradley R. 1980. *The Economics of Poverty and Discrimination*. Englewood Cliffs, N.J.: Prentice-Hall.

Tabb, William K. 1970. *The Political Economy of the Black Ghetto*. New York: W. W. Norton and Company.

Taeuber, Karl. 1975. Racial Segregation: The Persisting Dilemma. *Annals of the American Academy of Political and Social Sciences* 422 (November): 87–96.

———. 1983. Racial Residential Segregation, 28 Cities, 1970–1980. CDE Working Paper, University of Wisconsin-Madison (March).

Taeuber, Karl, and Alma F. Taeuber. 1965. *Negros in Cities: Residential Segregation and Neighborhood Change*. Chicago: Aldine.

Taggart, H. T., and K. W. Smith. 1981. Redlining: An Assessment of the Evidence of Disinvestment in Metropolitan Boston. *Urban Affairs Quarterly* 17: 91–107.

U.S. Bureau of the Census. 1979. *The Social and Economic Status of the Black Population in the United States: An Historical View, 1790–1979*. Washington, D.C.: GPO.

————. 1982. *State and Metropolitan Data Book 1982.* Washington, D.C.: GPO.

————. 1983. *America's Black Population 1970 to 1982: A Statistical View.* Washington, D.C.: GPO.

U.S. Commission on Civil Rights. 1970. *Home Ownership for Lower-Income Families: A Report on the Racial and Ethnic Impact of the Section 235 Program.* Washington, D.C.: GPO.

————. 1979. *The Federal Fair Housing Enforcement Efforts.* Washington, D.C.: GPO.

Wilson, Franklin D. 1979. *Residential Consumption, Economic Opportunity, and Race.* New York: Academic Press.

5

Housing Policy and Suburbanization: An Analysis of the Changing Quality and Quantity of Black Housing in Suburbia since 1950

Christopher Silver

Introduction

Suburbanization has been a process associated with urban growth since the nineteenth century (Singleton, 1973). In the past four decades, however, the excessively rapid pace of suburbanization has transformed the entire fabric of metropolitan life in the United States. The sum effect of this metamorphosis has been the "urbanization of the suburbs" or, as Muller (1981: x) puts it, the creation of an "outer city." According to Muller (1981: x), this "outer city" boasts not only the greatest share of the metropolitan populace but has all but "eliminated the regional economic dominance of the central city by attracting a critical mass of leading urban activities to relocate to the outer ring." Recently released evidence from the 1980 census indicates that the migration from city to suburbs and nonmetropolitan areas during the 1970s far exceeded the rate during the 1960s. The overall net migration loss for cities was 13 million of which 10 million persons were absorbed by the suburbs (Tucker, 1984). Moreover, the decentralization phenomenon affected some of the older fringe suburban communities and housing conditions, bestowing upon them demographic characteristics previously associated with deteriorating core city communities (Long and DeAre, 1981).

In the wake of this metropolitan demographic development and changing housing conditions, the suburbs have taken on a new and diverse social character not in keeping with traditional perceptions. Berry's (1973) concept of a "mosaic culture" in which homogeneous communities persist to offer residents distinctly different lifestyles still supplies an accurate portrayal of suburban society. Yet increasingly observable in the population mix of suburbs are black exiles from the center city. As Maxwell (1979) in a *Wall Street Journal* feature article noted, "Much Like Whites, Many Blacks Move Out to the Suburbs."

Nevertheless, the available evidence suggests that the progress made by blacks and other minorities in penetrating the suburbs must be regarded as a mixed success. One indication of a continuing disparity between white and black gains through suburbanization is the resegregation of blacks in suburbia along racial lines as rigidly drawn as in the urban core. Increased housing costs, the absence of services needed by low-income families, and the prospects of encountering white hostility also have posed a dilemma for blacks seeking to join the suburban stream in search of a better living environment. In addition, the movement of the black middle class to the suburbs has been viewed by some black leaders as potentially undermining recently acquired political power in the center city, especially in the face of white gentrification in selected core city neighborhoods.

The purpose of this chapter is to examine the dynamics of black suburbanization and its impact on black housing conditions since the 1950s. A number of issues flow from this general inquiry, such as: (1) to what extent has black suburbanization involved households in various income groupings; (2) is there a pattern of black suburbanization indicative of a segregation process or greater dispersion; and, (3) to what extent has public policy, most notably in the area of publicly assisted housing, fostered greater economic and racial diversity in suburbs. While drawing upon an abundant literature to sketch an historical overview of black suburbanization, six metropolitan areas—Atlanta, Chicago, Houston, Philadelphia, Richmond, and San Diego—are used as case studies to examine regional and inter-metropolitan variation in closer detail.

Demographic Trends since the 1950s

The enormous attention riveted on black suburbanization beginning in the late 1960s has tended to obfuscate the fact that since the 1930s there has been a steady increase in the number of blacks living in the suburbs of the nation's largest cities. Connolly (1973: 93) noted that "blacks have always lived within the suburban community, though often segregated by race and status from the white community." Schnore et al. (1976) contended that although the principal destination of blacks migrating from rural areas was the center city, the nonwhite population growth rate in the rings of the nation's twelve largest SMSAs after 1930 was far higher than that of whites—362.7 percent for blacks against 58.4 percent for whites. Yet, even with the sizable gain in the proportion of blacks since 1930, Schnore et al. (1970) concluded that the suburbs appeared to remain predominantly white, particularly because the modest growth in the black suburban population occurred largely in segregated suburban pockets.

Between 1950 and 1970, the proportion of suburban black population grew approximately from 4.1 to 4.8 percent, with the greatest growth occurring in the 1960s when 800,000 blacks entered suburbia (Guest, 1978; Muller, 1981). A vast out-migration of whites, coupled with a continuation of the flow of rural blacks to the central city diluted the statistical effect of this surge in black suburbanization, however. This can be seen from the modest growth in the proportion of urban blacks residing in suburbia between 1960 and 1970—from 15.1 to 16.2 percent. The flow of blacks from suburbs to the city helped, in part, to sustain an annual rate of increase of 2.97 percent in the center city black population during the 1960s, while the suburban black population, during the same period, grew at an annual rate of 2.53 percent (Lake, 1981: 16). Yet, the outward movement of blacks from the center city marked the 1960s as a watershed in the evolution of the metropolis.

The 1970s witnessed a significant acceleration of the black suburbanization process. The number of suburban blacks grew from 4.2 million in 1970 to 6 million by 1980. The proportion of blacks in suburbia increased in 44 out of the 50 largest SMSAs during the decade. Two factors are significant to note here. First, five of the six largest SMSAs where the proportion of blacks living in suburbs declined during the 1970s were in the Sunbelt area. As Frey (1978) noted, the population redistribution process at work in suburbs in the South tended to decrease the black suburban percentage more in that region than in any other. In the South, as well as in the West, a tremendous increase in white suburbanites coupled with continued black out-migration overshadowed otherwise significant increases in black suburban residents. Secondly, a total of twenty-three large SMSAs experienced less than 0.5 percent increase or no change at all in the proportion of black suburbanites during the 1970s. Three of these "no change" metropolitan areas—Albany, New York, Providence, Rhode Island, and Columbus, Ohio—represented the older industrial northeastern metropolitan areas. On the other hand, Newark, Chicago, Baltimore, St. Louis, and Cleveland experienced substantial absolute and relative increases in their black suburban population. Thus, in metropolitan areas plagued by central city housing decay, blacks joined whites in the march to the suburbs.

It may also be noted that the annual increases in black suburbanization fluctuated throughout the decade. Clark (1979) shows that the annual increase in black suburban migration reached a high of 4.5 percent during the 1970–1974 period, but fell to 3.8 percent during the years 1974–1977. The financial crisis in the housing market during this period may help to explain the downturn in black suburbanization. Reverse migration was also at work. From 1975 to 1978, Clark (1979: 24, 57) noted that 780,000 blacks moved from the central city to the suburbs. However, a simultaneous reverse flow sent 409,000 blacks to the central city, leaving a net gain of only 371,000 new suburban blacks. Clearly, the rate of black in-migration to central cities declined in the 1970s and blacks showed an increasing proclivity to choose the suburbs as a residence where better housing was available. Moreover, the variations in black suburbanization rates in the major urban areas serve as a further indication of the volatile nature of the movement during the 1970s (Nelson, 1979: 27). The suburbs in the 1970s were "a new racial frontier" but the process of black suburbanization was "more than a transient phenomenon" (Lake, 1981: 26).

Regional Variations

Intermetropolitan variation in the rate of black suburbanization reflected noteworthy regional dissimilarities in the migration patterns. Pendleton (1973) observed that the population base for potential suburbanization determined the degree of change during the 1960s. The greatest increase occurred in the West where the suburban portion of the metropolitan population increased from 25.6 to 29.5 percent by 1970, but where the overall black urban population was smallest. Black suburbanites increased from 11.6 to 12.8 percent in the North Central region; from 14.2 to 14.8 percent in the South, and remained constant at 18.7 percent in the Northeast during the 1960s (Pendleton, 1973: 173). These regional variations persisted into the 1970s. In certain metropolitan areas, in the South in particular, the 1970s witnessed a dramatic decline in black suburban proportions.

As Guest (1978) observed, the macro trends by region fail to provide a sufficient measure of the change taking place in neighborhoods or communities. His nine-part typology of suburban communities classified according to the mix and direction of racial occupancy between 1950 and 1970 underscores the variation in suburbanization by regions. Guest (1978) found that in 76 percent of the cases examined, the dominant white community remained most prominent in the North, as compared to 41.7 percent of the cases in the South. Only 7.0 percent of the suburban communities in the North, and 2.8 percent in the South exhibited traits of the invasion-succession process from 1950 to 1970. Numerous communities (10.7 and 16.1 percent in the North and the South, respectively) experienced simultaneous increases in blacks and whites.

Using eleven metropolitan areas drawn from various regions, Pendleton (1973) surmised that migration to the suburbs does make a positive difference for blacks, but to a much lesser extent than for whites. Only in the South did he find an appreciably high incidence of substandard black housing in the suburbs, owing to remnants of black rural residences being incorporated into an expanding metropolitan fabric.

Ghettoization of Suburbs

A major concern in the assessment of black suburban migration has been the extent that patterns of center city racial residential segregation have been transplanted along the urban fringe. Studies of black suburbanization covering the 1950s and 1960s contend that the central city ghetto social structure reemerged in the suburban context (Sutker and Sutker, 1974). Rose (1976) argues that in the case of Cleveland, black suburbanization followed two distinct spatial patterns that pushed the center city ghetto into the adjacent suburbs—black colony segregated by race and income in the industrial satellite cities, and the spillover from the expansion of the center city ghetto. Connolly's (1973) comparative analysis of ten large SMSAs during the 1960s substantiated the pervasiveness of these patterns. More recently, Lake and Cutter (1980) expanded the typology of black suburban settlements to six distinctive forms. This typology included not only the black colony and spillover models but also the metropolitan rural enclave, the subsidized housing community, the industrial-commercial mixed community, and the outer industrial community. The common attribute of all forms of black suburbanization is that it "tends to follow administrative boundaries in that the black suburban community grows within a defined area over time rather than spreading out randomly throughout the suburbs" (Stahura, 1983: 422).

Evidence from the 1970s suggests a continuation of segmented residential patterns along racial lines but within the context of a broader dispersion of black households in the suburbs. Marshall's (1982) study of 56 SMSAs with 20,000 or more blacks living in the center city showed that affluent blacks in the 1960s sought out suburbs "with many of the characteristics of ghetto areas, such as low quality housing." Farley et al. (1978) found that blacks in Detroit preferred racially mixed neighborhoods and were willing to move to these if there were no overt signs of white hostility. Lake (1981) confirms that in New Jersey suburbs in the 1970s, the largest increases in black suburbanites occurred in spillover communities, and those where there has been substantial subsidized housing construction.

Housing Policy and Black Suburbanization

The demographic transformations of the 1960s and 1970s that augmented black representation in suburbia did not occur in a public policy vacuum. Nor did they in the preceding era when blacks were virtually locked out of the newly-developing suburbs. From 1930s through the early 1960s, racially tinged housing policy flowed from the nation's capital to localities to ensure black exclusion from the suburbs. The discriminatory practices of the Federal Housing Administration through its mortgage insurance program and through segregation in public housing site selection have been fully documented.

The Kerner Commission (1968) report decried the effects of racial residential segregation, and the exclusion of blacks from better housing in the suburbs. It called for a massive infusion of federal funds for low income housing construction and rehabilitation outside the center city ghetto and enactment of an open housing law to end discrimination in the sale and rental of housing. Passage of the Fair Housing Act in 1968, coupled with new programs for production of subsidized housing, most notably the Sections 235 and 236 programs, signaled a new willingness to use housing policy to foster racial and economic integration in the central city and in the suburbs. The overall scale of subsidized housing construction from 1961 to 1977 indicates that there was no cessation of activity during President Nixon's administration. A total of 1.93 million subsidized units were started during this period, with an annual high of 188,000 occurring in 1970. This contrasts with only 33,000 subsidized housing units that started in 1960 (Murray, 1983: 592). Suburban communities absorbed a notable share of subsidized housing during the 1970s even though the general climate, as Danielson (1976) shows, was one of overt hostility.

In the face of hostility to open housing, Downs's *Opening Up the Suburbs* (1973) offered a rationale for socioeconomic and racial integration in the suburbs based upon a combination of enlightened self-interest and social justice. His strategy revolved around the concept of limited, controlled residential integration (to ensure the preservation of white middle-class dominance) through incentives to private housing developers and communities accepting a fair share of low-income housing. The Housing and Community Development Act of 1974 embraced the spirit of the Downs's proposal through the Section 8 subsidized housing program. Section 8 combined production incentives with consumption subsidies to foster new construction aimed at low and moderate income families (Solomon, 1974). By the early 1980s, the Section 8 program had become the nation's second largest low-income housing program (second to public housing program) with over one million units in the inventory. By 1980, the U.S. Department of Housing and Urban Development (HUD) was able to claim that three-quarters of new and rehabilitated Section 8 units were located outside of traditional ghetto areas. According to Cho and Puryear (1980), the distribution of Section 8 units was fundamentally different from that of previous low-income housing programs in that they were evenly distributed between cities and suburbs and across regions.

The limited effectiveness of federal housing initiatives in bringing about integration in the suburbs was not simply owing to white opposition to large-scale subsidized housing projects. A more important factor was that little of the low and moderate income housing being built in the suburbs ultimately benefited blacks. According to a 1980 HUD-sponsored study of subsidized housing in Boston, Houston, Detroit, St. Louis, New York, and Richmond, blacks made up only 18 percent of the residents in suburban projects. Even though HUD required a fair housing market plan to qualify for Section 8 subsidies, only eight of sixty projects investigated actively marketed for minority residents (Rodrique and Flourney, 1985). Thus, while subsidized housing represented a distinctly new feature on the suburban landscape during the 1970s and early 1980s, its relationship to increased black suburbanization was not so clear-cut (Jakubs, 1982).

Limited success also has characterized enforcement of the federal Fair Housing Act. Based simply upon the caseload of fair housing litigations, the federal law and complementary state and local ordinances have challenged a range of discriminatory practices in housing. As Clark (1982: 143) points out, one of the most sweeping decisions regarding an attempt to deny low-income access to the community came in the 1980 *United States v. City of Parma*, involving a predominantly white suburb of Cleveland. The *Parma* decision extended the scope of the 1976 Supreme Court decision in *Hills v. Gautreaux*, which found that HUD sanctioned the Chicago Housing Authority to restrict low-income housing to one segment of the housing market—the city—to the exclusion of the suburbs (Clark, 1982: 140). Use of the Section 8 program outside the city to achieve residential dispersion of low-income housing was the remedy arrived at by the court. Yet as Welfeld (1980) noted, the *Gautreaux* decision was no remedy to the existing patterns and practices. A weakening of political support for a policy of dispersion in Congress in the early 1980s, coupled with the cessation of new Section 8 construction, precluded effective implementation of the court mandate (Clark, 1982: 144). Thus, federal housing policy alone has not been a remedy to black exclusion from the suburbs. Rather, a combination of housing policy and market forces have engendered black dispersion in the last decade.

Case Studies

Data from Atlanta, Chicago, Houston, Philadelphia, Richmond, and San Diego suggest that black suburbanization accelerated in the past two decades. Clearly, interregional and intermetropolitan variations overshadow any consistent national trends apart from a steady absolute increase in the number of black suburbanites. Atlanta and Chicago exemplify the disparities in the black suburbanization process. Between 1960 and 1980, the black population in Chicago's suburbs increased three-fold, whereas in suburban Atlanta the growth was nearly five hundred percent. The suburban share of Atlanta's metropolitan black population grew from 19 percent in 1960 to 43 percent in 1980. By contrast, the suburban proportion of Chicago's blacks grew only from 9 percent in 1960 to 16 percent in 1980.

Table 5.1
Black Population outside Dominant Central City for Selected SMSAs in 1960,
1970, and 1980

SMSA	Total Black Population			% Black Total SMSA		
	1960	1970	1980	1960	1970	1980
Atlanta	45,010	85,581	215,915	19	28	43
Chicago	77,517	128,299	230,826	9	10	16
Houston	31,314	65,831	88,474	13	17	15
Philadelphia	142,064	190,509	245,527	21	23	28
Richmond	15,394	25,475	69,786	14	19	40
San Diego	4,972	9,067	26,752	13	15	26

Source: U.S. Bureau of the Census (1963, 1972, 1983).

The disparity is even more considerable when one takes into account the
sizable rural-to-urban migration of blacks in the Atlanta SMSA during this
period. As Table 5.1 shows, the major suburban gains made by blacks in
Chicago occurred in the 1970s, whereas in Atlanta they were spread over
the two decades. Smaller gains were recorded for blacks in suburbs of
Houston and Philadelphia during the 1970s. In Houston, the suburban
segment of the metropolitan black population actually declined during the
decade. Richmond and San Diego more closely approximate the Atlanta
pattern.

A closer examination of the suburbanization process in Chicago since
1950 reveals that black out-migration did not necessarily represent an escape
from ghetto housing conditions. Suburbanization of blacks in Chicago must
be viewed against a longstanding tradition of minority residence in the
industrial satellite cities that surround the central city. Black neighborhood
conditions in these satellite cities closely approximate those in the most
deteriorated sections of central Chicago (Felbinger, 1984). Yet it was into
these deteriorated suburban pockets that most blacks migrated during the
1960s. The initiation of a metropolitan open housing movement in the late
1960s did promote a wider dispersal of blacks throughout Chicago's suburbs. In 1968 alone, 353 units were occupied by blacks in suburban Chicago's communities that previously had resisted integration (Berry, 1979:
63). Yet the near doubling of Chicago's black suburban population in the
1970s reflected not only increased access to more affluent neighborhoods,

Table 5.2
Suburban Black Families with Income below Poverty Level for Selected SMSAs,
1970 and 1980*

	Number of Black Families		% Below Poverty	
SMSA	1970	1980	1970	1980
Atlanta	11,490	51,243	26	18
Chicago	26,671	52,335	13	16
Houston	13,360	19,941	35	18
Philadelphia	40,366	56,677	18	19
Richmond	5,390	14,838	19	13
San Diego	1,060	5,610	21	17

* Includes black families residing in center cities located
  in SMSA but beyond the corporate boundaries of the dominant
  city.

Source: U.S. Bureau of the Census (1972, 1983).

but also the suburbanization of poverty. As it may be seen in Table 5.2, suburban black families below poverty level increased from 26,671 in 1970 to 52,335 in 1980. Also, in the Philadelphia SMSA, the absolute and the relative size of suburban blacks below poverty level increased between 1970 and 1980. While this can be explained in part by black increases in the declining industrial suburbs, there is also evidence that poverty in the black belt of the inner city spilled over into other suburban communities.

The growth in black renters offers a further clue to suburbanization of poverty. Outside of Chicago, for example, the majority of blacks were renters in 1980, whereas in 1960 and 1970, the majority were home owners. In Philadelphia, the proportion of black home owners declined from 54 to 53 percent during the 1970s. In all six study areas, the increase in black renters exceeded the growth rate in black home owners in the suburbs during the 1970s (Table 5.3).

There was a decline in the proportion of suburban blacks in Chicago who paid less than 80 percent of the metropolitan median rent between 1970 and 1980, thereby suggesting either a more affluent black population, an increase in the availability of housing subsidies, or the absence of low cost housing. When compared to 1960 figures, there was actually a slight proportional increase in blacks paying rents 80 percent or less of the SMSA median rent by 1980. During this same period, the proportion of black

Table 5.3
Black Housing Units outside Dominant City for Selected SMSAs in 1960, 1970, and 1980

	1960		1970		1980	
SMSA	Owner	Renter	Owner	Renter	Owner	Renter
			Number			
Atlanta	4,060	5,908	6,921	6,330	32,136	34,485
Chicago	8,750	8,371	16,086	14,239	32,883	33,819
Houston	6,137	1,987	11,335	5,380	16,511	8,614
Philadelphia	18,293	16,439	26,976	22,549	40,461	35,567
Richmond	2,230	1,004	4,588	1,336	12,286	6,010
San Diego	844	1,459	500	865	1,953	5,517
			Percent			
Atlanta	41	59	52	48	48	52
Chicago	51	49	53	47	49	51
Houston	76	24	68	32	66	34
Philadelphia	53	47	54	46	53	47
Richmond	69	31	77	23	67	33
San Diego	37	63	37	63	26	74

Source: U.S. Bureau of the Census (1963, 1972, 1983).

suburbanites who owned homes valued at 80 percent or less of the median value increased from 58 to 64 percent. Moreover, blacks who lived in suburban Chicago were predominantly poor or of moderate income. In 1960, 85 percent of black families outside of Chicago had incomes 120 percent or less of the median income. By 1980, the proportion of suburban black families above 120 percent of the SMSA median income rose to 34 percent, thereby demonstrating an appreciable increase in the number of affluent blacks. Still, two-thirds of black suburban families could be classified either as moderate or low income in 1980.

The 1983 Annual Housing Survey shows a narrowing of the income gap between whites and blacks in suburban Chicago as a result of recent migration but it also shows the persistence of racial disparities in housing conditions. The median income of black suburban homeowners ($31,400)

Table 5.4
Year Structure Built of Owner-Occupied Housing Units in Non–Central City in Selected SMSAs by Race and Year

SMSA Year/Race	Year Structure Built				
	April 70 or Later	1965 to March 70	1960–64	1959 or Earlier	Total
Atlanta, 1982					
Black	7,400	8,900	7,100	8,700	32,100
Non-black	123,700	47,800	35,700	62,600	269,800
% black	23	28	22	27	100
% Non-Black	46	18	13	23	100
Chicago, 1983					
Black	7,900	4,200	4,900	23,200	40,200
Non-Black	228,000	123,200	118,000	493,900	963,100
% Black	22	10	12	56	100
% Non-Black	23	13	12	52	100
Houston, 1983					
Black	9,900	2,600	1,600	7,600	21,700
Non-Black	263,300	55,800	32,400	97,100	448,600
% Black	45	12	8	35	100
% Non-Black	59	12	7	22	100
Philadelphia, 1982					
Black	7,900	3,000	6,700	20,300	37,900
Non-Black	134,200	66,600	77,100	421,500	699,400
% Black	21	8	18	53	100
% Non-Black	19	10	11	60	100
San Diego, 1982					
Black	400	400	na	400	1,200
Non-Black	86,000	31,400	27,100	71,000	215,500
% Black	33	33	na	34	100
% Non-Black	40	15	12	33	100

na: Data not available

Source: HUD, and U.S. Bureau of the Census (1984a, 1984b, 1984c, 1985a, 1985b).

was only slightly less than that of suburbanites as a whole ($34,500). Although three-quarters of the black households moved into their 1983 dwelling after 1970, most of these structures had been built prior to 1960. A negligible number of blacks secured a share of the 53,300 new housing units built in suburban Chicago after 1979 (Table 5.4). Blacks secured only 600 of the 20,100 rental units erected in the suburbs. Thus, blacks remained outside the new housing market despite possessing incomes that were sufficient to absorb the cost. The disparity between whites and blacks in the value of suburban housing in 1983 also suggests the failure of suburbanization to redress shelter deficiencies. The median value of black owner-occupied suburban homes in 1983 was $55,500 while for the suburbs as a whole it was $78,200.

Black suburbanization in Chicago since 1970 demonstrates the static condition of housing patterns in a discriminatory market. The income profile of black suburbanites, the age and value of their housing, and limited dispersal into newly-built residential communities suggests that central city neighborhood patterns were transferred to the suburbs. In suburban Chicago during the 1970s and 1980s, there was an unloosening of the white noose that previously gripped the suburbs. Poor, center city blacks moved into selected suburban locations and secured better housing than that found in the city (but still inferior to that of suburban whites).

In contrast, the experience in metropolitan Atlanta in the 1970s radically altered traditional racial residential patterns. Prior to 1950, black presence in suburban Atlanta was largely a holdover of rural blacks. Over the next three decades, Atlanta's center city black community grew by 162,000 as a result of rural-to-urban migration. With the current exodus of whites, blacks became a majority of the city population in the early 1970s and soon acquired political dominance. More than 130,000 blacks were added to Atlanta's suburban communities during the 1970s, a growth rate greater than that of Chicago. Black penetration into suburban Atlanta occurred in part as a spillover of the ghetto. But what was most significant was that the suburban black population grew faster than that of the city during the decade (Thomas, 1984: 26), with the suburbs accounting for 43 percent of the total SMSA black population by 1980. The Atlanta metropolitan area, therefore, represents a unique case of black dominance in the center city where the majority of metropolitan black population may soon reside outside of the center city.

Thomas's (1984: 26) analysis of census tract data for 1970 and 1980 confirms that Atlanta's blacks "left more densely populated areas for the relatively spacious suburbs." Thus, black housing quality improved, as reflected in the incidence and value of owner-occupied units. Thomas (1984: 26) found that "blacks are not moving solely to neighborhoods of poor housing that just happen to be outside the central city boundaries." Nevertheless, a sectoring process by race remained a feature of suburbanization in this southern metropolis.

Black suburbanization produced greater social change in Atlanta than in Chicago between 1960 and 1980. Eighteen percent of Atlanta's black suburban families had incomes below the poverty line in 1980 (16 percent in Chicago). In Atlanta's suburbs, this represented a decline from 26 to 18 percent between 1960 and 1980. During this same period, black renters in Atlanta's suburbs declined from 59 to 52 percent. Most significantly, the proportion of black renters with units costing 80 percent or less of the median metropolitan rent declined appreciably—from 33 to 18 percent. In suburban Chicago, the decline was slight. The proportion of suburban blacks in Atlanta with an income in excess of 120 percent of the metropolitan median increased dramatically from 5 to 29 percent. While still less than that of blacks in suburban Chicago in 1980, the explosive growth of the black middle-class in Atlanta's suburbs during the 1970s demonstrates the dynamic quality of black suburbanization (Tables 5.2 and 5.3).

The 1982 Annual Housing Survey shows a greater disparity in the income of black and white home owners in Atlanta as compared to Chicago. Moreover, the gap between the value of black-white owner-occupied suburban housing in Atlanta was only slightly less than that in Chicago. The age of housing in Atlanta's black suburbanites suggests that conditions were significantly better in the southern metropolis. Only 27 percent of Atlanta's suburban home owners, as compared to 56 percent in Chicago, lived in units built prior to 1960. And, in Atlanta 51 percent lived in housing erected after 1964, as compared to 32 percent in Chicago (Table 5.4).

The difference in the age of housing was even more marked among black suburban renters. Overall, black home owners in Atlanta secured a modest (5 percent) share of the 65,500 housing units built after 1978, as compared to only one percent in Chicago. But the Annual Housing Survey data underscore the dynamic quality of black suburbanization in Atlanta over the past two decades that has resulted in narrowing the racial gap.

The remaining four study areas represent variations of the dynamic-Atlanta and static-Chicago models. In Richmond, the black suburbanization pattern closely resembles that of Atlanta, especially in the share of the SMSA's black population residing outside the center city (40 percent). In 1960, among the six SMSAs studied, Philadelphia had the largest proportion of blacks (21 percent) living in the suburbs. But, the relative size of black suburbanites in the Philadelphia SMSA remained constant over the followng two decades. By contrast, the suburban share of Houston's black population declined between 1970 and 1980. Finally, San Diego exemplified the western urban pattern of substantial proportional gains through black suburbanization, but within the context of a relatively small base of center city black community. In certain respects, San Diego affords a third model of black suburbanization because of its marked difference from both Atlanta and Chicago in the quality of black housing in the inner city. Black suburbanization in San Diego pushed the center city ghetto into the eastern fringes of the metropolis. Ford and Griffin (1979) indicate that barriers to black in-migration into white neighborhoods left an expansive and physically attractive area east of the central business district open to the black community. The "new ghetto" consisted of newly-built suburban style housing along the urban fringe, equal in quality to that for whites, but at more affordable prices. Although blacks moved into all-white areas in various parts of suburban San Diego during the 1970s, only 18 percent of the city's black population lives outside of the southeast sector which extends well into the suburban fringe.

Despite the attractiveness of new center city black neighborhoods, the growth rate of blacks outside the city since 1950 has been phenomenal. From a small base of 1,632 in 1950, San Diego's black population grew to 26,752 by 1980. In contrast to Atlanta and Chicago, San Diego's suburban black community consists largely of renters (74 percent). Income differentials may explain the preponderance of black renters in suburban San Diego. Seventy percent had incomes of 120 percent or less of the SMSA median in 1980—a smaller proportion than that in suburban Chicago. In addition, blacks secured only a limited number of newly-built rental units in San Diego's suburbs, but gained an impressive share (1,300 units) of owner-occupied units in the city.

Data derived from HUD inventories of subsidized housing in the six SMSAs offer an additional measure of the *opportunity* for suburbanization among low and moderate income black households. There has been no systematic effort to determine whether subsidized housing has benefited blacks, although available evidence suggests that the bulk of low and moderate income residents in suburban assisted housing have been drawn from the nonblack pool already living outside the center city (Rodrique and Flourney, 1985). Yet as Downs (1973) contends, increasing the opportunities for low income residents in suburbia while at the same time challenging discriminatory real estate practices is likely to benefit blacks over the long term. The critical question from this perspective is whether subsidized housing programs in the past two decades have enhanced the *opportunity mechanism*.

Available data on the Section 221(d)(3), Section 202, and Section 236 program indicate that between 1968 and 1978, there was considerable housing development in four of the six SMSAs studied. In Chicago, for example, subsidized housing was concentrated in the older industrial suburbs. Only a few Section 236 projects constructed in the late 1970s found their way into scattered sites. In Atlanta, 24 out of 31 projects were located in either Decatur, Jonesboro, or Marietta, thereby contributing to the concentration of low-income urban families in selected suburban locations. More than one-third of the subsidized units in suburban Philadelphia were built in a single township. Only in the case of San Diego, there was a wide dispersion of subsidized housing in suburbs. Its 35 projects (4,411 units) were scattered throughout 14 separate suburban communities. In Richmond and Houston, however, there was simply minimal participation in the subsidy program. Given the size of Houston's center city black population and the rapid expansion of the suburbs, its 730 units of Section 236 housing and 120 units of 221(d)(3) over the ten-year period suggest how vigorously its suburbs resisted integration along either race or class lines (Table 5.5).

In its involvement in the Section 8 program from 1976 to 1985, however, Houston exceeded both Richmond and San Diego, but fell considerably short of comparably-sized metropolitan areas to the north. Whereas Hous-

Table 5.5
Section 221 (d)(3) and Section 236 Housing Constructed outside Dominant Central City for Selected SMSAs, 1968–1978

SMSA	Section 221(d)(3)*		Section 236	
	No. of Project	No. of Units	No. of Project	No. of Units
Atlanta	9	769	22	2,782
Chicago	19	2,317	24	3,888
Houston	1	120	4	730
Philadelphia	4	613	12	2,411
Richmond	0	0	na	936
San Diego	3	746	32	3,665

* Also includes Section 202 for elderly units.

Source: HUD (1985a).

ton added 4,071 Section 8 units to its suburbs, Atlanta added 5,100 units, and Chicago and Philadelphia registered gains of just over 12,000 units each. What is significant to note in the cases of Atlanta, Chicago, and Philadelphia, however, is that between 45 and 52 percent of their new subsidized units were designed for the elderly. In other words, the Section 8 program enabled suburbs to increase their stock of subsidized units while ensuring that they could be filled largely with white needy clients. The Section 8 data indicate that there was a significant dispersion after 1976 of subsidized housing into suburban communities that previously had resisted economic and racial integration (Table 5.6). Due to the lack of data on racial occupancy in suburban subsidized housing, it is impossible to determine precisely whether the increased *opportunities* have translated into benefits for blacks. The impression, however, is that the incidence of black suburbanization through federal housing assistance has been minimal.

Conclusion

The process of black suburbanization since the 1950s has brought about a discernable demographic redistribution of blacks in most major metropolitan areas by opening up the moderate and middle income neighborhoods

Table 5.6

Non–Central City Section 8 Housing Units—New Construction, Rehabilitated,
Existing, and Mod-Rehabilitation, 1976 through June 30, 1985

SMSA	No. of Projects	Nonelderly Total Units	Elderly	% Elderly
Atlanta [a]	69	3,561	1,590	45
Chicago [b]	100	7,904	4,137	52
Houston [c]	33	3,047	1,024	34
Philadelphia [d]	87	8,038	4,005	50
Richmond	na	3,090	253	8
San Diego [e]	22	1,950	593	30

a: Includes Section 8 projects initiated by center city housing
    agency in non–central city areas.

b: Excludes 5 projects in Elgin (538 units, of which 100 are
    for elderly), and 4 projects in Joliet (585 units, of which
    134 are for elderly). Also includes Section 8 projects
    initiated by center city housing agency in non–central city
    areas.

c: Excludes 5 projects in Pasadena (335 units, of which 220 are
    for elderly). Also, includes Section 8 projects initiated by
    center city housing agency in non–central city areas.

d: Excludes 8 projects in Camden, N.J. (1,358 units, of which 576
    are for elderly). Also includes Section 8 projects initiated
    by center city housing agency in non–central city areas.

e: Excludes 2 projects in Chula Vista (119 units, of which 110
    are for elderly). Also includes Section 8 projects initiated
    by center city housing agency in non–central city areas.

na: Data not available

Source: HUD (1985a, 1985b; VHDA, 1985).

to black occupancy. The gap between the black and white communities persists, however. Federal housing policy since the 1960s has played a role in fostering race and class dispersion in the suburbs, although available evidence suggest that the full potential of the Fair Housing Act of 1968 and various housing subsidy programs has not been realized. It is clear that segregated racial residential patterns continue to characterize the suburbs even as large numbers of more affluent blacks join the center city exodus. It is also clear that the dynamics of the local housing market dictate the variations in the pace and scope of black entry into white suburban communities across the country. Yet as this analysis has suggested, the suburban *opportunities* in both publicly assisted and private housing have fostered social changes that have redounded to the benefit of blacks, particularly since 1970. Assuming that the trends of the past decade persist, there is a basis for cautious optimism that black suburbanization will continue to reduce urban racial disparities. Pursuing housing and neighborhood improvements rather than residential integration appears to be a more realistic objective of the suburbanization process over the next decade.

As a general assessment, the quality and quantity of black housing in suburbia have grown appreciably since 1950. Certainly the past fifteen years have witnessed an accelerated movement of blacks from deteriorated city neighborhoods to better quality housing along the urban fringe. When black suburbanization is examined within the context of metropolitan development in various parts of the nation, however, there is less basis to state that qualitative improvement in housing has been a universal experience. Even more affluent black migrants have been limited in their entry to newly constructed communities, settling instead for housing filtered through former white occupants. Blacks have not secured a share of new housing units commensurate with their population growth in suburbs. Even among the substantial number of poor blacks that have joined the migration to the suburbs, the increasing quantity of subsidized units largely has been closed off to them. Resegregation in the suburbs has perpetuated the qualitative inferiority of black housing as compared to that of whites. It would seem that the dispersal of increasingly larger numbers of blacks into white communities in selected metropolitan areas has opened doors that can only lead to future qualitative and quantitative gains. In the final analysis, however, if the current trends continue, the urbanization of the suburbs will most likely result in the maintenance of segregated residential patterns in the new urban frontiers.

References

Berry, Brian J. L. 1973. *Human Consequences of Urbanization: Divergent Paths in the Urban Experience of the Twentieth Century.* New York: St. Martin's.

———. 1979. *The Open Housing Question: Race and Housing in Chicago, 1966–1976.* Cambridge: Ballinger.

Cho, Yong Hyo, and David Puryear. 1980. *Distressed Cities: Targeting HUD Programs.* In *Urban Revitalization,* edited by Donald Rosenthal, 191–210. Beverly Hills, Calif.: Sage.

Clark, Thomas A. 1979. *Blacks in Suburbia: A National Perspective.* New Brunswick, N.J.: Rutgers University, Center for Urban Policy Research.

———. 1982. Federal Initiatives Promoting the Dispersal of Low Income Housing in Suburbs. *Professional Geographer* 34: 136–46.

Connolly, Harold X. 1973. Black Movement into Suburbs: Suburbs Doubling Their Black Population During the Sixties. *Urban Affairs Quarterly* 9: 91–111.

Danielson, Michael N. 1976. *The Politics of Exclusion.* New York: Columbia University Press.

Downs, Anthony. 1973. *Opening Up the Suburbs: An Urban Strategy for America.* New Haven: Yale University Press.

Farley, Reynolds, et al. 1978. Chocolate City, Vanilla Suburbs: Will the Trend Towards Racially Separated Communities Continue? *Social Science Research* 7: 319–44.

Felbinger, Clair L. 1984. Economic Development or Economic Disaster?: Joliet, Illinois. In *Urban Economic Development,* edited by Richard D. Bingham and John P. Blair. Beverly Hills, Calif.: Sage.

Ford, Larry, and Ernst Griffin, 1979. The Ghettoization of Paradise. *Professional Geographer* 69: 140–58.

Frey, William H. 1978. Black Movement to Suburbs: Potential and Prospects for Metropolitan-Wide Integration. In *The Demography of Racial and Ethnic Groups,* edited by Frank D. Bean and W. Parker Frisbie, 79–117. New York: Academic Press.

Guest, Avery. 1978. The Changing Racial Composition of Suburbs: 1950–1970. *Urban Affairs Quarterly* 14: 195–206.

HUD (U.S. Department of Housing and Urban Development). 1985a. *Multifamily Insured and Direct Loan Information System.* Unpublished Data (in the form of computer printouts), obtained from HUD, Housing Information and Statistics Division, Central Office. Washington, D.C.

———. 1985b. *Subsidized Housing Inventory.* Unpublished data (in the form of computer printouts), obtained from HUD, Housing Information and Statistics Division, Central Office. Washington, D.C.

HUD (U.S. Department of Housing and Urban Development) and U.S. Bureau of the Census. 1984a. *Housing Characteristics for Selected Metropolitan Areas: Atlanta, Ga. SMSA.* Annual Housing Survey 1982. Current Housing Reports H–170–82–21. Washington, D.C.: GPO.

———. 1984b. *Housing Characteristics for Selected Metropolitan Areas: Philadelphia, Pa-NJ. SMSA.* Annual Housing Survey 1982. Current Housing Reports H–170–82–33. Washington, D.C.: GPO.

———. 1984c. *Housing Characteristics for Selected Metropolitan Areas: San Diego, Ca. SMSA.* Annual Housing Survey 1982. Current Housing Reports H–170–82–38. Washington, D.C.: GPO.

———. 1985a. *Housing Characteristics for Selected Metropolitan Areas: Chicago,*

Il. *SMSA.* Annual Housing Survey 1983. Current Housing Reports H–170–83–22. Washington, D.C.: GPO.

————. 1985b. *Housing Characteristics for Selected Metropolitan Areas: Houston, Tx. SMSA.* Annual Housing Survey 1983. Current Housing Reports H–170–83–49. Washington, D.C.: GPO.

Jakubs, John F. 1982. Low-Cost Housing: Spatial Deconcentration and Community Change. *Professional Geographer* 34: 156–66.

Kerner Commission. 1968. *Report of the National Advisory Commission on Civil Disorder.* New York: New York Times Company.

Lake, Robert. 1981. *The New Suburbanites: Race and Housing in the Suburbs.* New Brunswick, N.J.: Rutgers University, Center for Urban Policy Research.

Lake, Robert, and Susan C. Cutter. 1980. Typology of Black Suburbanization in New Jersey since 1970. *Geographical Review* 70: 167–81.

Long, Larry, and Diana DeAre. 1981. The Suburbanization of Blacks: 1980 Census Trends. *American Demographics* 3: 16–21.

Marshall, Harvey. 1982. Black and White Upper-Middle Class Suburban Selection: A Causal Analysis. *Pacific Sociological Review* 25: 27–57.

Maxwell, Neil. 1979. Black Flight: Much Like Whites, Many Blacks Move to the Suburbs. *Wall Street Journal* (20 August) 1, 29.

Muller, Peter O. 1981. *Contemporary Suburban America.* Englewood Cliffs, N.J.: Prentice-Hall.

Murray, Michael P. 1983. Subsidized and Unsubsidized Housing Starts, 1961–1977. *Review of Economics and Statistics* 65: 590–97.

Nelson, Kathryn P. 1979. *Recent Suburbanization of Blacks: How Much, Who, and Where.* Washington, D.C.: HUD, Office of Policy Development and Research.

Pendleton, William. 1973. Blacks in Suburbs. In *The Urbanization of the Suburbs,* edited by Louis H. Masotti and Jeffrey K. Hadden. Beverly Hills, Calif.: Sage.

Rodrique, George, and Craig Flourney. 1985. Separate and Unequal: Illegal Segregation Pervades Nation's Subsidized Housing. *Dallas Morning News* (10–17 February).

Rose, Harold M. 1976. *Black Suburbanization: Access to Improved Quality of Life or Maintenance of the Status Quo?* Cambridge, Mass.: Ballinger.

Schnore, Leo F., et al. 1976. Black Suburbanization, 1930–1970. In *The Changing Face of the Suburbs,* edited by Barry Schwartz, 69–94. Chicago: University of Chicago Press.

Singleton, Gregory H. 1973. The Genesis of Suburbia: A Complex Historical Trend. In *The Urbanization of the Suburbs,* edited by Louis H. Masotti and Jeffrey K. Hadden, 29–50. Beverly Hills, Calif.: Sage.

Solomon, Arthur P. 1974. *Housing the Urban Poor: A Critical Evaluation of Federal Housing Policy.* Cambridge, Mass.: MIT Press.

Stahura, John M. 1983. Determinants of Change in the Distribution of Blacks across Suburbs. *Sociological Quarterly* 24: 421–33.

Sutker, Solomon, and Sara S. Sutker, eds. 1974. *Racial Transition in the Inner Suburb: Studies of the St. Louis Area.* New York: Praeger.

Thomas, Robert H. 1984. Black Suburbanization and Housing Quality in Atlanta. *Journal of Urban Affairs* 6: 17–28.

Tucker, C. Jack. 1984. City-Suburban Population Redistribution: What Data from the 1970s Reveal. *Urban Affairs Quarterly* 19: 539–49.

U.S. Bureau of the Census. 1963. Census of Population and Housing, 1960: Census Tracts. *Atlanta, Chicago, Houston, Philadelphia, Richmond, and San Diego SMSAs.* Washington, D.C.: GPO.
———. 1972. Census of Population and Housing, 1970: Census Tracts. Final Report PHC(1)–14 *Atlanta*, Ga. SMSA; PHC(1)–43 *Chicago*, Il. SMSA; PHC(1)–89 *Houston*, Tx. SMSA; PHC(1)–159 *Philadelphia*, Pa. SMSA; PHC(1)–173 *Richmond*, Va. SMSA; PHC(1)–188 *San Diego*, Ca. SMSA. Washington, D.C.: GPO.
———. 1983. Census of Population and Housing, 1980: Census Tracts. Report PHC80–2–77 *Atlanta*, Ga. SMSA; PHC80–2–119 *Chicago*, Il. SMSA; PHC80–2–184 *Houston*, Tx. SMSA; PHC80–2–283 *Philadelphia*, Pa.-NJ. SMSA; PHC80–2–302 *Richmond*, Va. SMSA; PHC80–2–320 *San Diego*, Ca. SMSA. Washington, D.C.: GPO.
VHDA (Virginia Housing Development Authority). 1985. *Subsidized Housing Inventory: Housing Opportunities Made Equal.* Unpublished data obtained from VHDA, Richmond, Virginia.
Welfeld, Irving. 1980. The Courts and Desegregated Housing: The Meaning (if any) of the Gatreaux Case. In *Housing Urban America*, edited by Jon Pynoos, Robert Schafer, and Chester Hartman. Chicago: Aldine.

6

The Housing Conditions of Black Female-headed Households: A Comparative Analysis

Jamshid A. Momeni

It is axiomatic that America will attain neither national maturity nor un-
qualified international respect until minority groups share, in actuality, our
cherished and vaunted democratic way of life. Still on the list of problem
areas where inequities exist is the field of housing for minority groups.

Hubert M. Jackson, 1958

In 1949, the U.S. Congress proclaimed the national goal of "a decent home
and suitable living environment for every American family." Housing quantity, quality, discrimination, and affordability have been the major areas of
concern in the past thirty years for Americans in general, and minorities in
particular. As several chapters in this book document, since the enunciation
of the national housing goal the nation has significantly succeeded in solving
the housing problems of the 1940s and the 1950s by eliminating both severe
shortages and substandard units.

Despite the achievements, however, there is much more to be done if the
national goal of a decent home and living environment for every American
family is to be fully realized. By all standards of measurement, a substantial
disparity in housing conditions by race, ethnicity, and income persists, pointing to the relative deprivation of certain socioeconomic groups in the society.
Davis (1967) states: "Too many people in our country are badly housed.
According to the 1960 census, 10.6 million units of the 58.3 million housing
units were considered substandard.... Except where aided by grants or
subsidies, the *poor* [emphasis mine] of the nation are found in substandard
housing." The U.S. Commission on Civil Rights (1971: vii) pointed out the
following:

The national housing goal has not been achieved for all Americans nor have the benefits of homeownership been made equally available to all. For the nation's poor, decent housing often has been beyond their means.... As of 1970 nearly two out of every three white families owned their own homes, but only two out of every five black families were homeowners. For this group of Americans the national housing goal remains largely a shadowy slogan without substance.

Manning Marable, a black sociologist, as recently as March 30, 1985 wrote: "The heart of the great American Dream has for generations been the ownership of a home." Marable (1985) emphasizes that while 67 percent of whites were home owners by the late 1970s, the "black Americans' dreams have generally been deferred in this area. Barely one in five black families owned their own homes from 1890 through World War II. During the 1960s and 1970s, however, the percentage of black home owners doubled up to 44 percent in 1975." Black female householders (BFHHs) are a growing minority. In 1970, 34.7 percent of black households were headed by women. By 1980 their proportion had risen to 43.7 percent—a full nine percentage point increase. In terms of absolute numbers, BFHHs increased from 2,161,000 in 1970 to 3,751,000 in 1980.

Female householders (FHHs), in general, and BFHHs, in particular, are among the most poorly housed groups in the United States. Statistics published by the U.S. Department of Housing and Urban Development (HUD) affirm this contention. According to HUD (1978:12), "the poor female headed household has 1 chance in 5 (.2) of being inadequately housed." Donna Shalala, assistant secretary for Policy Development and Research, stated: "The households of black and Hispanic women have considerably greater chances of being inadequately housed than the total population does. And we estimate that female heads of household, no matter what their race or ethnic background, must pay inordinate fractions of their incomes for housing adequate to their needs. There is much to consider; much to be done" (HUD, 1978: Foreword).

The purpose of this chapter is to examine the housing conditions of the BFHHs, and assess the changes/trends in recent years. The analysis will include an examination of differentials in adequacy, quality, affordability, and home ownership by the BFHHs. Relative to future trends, expected demographic factors that affect housing shall be examined. The data for this study are partly drawn from the 1970 Public Use Samples and the 1980 Public Use Microdata Samples. We have also utilized relevant published census data whenever such information were available. The unit of analysis is household (a group of people, related or unrelated, who live in the same housing unit more than 50 percent of the time) as opposed to a family. Relative to the method of analysis, we have controlled for tenure (owner v. renter), household type, household size, structure type, and race.

Geographic Distribution

The geographic distribution of the black female-headed households by regions and divisions for 1970 and 1980 follow (U.S. Bureau of the Census, 1972, 1983):

Regions/Divisions	1970	1980
I. North	22.8	21.9
1. New England	1.8	2.0
2. Middle Atlantic	21.0	19.9
II. North Central	20.1	21.2
3. East North Central	16.8	18.1
4. West North Central	3.3	3.1
III. South	49.0	48.4
5. South Atlantic	25.7	26.8
6. East South Central	10.7	9.9
7. West South Central	12.6	11.7
IV. West	8.1	8.6
8. Mountain	0.7	0.8
9. Pacific	7.4	7.8

About 23 percent in 1970, and 22 percent of all black female-headed households in 1980 were in the North; 20.1 percent in 1970, and 21.2 percent in 1980 were in the North Central region; 49.0 percent in 1970, and 48.4 percent in 1980 resided in the South; the West, with 8.1 percent in 1970 and 8.6 percent in 1980, housed the smallest proportion of the black female-headed households. Four of the nine divisions namely, the Middle Atlantic, East North Central, South Atlantic, and West South Central divisions, housed more than three quarters of the BFHHs both in 1970 (76.1 percent) and in 1980 (76.5 percent). The South (region) plus the Middle Atlantic and East North Central divisions housed nearly nine out of every ten black female-headed households both in 1970 and 1980.

As these data indicate, there was only a small shift in the geographic distribution of the black female-headed households between 1970 and 1980. For example, in 1970, the five divisions with the highest proportion housed 86.8 percent of all BFHHs; the same geographic divisions in 1980 housed 86.4 percent of all BFHHs. The minor difference between the two years could very well be due to sampling variability. Nevertheless, between 1970 and 1980, the Northern and the Southern regions lost some of their BFHHs to the North Central and West regions.

Location

Discussions on metropolitan and nonmetropolitan, or central city living relate to limited choice in location. Dahmann (1985: 511) states: "Conventional wisdom tells us that the quality of residential environment declines with increasing size of settlements and with increasing centrality within settlements. The perception that large settlements and inner-city neighborhoods provide residential environment *that are less than desirable* [emphasis mine] is both long standing and widespread." This contention is supported by popular and scholarly accounts in the past and in recent years. According to Dahmann (1985), during the 1970s the United States witnessed a restructuring of its settlement pattern (system) towards deconcentration and suburbanization. Central city areas often represent units occupied by persons in service works, laborers, or those who had received no more than elementary education; and most housing units are rented units in old and dilapidated structures. As pointed out by Berry and Kasarda (1977: 221), older cities often bear the stamps of "obsolescence, high density, high industrialization, and aging inhabitants." Gorham and Glazer (1976: 5) point out that "housing is more than shelter. It is fixed in a neighborhood. The place and the neighborhood supplement the shelter of the house by meeting other needs and desires: personal security, information, access to jobs, credit, friends, as well as standard public services. It is infinitely more difficult to improve neighborhoods than it is to improve shelter."

In 1970, 87.3 percent of all black female-headed households were located in the urban areas. By 1980, this proportion had risen to 90.3 percent. The proportion residing in the central city component of the urban areas also increased from 64.5 percent in 1970 to 65.4 percent in 1980. These statistics show that black female-headed households today are more likely to be found in the central city locations. The increased concentration of the black female-headed households in the urban areas on the one hand, and in the central city component on the other hand, is regarded as having a worsening impact on their housing conditions during the intercensal period. Many observers have alluded to the fact that city-to-suburb migration is closely related to the personal income of the residents. Those with higher income have a much greater flexibility in choice of residential location than those with limited income, who are socially and economically forced to be confined to the central city location (Berry and Kasarda, 1977: 221). If central city location is any indicator of housing quality, it certainly points to the increased plight of the black female-headed households, the majority of whom not only are confined to the inner city location, but whose concentration in the central city has increased between the two censuses.

Aside from the metropolitan–nonmetropolitan or central city/suburban location, structure type is an important variable, for there is a wide black–

white differential in the socioeconomic and demographic features and housing conditions of those residing in various structure types (Momeni and
Brown, 1986). The following data from the Public Use Samples show the
pattern of occupancy of the BFHHs in 1970 and 1980, by structure type
(U.S. Bureau of the Census, 1972, 1983):

Structure Type	Number		Percent	
	1970	*1980*	*1970*	*1980*
1 family unit, detached	9,102	13,749	43.2	37.0
1 family unit, attached	1,686	3,591	8.0	9.7
2 family building	2,512	3,874	11.9	10.4
3–4 family building	2,152	3,509	10.2	9.5
5–9 family building	1,745	3,273	8.3	8.8
10–19 family building	1,464	2,890	7.0	7.8
20–49 family building	1,067	2,009	5.1	5.4
50 or more family building	1,222	3,668	5.8	9.9
Mobile home or trailer, etc.	104	551	0.5	1.5

According to the 1980 census, about two-thirds of all year-round housing
units in the United States are single family homes (54 million one family,
detached units, and 3.5 million one-family, attached units). The proportion
of BFHHs living in single-family housing (SFH) units, however, is far less
than the national average.

As the above data show 43.2 percent of all BFHHs (owner- and renter-
occupied units combined) in 1970 and only 37.0 percent in 1980 lived in
one-family, detached housing units. Another 8.0 percent in 1970, and 9.7
percent in 1980 were in the one-family, attached units (town- or row-
houses). That is, a total of 51.2 percent in 1970 and 46.7 percent in 1980
resided in the SFH units. The mere fact that two-thirds of all housing units
in the United States are SFH units is an indication of preference for such
units. According to the foregoing statistics, between 1970 and 1980, the
proportion of BFHHs (and thus, households) residing in the SFH units not
only did not increase, but declined from 51.2 to 46.7 percent.

Between 1970 and 1980, the relative proportion of BFHHs living in
mobile homes and/or trailers (the cheapest form of housing) tripled—from
0.5 to 1.5 percent. It is also interesting to note that the relative proportion
of BFHHs in buildings with 50 or more housing units nearly doubled—5.8
percent in 1970 to 9.9 percent in 1980.

As to the number of stories in a building, 88.7 percent of the BFHHs in
1970 and 87.8 percent in 1980 lived in buildings with 1 to 3 stories; the
remaining 11.3 percent in 1970 and 12.2 percent in 1980 lived in buildings
with 4 or more stories. If buildings with 13 or more stories are defined as

"high rise" apartment buildings, then the proportion of the BFHHs in such structures increased from 1.8 percent in 1970 to 3.4 percent in 1980.

Socioeconomic and Demographic Characteristics

It is contended that black female householders do not have the economic power necessary to enable them to secure adequate housing. Thus, it is important to examine the socioeconomic and demographic factors which may act as strong predictors of home ownership and housing condition.

Economic Status

As indicated earlier, the inner city residence of the majority of the BFHHs is associated with their economic conditions. Table 6.1 contains data on selected socioeconomic and demographic variables of households in 1980 by tenure, household type and size, and race for those residing in the *detached* SFH units. As it may be noted from the data, the black female-headed householders had significantly lower median income than whites. Among owners, in the multi-person category, the median income for black female householder was $11,200 annually, as compared to $21,700 for all white householders. Among renters, the median income for the black female head of a multi-person household was $6,500 as compared to $9,900 for her white counterpart, or $13,300 for all white renters. Among renters, in the one-person householder category, the median income was only $3,300 for BFHHs as compared to $13,300 for all white householders.

Relative to the level of poverty, data reveal that depending on household size (multi- or one-person), 19.1 (all black households) to 63.3 percent of BFHHs' income in 1979 was below poverty. The parallel figures for white householders ranged only between 6.5 and 35.5 percent, pointing at the significantly high degree of economic deprivation among the BFHHs. BFHHs in general, and renters in particular, are at the bottom of income stratum. Today, even an annual income of $15,000 is not enough for a multi-person household to pay rent and maintain the unit, let alone enabling the householder to purchase adequate housing. The income of BFHHs, with majority below $10,000 annually, is definitely not enough to pay rent and keep up with the needed repairs. Investigators have indicated that a major factor in the deterioration of rental housing is the tenants' growing inability to take care of the property, or their inability to pay the landlord enough rent to save the unit from ruin. While the purchasing power or the real income has either declined or has remained constant during the past years, rents have gone up. As a result, even the rental housing situation of many low income households has taken a serious turn for the worse.

Table 6.1
Selected Socioeconomic and Demographic Characteristics of Householders: Single Family Detached Units, 1980

SE/D Chars.*	Owner-Occupied			Renter-Occupied		
	All House-holds	Multi-Person FemHH*	One-Person FemHH*	All House-holds	Multi-Person FemHH*	One-Person FemHH*
Median Income ($1000s)						
White	21.7	15.0	6.4	13.3	9.9	4.9
Black	15.6	11.2	4.1	7.6	6.5	3.3
Percent Below Poverty						
White	6.5	13.2	22.5	18.4	34.2	35.5
Black	19.1	29.2	49.8	43.3	57.0	63.3
Percent HHs 16+ Years Old in Labor Force						
White	73.7	60.1	31.1	77.2	66.0	43.3
Black	69.0	60.7	35.7	61.1	52.9	35.6
Percent HHs* 16+ Year Old in Manag./Prof. Occupations						
White	29.9	25.4	26.5	20.5	19.6	27.0
Black	16.2	18.8	22.4	9.0	9.6	11.8
Median Age of Householders						
White	50.5	51.8	69.0	35.8	35.4	64.2
Black	50.5	49.6	66.8	42.5	38.3	63.2
Median No. of Years of School Completed, HHs 16+ Years Old						
White	12.6	12.4	12.1	12.4	12.3	11.4
Black	11.8	11.8	9.3	10.3	11.0	8.1

* FemHH: Female householder, no husband present;
  HHs: householders; SE/D Chars.: Socioeconomic and
  Demographic Characteristics

Source: U.S. Bureau of the Census (1984a).

Labor Force Participation and Occupational Status

Income, labor force participation (LFP), and occupation are often used as three objective criteria determining social class. In the previous paragraphs it was shown that BFHHs had, on the average, a much smaller annual income than an average white householder. It is a truism that income, the LFP, and occupational status are highly interrelated. Thus, as it may be predicted, the lower income of the BFHHs is associated with lower rates of employment (or higher unemployment rates) and lower occupational status.

Table 6.1 shows the percent of householders sixteen years of age and older in the labor force. As predicted, the LFP rate is much lower for the FHHs in general, and for the BFHHs, in particular. For example, among owners, the proportion in labor force was 60.7 percent for the BFHHs as compared to 73.7 percent for the total white population—that is, a difference of 13.0 percentage points. The gap is even wider if we compare the one-person black female householders with the average white householders. As a glance at Table 6.1 indicates, the rate for the one-person female householders is less than one half of the rate for the total white population. The differences in the LFP rate may be summarized as follow: (a) the LFP rate of the FHHs, regardless of race and tenure, is substantially lower than that for the total white population; and, (b) the LFP rate of the one-person householders is generally lower than the LFP rate of multi-person householders.

Due to the lack of space, we cannot present detailed data on occupational status of the BFHHs. Thus, we have chosen to present data only relative to those in managerial and professional occupations as an indicator of occupational status. Table 6.1 provides such data by tenure, household type and size, and race. These data reveal a significantly lower occupational status for the BFHHs than any other category shown in the table. The rate is much lower among renters than among owners. Among owners, nearly 30 percent of all whites, as compared to 18.8 percent of the BFHHs in the multi-person category, were in the managerial and professional occupations.

Median Age

Age is an important variable. It is, for example, positively associated with income, occupational status, and tenure since older individuals have had more time than younger people to purchase their own home. As it may be noted from the data in Table 6.1, generally speaking, the median age of renter-occupied householders, regardless of race, household size or type, is lower than the median age of owners. There is a significant difference between median age of householders in the multi- as opposed to one-person householders—while the former is in the mid to upper 30s among renters, the median age for the latter category is in mid to upper 60s among owners.

A third major difference is that, on the average, BFHHs are somewhat younger than white householders. This is not an unexpected finding, because of lower age at marriage, and thus earlier family formation among blacks than whites.

Level of Education

Black female householders are generally less educated than all female householders, or their white counterparts. The overall educational attainment of the BFHHs in 1970 and 1980 follows (U.S. Bureau of the Census, 1972, 1983):

Level of Education	1970	1980
Never attended school	2.6	1.1
Elementary school	39.5	22.9
High school	48.4	53.3
More than 12 years of formal schooling	9.5	22.7

As these figures show there was a significant increase in the level of education of the BFHHs during the intercensal period. The proportion with more than 12 years of education (beyond high school) rose from 9.5 in 1970 to 22.7 percent in 1980—a 2.4-fold increase.

Despite this increase, however, the level of education attained by the BFHHs lagged behind the educational attainment of their white counterparts to a significant degree. A cursory examination of these data in Table 6.1 points to the wide disparity in educational attainment of the BFHHs and their white counterparts or the total white population. As it may be noted, among home owners, the median number of years of school completed by the BFHHs was 9.3 years (less than high school), as compared to 12.1 years (above high school) for their white counterparts or 12.6 years for the total white population. Among renters, the gap was even wider—8.1 years for BFHHs as compared to 11.4 years for their white counterparts—that is, more than 3 years difference in the median number of years of education completed.

Marital Status

Marital status is often associated with the person's status as a householder. Female householders are often individuals who are separated, divorced, or widowed. There is a significant differential in the marital status of the female householders, as compared with all householders combined. Statistics on separation, divorce, and widowhood are often used as a measure (or index) of family disorganization. As described by Momeni (1984: 41), for the white population of the nation as a whole in 1980, 21.4 percent of the female population age 15 and older were either separated, divorced, or widowed; the corresponding figure for blacks was 30.5 percent. Based on aggregate data, in 1970 the marital status of the BFHHs were: married, spouse absent, 3.9 percent; widowed, 38.1 percent; divorced, 15.1 percent; separated, 26.0 percent; never married, 16.9 percent. That is, 79.2 percent were either separated, divorced, or widowed. In 1980, the parallel figures were: now married, 8.4 percent; separated, 18.5 percent; widowed, 27.5 percent; divorced, 20.0 percent; never married, 25.7 percent, with the sum of separated, divorced, and widowed equal to 66 percent. These data show that about eight-tenths (0.8) of the black female householders in 1970 and nearly seven-tenths (0.7) in 1980 were either separated, divorced, and/or widowed. During the ten-year period, the relative size of the index of family disorganization declined by 13.2 percentage points; but this was primarily due to the substantial increase in the proportion of "never married" householders in 1980 (25.7 percent as compared to 16.9 percent in 1970). That is, the decline is due to the shift in the proportion never married in the 1970s, when a large number of eligible men and women remained single and thus were not subjected to the risk of becoming separated, divorced, or widowed.

The 1980 census data reveal that the great majority of the female householders, including blacks, were either separated, divorced, or widowed. It was also interesting to note that the index of family disorganization was much higher among owners than among renters, both in black and white groups. As an example, for BFHHs, the index was 86.4 percent among home owners as against 70.6 percent among renters in 1980.

Number of Own Children

A child is defined as a son, daughter, stepchild, or adopted child of the householder irrespective of the child's age or marital status. Using the Bureau of the Census definition, the term "own children" refers to sons and daughters, including stepchildren and adopted children of the householder, who are single (never married) and under 18 years old. Larger numbers of children are often associated with lower socioeconomic status. Researchers have tested this hypothesis using both national and crosscultural data, and the findings appear to consistently show an inverse association between these two variables. Parcel (1982: 206), states: "Concerning number of children, the negative sign [negative or inverse association] suggests either that the presence of children in a white family hinders housing investments, or that larger families must take out larger mortgages which result in lower accumulation of housing assets."

The data from the 1980 census lend support for the above hypothesis. Among home owners, 56.1 percent of all black married couples and 47.9 percent of the BFHHs in the multi-person households had children of their own. The corresponding figures for whites were 50.1 and 41.2 percent, respectively. Among renters, a significantly higher proportion both in the black and white groups had children of their own. For instance, 70.1 percent of BFHHs in the multi-person households and 60.0 percent of white female householders in the multi-person households had children of their own. These data lend support for the hypothesis that the presence of children may hinder home ownership. The data also show a higher dependency load for BFHHs which results in hindering housing investment. Or, if the investment is made, due to the necessity of taking up larger mortgages, it will result in lower home equity.

Housing Quality and Quantity

Every housing unit has a quantitative and qualitative dimension. Indexes of quality deal with some aspects of the dwelling unit structures, and micro-neighborhoods. Housing quality is difficult to measure. But it may be defined as the total of some bundles of structural characteristics and services consumed by the urban households. Kain and Quigley (1970: 532) concluded that "the quality of the bundle of residential services has about as much effect on the prices of housing as such objective aspects as the number of rooms, number of bathrooms, and lot size."

Home Value

Value is usually measured by the respondent's estimate of how much the property (house plus lot plus neighborhood) would sell for, if it were for sale on the day census questionnaires were completed. As pointed out earlier, in buying housing, "families jointly purchase a wide variety of services at a particular location. These include a certain number of square feet of living space, different kinds of rooms, a particular structure type, [interior design], an address, accessibility to employment, a neighborhood environment, a set of neighbors, and a diverse collection of public and quasipublic services including schools, garbage collection, and police protection" (Kain and Quigley, 1970: 532). Many researchers have attempted to devise statistical estimates of the contribution of these individual attributes to the total payment (rent or purchase price), but as pointed out by some researchers, the complexity of the subject matter has prevented most researchers from arriving at any viable estimate. "Difficulty in measuring the physical and environmental quality of the dwelling unit and surrounding residential environment is perhaps the most vexing problem encountered in evaluating the several attributes of bundles of residential services. These problems are so serious that the U.S. Bureau of the Census omitted all measures of dwelling quality from the 1970 housing census" (Kain and Quigley, 1970: 532). However, the actual "market value" of a unit provides an overall estimate of housing quality (the dollar value of the house plus the lot plus the micro-environmental quality).

Homes occupied by blacks have a much smaller average value than those occupied by whites. The following are the values of owner-occupied housing units by race and place of residence in 1980 in thousands of dollars (U.S. Bureau of the Census, 1984a).

Place of Residence	All Races	White	Black
United States	55.8	57.3	33.8
Female householders	43.0	45.1	27.2
Inside SMSAs	61.0	62.7	36.4
Female householders	47.6	50.1	29.5
Central cities of SMSAs	53.2	56.4	33.0
Female householders	42.1	45.6	27.9

The above figures reveal that an average house owned by a black in the United States in 1980 was worth about $23,500 less than an average housing unit owned by whites. As for the BFHHs, the average value was 47.5 percent of the value of an average house owned and occupied by whites in the United States. Inside the SMSAs, the average value of a house owned by a BFHH was worth only 47.0 percent of an average house owned and occupied by whites inside the SMSAs; and, in the central cities of SMSAs, the average value of a housing unit owned by a BFHH was 49.5 percent of the value of an average house owned and occupied by whites in the central cities of SMSAs. These figures clearly show the wide disparity in the average value of owner-occupied housing units by race and place of residence. Assuming that these differences reflect the combined differentials in micro-environment and the quality/quantity of the structure itself, then, black home owners in general, and BFHHs, in particular, live in much lower level housing and neighborhoods than do whites.

Home Ownership

A housing unit is regarded as "owner-occupied" if the owner (or co-owner) lives in the unit, regardless of the mortgage status. Any unit not classified as "owner-occupied," is classified as "renter-occupied," regardless of the method of payment of rent (in cash or in kind). Social scientists interested in the relationship between social status and race have looked at some variables indicative of social class position. In such studies, however, the use of annual income and occupational status have overshadowed the use of financial holding and the asset accumulation, such as home equity, which should play a major role in determining the economic power and the social standing of the families. Some studies (Lampman, 1959; Kolko, 1962), however, have emphasized the need and the importance of wealth accumulation through home ownership and home equity as a significant factor in determining one's social and economic position. Henretta and Campbell (1978), Parcel (1982), and Jackman and Jackman (1980, reprinted in this book) discuss various benefits of home ownership and argue that asset accumulation is an important aspect of social and economic status, and that the differential in home investment by race significantly contributes to the difference in wealth, and thus, social class.

The following data show the pattern of home ownership in 1980 and 1970 for blacks and *all* female householders (U.S. Bureau of the Census, 1972, 1983).

	Black FHHs		**All FHHs**	
Tenure	*1970*	*1980*	*1970*	*1980*
Owner-occupied	30.2	33.6	46.9	49.0
Rented (cash)	66.2	64.4	49.4	48.8
Rented (no cash)	3.0	2.0	2.8	2.2
Cooperative or condominium	0.6	0.0	0.8	0.0

These data show that the proportion of owner-occupied units by the BFHHs increased from 30.2 percent in 1970 to 33.6 percent in 1980—a small, but nonetheless modest increase in homeownership. The data also show that the chance for a black female householder to own a home is one half of that of an average white householder. Similar intercensal gain is registered for *all* female householders (2.1 percent). But the 1980 data show a wide discrepancy in home ownership between BFHHs and all female householders—33.6 vs. 49.0 percent in 1980. To investigate black home ownership, Kain and Quigley (1972) developed models relating the probability of home ownership to socioeconomic status of a sample of 401 blacks and 784 whites in the St. Louis metropolitan area and concluded that after controlling for several independent variables, housing market discrimination limits black home ownership. Jackman and Jackman (1980) examined black-white differences in home ownership and concluded that "the probability of homeownership is considerably lower for blacks than it is for comparable whites, throughout the United States," and that black-owned homes outside the South were "worth considerably less than the homes of comparable whites." The above data confirm Jackman and Jackman's findings.

Year Structure Built (Age)

The age of the housing unit is an indicator of the quality of housing. It is a factor causing decay and dilapidation. In addition, older structures often do not have the kind of equipment (e.g., gas line, dishwasher, garbage disposal, etc.) that are placed in the newer buildings as standard equipment.

Based on the 1970 census data, 52.1 percent of BFHHs, as compared to 51.3 percent of all female householders, lived in units built in 1939 or earlier—i.e., in units 30 or more years old. However, the figures for 1980 were 47.3 percent for blacks, as compared to 43.9 percent for all female householders. These figures show a nearly five percent reduction for black females and seven percent reduction for all female householders who lived in units 30 or more years old. The gap between black females and all females combined not only did not narrow between the two censuses, but widened from a difference of less than 1 percent in 1970 to 3.4 percent in 1980.

Table 6.2 presents data for selected structural characteristics of housing units. As these data show for every category in the table, the proportion of black female householders occupying structures that are more than 30 years old is higher than the corresponding proportions for either their white counterparts, or the total white population.

Number of Rooms

"Rooms" refers to the number of whole rooms used for living purposes. Strip or pullman kitchens, bathrooms, open porches, balconies, halls, half rooms, utility rooms, and unfinished attics or basements are not regarded as "rooms" (U.S. Bureau of the Census, 1984b: A–6).

Number of rooms in a housing unit is a *quantitative* measure of space available to the household. Generally speaking, units with more rooms are preferred over units with fewer rooms which provide little space for the occupants. Of all black female-headed households in 1970, 7.2 percent resided in 1–2 room units; 48.6 percent in 3 or 4 room units; 36.4 percent in 5 or 6 room units; and, only 7.7 percent lived in 7 or more room units. The corresponding figures for *all* female-headed households in 1970 were: 8.4, 44.2, 37.1, and 10.3 percent, respectively. Data comparing BFHHs with whites are presented in Table 6.2. As these data show, there is a wide discrepancy between the amount of housing space available to black female-headed households as compared to whites. For example, among owner-occupied units, 86.5 percent of BFHHs in the multi-person household category, as compared to 89.6 percent of their white counterparts had 5 or more rooms available to them. Among the one-person householders who owned their homes, 71.1 percent of blacks, as against 75.7 percent of their white counterparts, had 5 or more rooms. Among renters, the black-white discrepancy was much higher, pointing to the fact that black female householders had significantly less housing space available to them than either their white counterparts or an average white household.

Table 6.2

Selected Structural Characteristics: Single Family Detached Housing Units, 1980

	Owner-Occupied			Renter-Occupied		
STC* & Race	All Households	Multi- Person FemHH*	One- Person- FemHH*	All Households	Multi- Person FemHH*	One- Person FemHH*
Percent Units 30 or More Years Old						
White	34.9	43.0	56.5	52.0	51.6	61.6
Black	39.8	44.2	57.9	52.9	51.7	61.2
Percent Units with 5 or More Rooms						
White	89.1	89.6	75.7	67.4	70.1	45.8
Black	85.8	86.5	71.1	56.8	63.9	35.8
Percent Units with 4 or More Bedrooms						
White	22.0	23.0	8.8	12.1	13.2	4.5
Black	18.6	20.7	6.3	9.2	12.0	2.5
Percent Units Lacking Complete Plumbing						
White	0.9	1.2	1.8	3.4	2.8	4.2
Black	3.7	4.5	6.6	15.8	13.2	8.7
Percent Units Without Telephone						
White	2.0	2.2	2.3	13.3	13.4	8.9
Black	6.9	7.2	8.4	29.8	26.3	25.9
Percent Units Without Complete Kitchen Facilities						
White	0.9	1.1	1.4	3.0	2.6	3.3
Black	3.8	4.4	6.3	14.1	11.7	14.9
Percent Units Lacking Public Sewer						
White	35.4	28.6	29.3	37.2	26.4	31.4
Black	22.5	21.0	24.0	25.8	20.6	23.3

* FemHH: Female Householder, no husband present; STC: Structural Characteristics.

Source: U.S. Bureau of the Census (1984a).

Bedrooms

"Bedrooms" refers to the number of rooms designated mainly for sleeping
purposes. A living room with a sofa bed in it, although it could be used for
sleeping, is not considered as "bedroom." On the other hand, a room used
as guest room, though not used frequently, is regarded as "bedroom" (U.S.
Bureau of the Census, 1984b: A–6). Number of bedrooms in a housing unit
is another *quantitative* measure of space available to the household. The
1970 and 1980 data on the number of bedrooms for black female-headed
households and *all* female-headed households combined were as follow (U.S.
Bureau of the Census, 1972, 1983):

Number of Bedrooms	1970 Black FHHs	1970 All FHHs	1980 Black FHHs	1980 All FHHs
No bedroom	2.4	4.0	2.2	2.8
1–2 bedrooms	65.7	64.9	59.7	61.5
3 or more bedrooms	31.9	31.1	38.1	35.7

The above aggregate data on the number of bedrooms show no significant
difference between black females and all female-headed households combined, both in 1970 and 1980. However, the data show some improvements
for both categories during the intercensal period, as the proportion of units
with 4 or more bedrooms increased from 7.4 percent in 1970 to 9.2 percent
in 1980 for blacks, and from 7.7 percent in 1970 to 8.4 percent in 1980
for all female-headed households. The differences in the number of bedrooms in units occupied by BFHHs as compared to whites are quite apparent
from the data presented in Table 6.2, which shows the number of bedrooms
in the single family detached units by tenure, household type and size, and
race. The following observations may be made from Table 6.2: (a) units
occupied by blacks, regardless of household size (one-person v. multi-person), had fewer bedrooms; (b) the number of bedrooms for all categories,
including blacks, were fewer among the renter- than among the owner-
occupied units; (c) the black-white gap in the number of bedrooms was
much wider among the renters than owners; and, (d) roughly, for every
two black female householders who owned their unit and who had 4 or
more bedrooms, only one BFHH in the renter category had 4 or more
bedrooms.

Overcrowding

Number of "persons per room" is calculated by dividing the number of
persons in each occupied housing unit by the number of rooms in the unit.

Overcrowding is a serious problem for some groups, and it generally means lowering the quality of housing and life. It happens among groups who cannot afford adequate space for their household size. Units with more than 1.00 person per room are defined as "overcrowded." Based on the 1980 census data, the median number of persons per room is larger for black female-headed households than for whites. For instance, among home owners, the median was 3.2 for blacks in the single-family, detached units, as compared to 2.5 persons for their white counterparts. Within the renter-occupied units, the black-white gap was even wider—3.6 for blacks as compared to 2.8 persons per household for their white counterparts.

Consistent with these findings, black households in general and black female-headed households in particular were more overcrowded than the corresponding white households. The rate of overcrowding is particularly high among renters as compared to owners. As an example, according to the 1980 census data, 10.6 percent of the single-family, detached units owned by BFHHs, and 20.5 percent occupied by renters, were classified as overcrowded. This compares with only 1.6 percent and 4.5 percent of their white counterparts.

Plumbing Facilities for Exclusive Use

Housing units with "complete plumbing facilities for exclusive use" consist of those units which have cold and hot piped water, a flush toilet, and a bathtub or shower inside the housing unit for the exclusive use of the household. "Lacking complete plumbing for exclusive use" refers to units when: (a) all three specified plumbing facilities are present inside the unit, but are also shared by another household; and, (b) some or none of the specified facilities is available. The degree of completeness of plumbing facilities is another indicator of housing quality. Overall, in 1970, 83.6 percent of black female-headed households, as against 92.8 percent of *all* female-headed households, did have complete plumbing facilities. The corresponding proportions for 1980 were 94.8 and 97.5, respectively, pointing to substantial improvements during the decade.

The data in Table 6.2 reveal that a higher proportion of units occupied by blacks in general, and black female-headed households in particular, were found to lack complete plumbing facilities. In the owner-occupied multi-person category, 4.5 percent of black female-headed households in contrast to only 0.9 percent of whites lacked complete plumbing facilities. In the owner-occupied one-person category, 6.6 percent of black female-headed households, as compared to 1.8 percent of their white counterparts, and 0.9 percent of all whites lacked complete plumbing facilities. Among the renter-occupied units, the differential was even greater. For instance, in the multi-person renter-occupied units, 13.2 percent of black female-headed households as compared to 2.8 percent of their white counterparts lacked complete plumbing facilities.

Households without a Telephone

Today, a telephone is a necessity rather than a luxury item. If people do not have a telephone in their homes, it is most probably due to the fact that they cannot afford it. The lack of a phone may be used as an indicator of poor financial status.

In 1970, 68.4 percent of BFHHs, as compared to 84.7 percent of all female householders, did not have phones in their homes. The proportion of households with a phone increased dramatically between the two censuses. As depicted in Table 6.2, there is a great deal of variation by tenure, structure type, and race. A significantly higher proportion of renters than owners were without phone—e.g., 25.9 percent of renters in the one-person households, as opposed to 8.4 percent of owners. The incidence of householders without a phone was higher among blacks in general, and BFHHs, in particular, than among the total white population.

Kitchen Facilities

In 1970, 89.3 percent of the BFHHs, as compared to 96.1 percent of all female householders, did have complete kitchen facilities. An additional 0.5 percent of the blacks and 0.3 percent of all female householders reported that they did have complete kitchen facilities, but they were being shared by another household. That is, in 1970, 10.2 percent of the BFHHs and 3.7 percent of all female householders did not have complete kitchen facilities. In 1980, only 4.7 percent of BFHHs and 2.2 percent of all female householders reported not having complete kitchen facilities, pointing to significant improvements during the intercensal years. Table 6.2 provides data relative to black female-headed households without complete kitchen facilities in 1980 in the single family units. The pattern can be summarized as such: the proportion of householders without complete kitchen facilities was higher among blacks than among whites; higher among renters than among owners.

Public Sewer

The availability of public sewer system in the neighborhood and in the unit greatly enhances the value and the quality of living environment. Based on data shown in Table 6.2, the proportion of units without public sewer occupied by blacks was lower than those occupied by whites. This is perhaps the only dimension of housing quality that blacks seem to have an edge over whites. The relatively lower incidence of units occupied by the BFHHs without public sewer is believed to be due to the fact that central city locations, where the majority of the BFHHs live, do have a sewer system.

Relative to the availability of central air conditioning, type of heating equipment, and house heating fuel BFHHs are also at a significant disadvantage. As to the availability of air conditioning (AC), 13.4 percent of BFHHs, as compared to 37.4 of all white households, had a central AC system. Lack of a central AC system in some parts of the country, such as Maine, may not have much impact on the quality of living; but, in the south where almost one-half of all BFHHs reside, it is a major factor affecting housing quality.

The availability of a central warm-air furnace or an electric heat pump in the housing unit greatly impacts housing quality, for they constitute the most desirable home heating equipment today. Based on the 1980 census data, 34.6 percent of the one-person BFHHs in the owner-occupied, *detached* SFH units, as compared to 52.7 percent of their white counterparts and 61.5 percent of all whites, had a central warm-air system. In multiperson owner-occupied, *detached* SFH units, 41.7 percent of BFHHs as opposed to 58.1 percent of their white counterparts had a central warm-air system (U.S. Bureau of the Census, 1984a).

In addition to the above qualitative and quantitative differentials in the units occupied by the BFHHs, a higher proportion of BFHHs' income than that of whites is paid for rent. In 1980, one-half of all white renters of *detached* SFH units in the United States paid more than 24.0 percent of their 1979 annual income for rent; and, one-half of white female householders renting *detached* SFH units paid more than 34.8 percent of their 1979 annual income for rent. Relative to blacks, the corresponding figures were 29.5 percent and 38.1 percent, respectively, indicating that female householders in general, and BFHHs in particular, have to pay an inordinate proportion of their annual income for subaverage housing in the United States.

Overall, the analyses show some improvements in housing conditions between 1970 and 1980. However, the wide black-white gaps continue to persist. The major factor responsible for the black-white differential seems to stem from the wide income differences between the two groups. It is concluded that BFHHs, the majority of whom have an annual income below poverty level, cannot afford the housing adequate for their needs; and, even those with an annual income technically above the poverty line do not make enough to enable them to attain the national goal of a decent home for every American family set in 1949. The black-white disparities in housing are expected to continue as long as the income gaps remain.

Acknowledgments

This research was partially supported by a grant from the Institute of Urban Affairs and Research, Howard University. The substance and findings of this study are solely those of the author.

References

Berry, Brian J. L., and John D. Kasarda. 1977. *Contemporary Urban Ecology*. New York: Macmillan Publishing Co.

Dahmann, Donald C. 1985. Assessments of Neighborhood Quality in Metropolitan America. *Urban Affairs Quarterly* 20 (4): 511–35.

Davis, Tom L. 1967. Cooperative Self-help Housing. *Law and Contemporary Problems* 32 (2): 409–15.

Gorham, William, and Nathan Glazer, eds. 1976. *The Urban Predicament*. Washington, D.C.: The Urban Institute.

Henretta, John C., and Richard T. Campbell. 1978. Net Worth as an Aspect of Status. *American Journal of Sociology* 83 (March): 1204–23.

HUD (U.S. Department of Housing and Urban Development). 1978. *How Well Are We Housed? 2. Female-Headed Households*. HUD-PDR–344. Washington, D.C.: GPO.

Jackman, Mary R., and Robert W. Jackman. 1980. Racial Inequalities in Home Ownership. *Social Forces* 58: 1221–34.

Jackson, Hubert M. 1958. Public Housing and Minority Groups. *Phylon* 19 (1): 21–30.

Kain, John F., and John M. Quigley. 1970. Measuring the Value of Housing Quality. *Journal of the American Statistical Association* 65 (330): 532–48.

———. 1972. Housing Market Discrimination, Homeownership, and Savings Behavior. *American Economic Review* 62 (3): 263–77.

Kolko, Gabriel. 1962. *Wealth and Power in America*. New York: Praeger.

Lampman, Robert J. 1959. Changes in the Share of Wealth Held by Top Wealth-holders, 1922–1956. *Review of Economics and Statistics* 41 (November): 379–92.

Marable, Manning. 1985. The Housing Crisis. *Washington Afro-American* (newspaper) (30 March): 4.

Momeni, Jamshid. 1984. Demography of Racial and Ethnic Minorities in the United States: A Political and Sociodemographic Review. In *Demography of Racial and Ethnic Minorities in the United States*, by Jamshid A. Momeni, 3–44. Westport, Conn.: Greenwood Press.

Momeni, Jamshid A., and Diane R. Brown. 1986. *Housing Characteristics of Black Female Householders: An Analysis of Data from the 1970 and 1980 Censuses*. Washington, D.C.: Institute for Urban Affairs and Research, Howard University.

Parcel, Toby L. 1982. Wealth Accumulation of Black and White Men: The Case of Housing Equity. *Social Problems* 30 (2): 199–211.

U.S. Bureau of the Census. 1972. *Public Use Samples of Basic Records from the 1970 Census* (5 percent Sample).

———. 1983. *Public Use Microdata Samples*. Census of Population and Housing, 1980 (File C Tape).

———. 1984a. *Metropolitan Housing Characteristics*. 1980 Census of Housing: United States Summary HC80–2–1. Washington, D.C.: GPO.

———. 1984b. *Structural Characteristics of the Housing Inventory*. 1980 Census of Housing. Subject Reports HC80–3–4. Washington, D.C.: GPO.

U.S. Commission on Civil Rights. 1971. *Home Ownership for Lower Income Families: A Report on the Racial and Ethnic Impact of the Section 235 Program*. June 1971.

7

Accessibility to Housing: Differential Residential Segregation for Blacks, Hispanics, American Indians, and Asians

Joe T. Darden

Introduction

Residential segregation is clearly one of the most significant, sensitive, and difficult problems facing American society. It remains an American dilemma. Residential segregation can be conceptualized as an adaptation of a particular group to certain spatial constraints within the urban environment. Since individual access to housing within the residential marketplace is constrained by numerous factors, including ability to pay, segregation occurs between groups (Hawley, 1950; Alonso, 1960). Implicit in ecological theory is that a group's status strongly influences its ability to obtain access to housing and that those structural features of metropolitan areas which affect housing supply and demand influence the level of segregation.

According to theories of human ecology, variation in segregation between groups relates directly to measurable differences on social and economic variables (Burgess, 1923; Park, 1926; Massey, 1981: 316). Thus, low status groups tend to be spatially segregated from higher status groups, partly because high status persons avoid locating their residences in the same areas, and partly because low status persons are less able to compete for the more expensive residential homes occupied by high status groups (Marshall and Jiobu, 1975: 449). The relationship between socioeconomic status of ethnic and racial groups and residential segregation has been examined by several studies.

Socioeconomic Status and Ethnic Residential Segregation

Most past research has shown an inverse relationship between the level of an ethnic group's socioeconomic status and that ethnic group's level of residential segregation.

Bleda (1975) used 1970 census data on fifteen Standard Metropolitan Statistical Areas to test the ethnic group socioeconomic status and residential segregation hypothesis. Her findings provided support for the socioeconomic status—residential segregation relationship. Further support for the socioeconomic status hypothesis was provided by Guest and Weed (1976) who examined residential segregation for Chicanos, blacks and Puerto Ricans in 1960 and 1970 for Cleveland, Boston, and Seattle as part of a comparison of relative segregation of "old immigrant groups" (Western Europe and Canada), "new immigrant groups" (Eastern and part of Southern Europe), and non-European immigrants. Guest and Weed found support for the socioeconomic status—ethnic residential segregation relationship.

Finally, Massey (1979) examined Spanish American residential segregation in the twenty-nine largest urbanized areas in the United States and found a negative relationship between socioeconomic status and the degree of Spanish-white residential segregation. He concluded that whether measured in terms of education, income, or occupation, Spanish-white segregation declines unambiguously with increasing socioeconomic status (Massey, 1979: 1017).

In sum, past studies generally confirm the ecological theory that residential segregation between ethnic groups is inversely related to socioeconomic status or ability to pay variables. However, the viewpoint that the degree of residential segregation between racial groups is a result of racial differences in the "ability to pay" has been discredited by a number of studies.

Socioeconomic Status and Racial Residential Segregation

During the seventies, Darden (1973) tested the relative effects of housing cost on black residential segregation in a longitudinal study of the city of Pittsburgh. The study period was from 1940 to 1970, because data on economic factors by race and census tract were not available prior to 1940. As a means of preliminary exploration, indices were calculated showing the segregation of low-value from high-value housing and of low-rent from high-rent housing for each decade, and these were compared with the indices for racial residential segregation. The results showed that segregation on the basis of housing value and segregation on the basis of rent were much lower than segregation on the basis of race. Had all blacks in Pittsburgh lived in low-value or low-rent housing and all whites in high-value or high-rent housing from 1940 to 1970, the amount of segregation between blacks and whites could not have been higher than 34.8 to 39.3 percent from 1940 to 1970. Therefore, if black residential segregation in Pittsburgh was solely a result of segregation between low-value housing and high-value housing for homeowners and between low-rent and high-rent housing for those who rent, the maximum possible level of black residential segregation would have been far below the 70.5 to 75.7 percent level actually observed.

Farley (1977) analyzed 1970 census data for twenty-nine urbanized areas using the index of dissimilarity. He was interested in answering the question, "To what extent are blacks in a given social group residentially segregated from whites in that same social group?" Farley measured the residential segregation between blacks and whites controlling for social class. His findings were in agreement with those mentioned above, namely that black residential segregation in the United States is not primarily a function of racial differences in socioeconomic status. He found that the levels of racial residential segregation did not vary spatially by class.

Massey's (1979) analysis of twenty-nine urbanized areas revealed little or no relationship between socioeconomic variables and black-white residential segregation. The high degree of residential segregation between blacks and whites could not be accounted for by socioeconomic factors alone.

Finally, Farley (1983) using 1980 census data on blacks in metropolitan St. Louis, Missouri found that the segregated distribution pattern of blacks was not strongly related to the cost of housing. Socioeconomic differentials between blacks and whites can account for less than 15 percent of the segregation among suburbs and less than 25 percent of the segregation in the central city of St. Louis. In short, if blacks and whites were residentially distributed only according to their socioeconomic status, with no independent effect of race, St. Louis would be a very integrated area, in sharp contrast to the highly segregated area that exists in reality.

In sum, the review of the literature on socioeconomic status and ethnic residential segregation seems to suggest that an inverse relationship does indeed exist. On the other hand, no such relationship seems to exist between socioeconomic status and racial residential segregation. The implications are clearly different for ethnic groups vis-à-vis racial groups. For the former groups, socioeconomic mobility leads to significantly reduced levels of residential segregation and ultimately to greater assimilation (Massey, 1979: 1021). For the latter groups, socioeconomic mobility is no guarantee of freedom of spatial mobility, that is, freedom to move into the residential area of one's choice subject only to ability to pay. Thus, the opportunity for assimilation is less and so are the opportunities for socioeconomic advancement.

The Social and Economic Consequences of Residential Segregation

Economist Steger (1973) has estimated that the income opportunity deprived due to residential segregation exceeds $10 billion annually. He further concluded that segregation reduces job opportunities for black families by restricting them to areas that are job deficient. Blacks remain disproportionately concentrated in central cities where job opportunities are fewer. Since 1948, suburban areas have received over 80 percent of the new employment in manufacturing, retail and wholesale trade, and selected services (Gold, 1972). Thus, newer and better job opportunities are locating further away from the places of black residence forcing black families to spend more time and money commuting to work or looking for work. Residential segregation also reduces the representation of blacks in certain occupations and restricts black labor force participation (Marston and Van Valey, 1979).

As a result of residential segregation, blacks generally pay more than whites for housing of comparable quality (Kain and Quigley, 1975; Jackman and Jackman, 1980; Villemez, 1980). Residential segregation also facilitates discrimination in the distribution of mortgage and home improvement loans (Darden, 1985a).

In sum, given the important impact of residential segregation on individual life chances, racial segregation cannot be ignored as a salient dimension of social stratification in the United States (Massey and Mullan, 1984). Yet residential segregation of racial groups remains high in American cities and has been for sometime. In 1950, the average level of segregation by block in the 25 largest cities with 100,000 or more blacks was 88 percent. Between 1950 and 1970, there was virtually no reduction in the average level of segregation. In fact, only between 1970 and 1980 was there any visible change. The index of dissimilarity dropped from 87 percent in 1970 to 81 percent in 1980. Thus, over a 30 year period, the average level of residential segregation between blacks and whites in the nation's 25 largest cities with over 100,000 or more blacks declined by only 7 percentage points (Citizens Commission on Civil Rights, 1983; Sorenson, Taeuber and Hollingsworth, 1975; Darden, 1984a).

The purpose of this chapter is two-fold; (1) to determine the degree to which blacks, Hispanics, American Indians, and Asians are residentially segregated from whites in metropolitan areas of Michigan and (2) to determine how much of each group's residential distribution can be explained by housing cost. The four groups in this chapter represent racial and/or ethnic urban minorities with a history of discrimination and socioeconomic inequality. Yet, it is reasonable to assume that segregation in housing has not been experienced equally by these groups. Instead these minorities have been placed on a continuum, i.e. the white population has been more willing to share residential space with one group than with the other. Such differential sharing of residential space has important consequences for *spatial assimilation*. Spatial assimilation is the process whereby a group attains residential propinquity with members of the host society (Massey and Mullen, 1984: 837). In the United States, it has generally involved the movement of minority groups out of established racial or ethnic neighborhoods into a larger urban environment inhabited primarily by "nonethnic" native whites (Kiang, 1968). Thus, overall segregation of the minority group declined.

Data and Methods of Analysis

Data for this chapter were obtained from the U.S. Bureau of the Census's Population and Housing Summary Tape Files 1-A and 4-A (U.S. Bureau of the Census, 1982, 1983). The data consisted of (1) the number of whites, blacks, Hispanics, American Indians and Asians by census tracts and (2) the median housing value and rent by census tracts for the twelve Standard Metropolitan Statistical Areas (SMSAs) in Michigan.

The method employed to measure residential segregation, which is defined as the overall unevenness in the spatial distribution of two racial/ethnic groups is the index of dissimilarity. The index is simple to compute, easy to understand and is considered the standard measure of residential segregation (Massey, 1981: 313). It can be stated mathematically as

$$D = 100 \left(1/2 \sum_{i=1}^{k} \left| x_i - y_i \right| \right)$$

where

x_i = the percentage of the Standard Metropolitan Statistical Areas' white population living in a given census tract;

y_i = the percentage of the Standard Metropolitan Statistical Areas' black, Hispanic, American Indian or Asian population living in the same census tract;

D = the index of dissimilarity, or one-half the sum of the absolute differences (positive and negative) between the percentage distribution of the white, black, Hispanic, American Indian or Asian population in the Standard Metropolitan Statistical Areas (Darden and Tabachneck, 1980).

The index value may range from "0" indicating no segregation to "100" indicating total segregation. Whatever the value of the index, it reflects the minimum percentage of either group that would have to move from one tract to another to achieve an even spatial distribution throughout the SMSAs.

Despite its widespread use in residential segregation research, the index of dissimilarity has certain limitations. Among such limitations is the fact that the index is sensitive to the size of the spatial units used (Darden and Haney, 1978: 24). Since census tracts were chosen as the spatial units for this chapter, the degree and magnitude of segregation by block could not be determined. The segregation indices in this chapter take into account only differences in the spatial distribution of groups between census tracts and reveal nothing about the distribution of the same groups between blocks.

Once the extent of residential segregation was determined, the second objective was to determine whether the segregated distribution patterns were related to the cost of housing. Pearson correlation coefficients were computed between the percentage distribution of blacks, Hispanics, American Indians and Asians and median housing value and rent for all census tracts in each SMSA examined.

The Accessibility for Blacks to Nonsegregated Housing

Most blacks in Michigan continue to live in racially segregated housing. In Michigan's SMSAs, central cities, and suburbs, the majority of blacks are residentially segregated.

In 1980, 1,167,728 blacks, representing 97.4 percent of the state's total black population, lived in Michigan's 12 SMSAs. As indicated in Table 7.1, residential segregation was high (i.e., above 50 percent) between blacks and whites in each SMSA except Ann Arbor (44.5 percent) and Lansing (44.7 percent). The mean level of segregation for the 12 SMSAs was 66.8 percent. However, the level of black segregation was above 80 percent in metropolitan Detroit (85.8), Flint (83.3), Saginaw (83.0), and Benton Harbor (82.1). These four SMSAs were the most segregated in the state.

Although black residential segregation in Michigan's metropolitan areas remains very high, a slight declining trend can be observed over the last two decades. In 1960, the mean level of black segregation for all of Michigan's metropolitan areas was 80.3 percent. From 1960 to 1970, segregation declined to 76.9 percent. From 1970 to 1980, black segregation dropped to 66.8 percent, reflecting a −13.5 percentage point change from 1960 to 1980 (Table 7.1).

Clearly, most blacks are not evenly distributed within SMSAs. Instead, most blacks are residentially segregated within central cities. In 1980, 950,774 blacks, representing 79.3 percent of the state's black population, lived in Michigan's twelve central cities.

Blacks in the Suburbs

Although black suburbanization has been increasing, relatively few blacks compared to whites lived in the suburbs in 1980. The 214,424 suburban blacks represented only 17.8 percent of the state's black population, whereas 64.7 percent of the state's white population lived in the suburbs. Ann Arbor had the highest percentage (11.6 percent) of blacks living in the suburbs. The suburban areas with the least percentage of blacks were Bay City (0.4 percent) and Grand Rapids, 0.8 percent.

The percentage increase in the suburban population of Michigan's SMSAs was greater for blacks than for whites between 1960 and 1980, but black suburbanization in Michigan has not generally been synonymous with black

Table 7.1
Changes in Black Residential Segregation in Metropolitan Areas of Michigan,
1960–1980

SMSA	Index of Dissimilarity			% Change 1960–1980	Suburban Index of Dissimilarity
	1960	1970	1980		
Detroit	87.1	88.9	85.8	-1.3	83.9
Flint	83.0	86.4	83.3	+0.3	54.6
Saginaw	81.6	83.7	83.0	+1.4	32.4
Benton Harbor	na	na	82.1	na	48.8
Grand Rapids	83.9	84.6	71.9	-12.0	42.0
Jackson	80.2	80.9	71.5	-8.7	82.4
Muskegon	74.5	80.5	63.0	-11.5	78.1
Battle Creek	na	na	61.5	na	56.9
Kalamazoo	76.2	71.3	59.1	-17.1	20.9
Bay City	na	76.4	52.2	na	27.8
Lansing	83.3	64.8	44.7	-38.6	31.6
Ann Arbor	72.6	51.9	44.5	-28.1	45.7
Mean	80.3	76.9	66.8	-13.5	58.9

na: Data not available and/or not applicable.

Source: Computed by the Author using the 1960 and 1970 Census
data, and the Summary Tape File 1-A, for Michigan, 1982.

residential desegregation. Blacks living in the suburbs of Benton Harbor,
Detroit, Jackson, and Muskegon were more residentially segregated in 1980
than blacks living in the central cities of those areas (Darden, 1985a: 12).
Blacks in the suburbs of Detroit were the most residentially segregated (83.9
percent) of all suburban blacks in Michigan SMSAs. The least segregated
blacks in suburban areas were in Kalamazoo (20.9 percent). The mean level
of segregation for the 12 suburban areas was 58.9 percent.

Housing Cost as a Factor in Black Residential Segregation

What role does housing cost play in black residential segregation? An
important factor which is expected to influence the spatial distribution of
a population in a truly open market economy is the cost of housing. The

cost of housing also varies by census tracts. Thus, if blacks locate disproportionately in census tracts where the housing value and rent are low, it
would be reasonable to conclude that segregation of blacks may be related
to the cost of housing. If, on the other hand, little or no relationship exists,
it would be reasonable to conclude that housing cost is probably not an
important variable in explaining black residential segregation (Table 7.2).
The same reasoning applies as we assess the housing cost factor for the
remaining minority groups with the use of correlation coefficients. The
relationship between the spatial distribution of blacks and the median value
of owner-occupied housing was weak in seven, or 58.3 percent of the twelve
SMSAs. The correlations ranged from − .23 for metropolitan Lansing to
− .69 for metropolitan Benton Harbor. Housing cost had its strongest relationship to the spatial distribution of blacks and housing value in metropolitan Benton Harbor. Even there, however, housing cost could explain
only 47 percent of the spatial variation of the black population, leaving 53
percent unexplained (Table 7.3). The importance of housing cost was neg-
ligible in explaining the spatial distribution of the black population in metropolitan Ann Arbor and Lansing. In both metropolitan areas, only 5 percent
of the spatial variation of the black population could be attributed to housing
cost, leaving 95 percent unexplained or attributed to other factors. The data
indicate, then, that housing cost is not the major reason most blacks in
owner-occupied housing in metropolitan areas of Michigan live in racially
segregated housing.

The relationships between the spatial distribution of blacks and median
housing rent were even weaker than those of median owner-occupied housing value. Housing rent had its strongest relationship to the spatial distribution of the black population in metropolitan Detroit. Even there, however,
the cost of rental housing could explain only 28 percent of the spatial
variation of the black population, leaving 72 percent unexplained (Table
7.3). The cost of rental housing is clearly not an important factor in explaining the spatial distribution of blacks in ten (83 percent) of the twelve
metropolitan areas. That is, most blacks in Michigan live in racially segregated housing, and the cost of home ownership or renting is not the
primary reason for such segregation (Darden, 1985a: 15).

The Accessibility for Hispanics to Nonsegregated Housing

Like the black population, Hispanics represent a large, highly visible,
urban minority with a history of discrimination and socioeconomic ex-
ploitation (Massey, 1979; Darden, 1983). But the Hispanic population has
had more of a language barrier—similar to the earlier European immigrants—and less of a color barrier than blacks. Therefore Hispanics generally have greater accessibility than blacks to nonsegregated housing.
Previous studies on Hispanic segregation suggest that patterns are similar

Table 7.2
Correlation Coefficient *(r)* between Percent Black and Median Housing Value and between Percent Black and Median Rent in Michigan's SMSAs, 1980

SMSA	Median Value		Median Rent	
	r	N	r	N
Ann Arbor	-.24**	83	-.19**	84
Battle Creek	-.45*	62	-.14	62
Bay City	-.50*	34	-.22	34
Benton Harbor	-.69*	66	-.27**	67
Detroit	-.52*	903	-.53*	910
Flint	-.48*	127	-.25	126
Grand Rapids	-.38*	149	-.18*	150
Jackson	-.41*	43	-.21	43
Kalamazoo	-.44*	94	-.23**	15
Lansing	-.23*	134	-.08	138
Muskegon	-.52*	65	-.22**	65
Saginaw	-.62*	56	-.39*	56

* and ** significant at 0.01 and 0.05 levels, respectively.

N: Number of census tracts on which the analysis is based.

to those observed among earlier European ethnic groups and are generally unlike those of blacks (Massey, 1981; Lopez, 1981; Darden, 1983). Specifically, Hispanic–white segregation ranges from moderate to high but rarely reaches the very high levels that characterize black–white segregation. Hispanics are usually more segregated from blacks than from whites. Finally, patterns of Hispanic segregation seem to be more influenced by social class than the pattern of black segregation.

The Hispanic population represents the second largest minority group in the United States. It is also the fastest growing minority group. In 1980, more than 1.2 million Hispanics lived in the north central states with approximately 162,000 living in Michigan (U.S. Bureau of the Census, 1981). Within Michigan, they are concentrated primarily in the 12 Standard Metropolitan Statistical areas. The Hispanic population ranges from 1,807 in metropolitan Jackson to 71,589 in metropolitan Detroit (Table 7.4). In general, Hispanic–white residential segregation is moderate to low and does

Table 7.3

Population and Racial Minority Group Segregation in SMSAs of Michigan, 1980

Index of Dissimilarity

SMSA	Asian Vs. White	Indian Vs. White	Black Vs. White	Hispanic Vs. White
Ann Arbor	31.3	24.1	44.5	25.0
Battle Creek	41.5	33.6	61.5	26.0
Bay City	15.2	31.0	52.2	33.4
Benton Harbor	29.8	26.3	82.1	38.5
Detroit	26.1	36.3	85.8	43.6
Flint	25.3	30.0	83.3	33.4
Grand Rapids	27.1	40.8	71.9	48.9
Jackson	26.0	46.1	71.5	39.4
Kalamazoo	22.9	30.7	59.1	29.0
Lansing	33.0	38.6	44.7	37.8
Muskegon	27.2	36.9	63.0	34.2
Saginaw	18.9	44.1	83.0	54.6
Mean	27.0	34.8	66.8	36.9

Source: Computed by the author based on data from U.S. Bureau of the Census (1982).

not reach the high levels that characterize black–white segregation in any metropolitan area. The mean level of Hispanic–white residential segregation is 36.9 percent compared to 66.8 percent for black–white segregation (Table 7.3). Furthermore, in Battle Creek, Benton Harbor, Flint, and Kalamazoo, black–white segregation is more than twice the level of Hispanic–white segregation.

Hispanics are also more suburbanized than blacks. An average of 58 percent of the Hispanic population of metropolitan areas live in the suburbs of Michigan's central cities compared to 34.3 percent of blacks (Table 7.4). Research has shown that there is an inverse relationship between the percentage of a minority group's population living in the suburbs of metropolitan areas and the level of minority group residential segregation from

Table 7.4
Percent of Each Racial Group's Population Living in the Suburbs of Michigan's SMSAs, 1980

Suburbs	White	Asian	Indian	Hispanic	Black	Total SMSA@
Benton Harbor	98.7*	99.1*	93.6*	93.3*	48.9	91.4
Battle Creek	84.3*	80.6	67.9	76.2	40.3	80.9
Muskegon	80.2*	67.8	75.8	69.3	54.5	77.3
Jackson	76.3*	76.1*	57.9	55.3	43.3	73.8
Detroit	87.7*	80.1*	72.6*	59.5	14.8	72.4
Kalamazoo	74.3*	59.4	70.4	63.8	40.5	71.4
Grand Rapids	73.5*	63.2	49.3	58.2	10.9	69.8
Flint	79.3*	69.6*	67.8	53.1	16.2	69.4
Saginaw	75.6*	77.2*	56.4	42.8	23.1	66.0
Bay City	66.1*	76.1*	60.9	38.4	27.2	65.3
Lansing	75.6*	75.8*	50.2	41.3	26.9	63.7
Ann Arbor	59.8*	31.5	62.6*	44.5	64.7*	59.5
Mean	77.6	71.4	65.5	58.0	34.3	71.7

@ Percent of SMSA's population suburbanized.

* Higher than the percent of the total SMSA's population
  living in the suburbs (last column in this table).

Source: Computed by the author based on data from the U.S.
  Bureau of the Census (1981).

whites. In other words, minority groups with the greatest suburbanization have the lowest level of residential segregation (Darden, 1985b).

Housing Cost as a Factor in Hispanic Residential Segregation

Does housing cost explain why Hispanics are residentially segregated? The correlation analysis revealed a negative relationship between the spatial distribution of Hispanics and the spatial distribution of median housing value. The relationship is very strong in Bay City (−.74). As it may be noted from table 7.5, strong relationships exist in Flint (−.52), Jackson

(−.56), and Saginaw (−.68). However, no strong relationship exists in eight or 66 percent of the SMSAs.

The correlation coefficients between the spatial distribution of Hispanics and the cost of rental housing were weaker than those for owner-occupied housing value. No strong correlation exists in any SMSA. Clearly, the cost of housing is not the primary reason for Hispanic residential segregation.

The Accessibility for American Indians to Nonsegregated Housing

Like Hispanics, American Indians have greater accessibility to nonsegregated housing than blacks. As a result, American Indian–white residential segregation is generally lower than black-white residential segregation (Darden, 1984b). Furthermore, American Indians are usually more segregated from blacks than from whites.

Of the 1,364,033 American Indians in the United States, slightly more than half live in urban areas (i.e., off reservations). The American Indian population increased 72 percent between 1970 and 1980. This increase took place in states and regions throughout the country. More than 248,000 American Indians lived in the North Central states in 1980, and 40,000 lived in Michigan (U.S. Bureau of the Census, 1981) which ranks tenth in American Indian population. Within Michigan, 66 percent reside in Michigan's twelve Standard Metropolitan Statistical Areas. Although an urbanized racial–ethnic group, little is known about the residential pattern of American Indians.

In 1980, 26,582 American Indians resided in Michigan's twelve SMSAs. Jackson had the lowest number of American Indians (496) but the lowest percentage lived in Ann Arbor (.27 percent). Although Detroit had the greatest number with more than 12,000, Benton Harbor had the greatest percentage (2.38 percent). In fact, the American Indian percentage of the total population was less than 1 percent in every SMSA except Benton Harbor. Among all the census tracts examined, the mean level of segregation between American Indians and whites was 34.8 percent. The level of segregation ranged from a high of 46.1 percent in Jackson to a low of 24.1 percent in Ann Arbor (Table 7.3).

As expected, American Indian–white segregation was lower than black–white segregation. The mean level of black–white segregation was 66.8 percent compared to only 34.8 percent for American Indian–white segregation, a difference of 32 percentage points. Black-white segregation was higher than American Indian–white segregation in each SMSA examined.

American Indians are also more segregated residentially from blacks than from whites (Darden, 1984b). Furthermore, American Indians are more suburbanized than either blacks or Hispanics. Sixty-five percent live in Michigan's suburbs.

Table 7.5

Correlation Coefficient *(r)* between Percent Hispanic and Median Housing Value
and between Percent Hispanic and Median Rent in Michigan's SMSAs, 1980

SMSA	Median Value		Median Rent	
	r	N	r	N
Ann Arbor	+.34*	83	+.16	84
Battle Creek	-.38*	62	-.17	62
Bay City	-.74*	34	-.37**	34
Benton Harbor	+.07	66	-.11	67
Detroit	-.21	903	-.20*	910
Flint	-.52*	127	-.27	126
Grand Rapids	-.38*	149	-.17*	95
Jackson	-.56*	43	-.24	43
Kalamazoo	-.49*	94	-.43*	150
Lansing	-.38*	134	-.08	138
Muskegon	-.37*	65	-.37*	65
Saginaw	-.68*	56	-.34*	56

* and ** significant at 0.01 and 0.05 levels, respectively.

N: Number of census tracts on which the analysis is based.

Housing Cost as a Factor in American Indian Residential Segregation

What role does housing cost play in the residential segregation of American Indians? Like the pattern of blacks and Hispanics, the spatial distribution of American Indians is not strongly related to the cost of housing. Although as data in Table 7.6 show, a negative relationship exists in every SMSA between the distribution of American Indians and the median value of owner-occupied housing, the relationship was weak in every metropolitan area except Bay City.

The correlation coefficients between the distribution of American Indians and median housing rent generally indicated weaker negative relationships than those for owner-occupied housing value. No strong correlation exists in any SMSA. Therefore, the segregated distribution pattern of American Indians can hardly be explained by the cost of housing.

Table 7.6
Correlation Coefficient (r) between Percent American Indian and Median Housing
Value and between Percent American Indian and Median Rent in Michigan's
SMSAs, 1980

	Median Value		Median Rent	
SMSA	r	N	r	N
Ann Arbor	-.19**	83	-.14	84
Battle Creek	-.44*	62	-.26**	62
Bay City	-.61*	34	-.42*	34
Benton Harbor	-.14	66	-.25**	67
Detroit	-.25*	903	-.11*	910
Flint	-.14	127	-.06	126
Grand Rapids	-.49*	149	-.32*	150
Jackson	-.42*	149	-.18	43
Kalamazoo	-.45*	94	-.44*	95
Lansing	-.44*	134	-.21*	138
Muskegon	-.40*	65	-.36*	65
Saginaw	-.23**	56	-.28**	56

* and ** significant at 0.01 and 0.05 levels, respectively.

N: Number of census tracts on which the analysis is based.

The Accessibility for Asian Americans to Nonsegregated Housing

The Asian population in this study includes Chinese, Filipinos, Japanese, Asian Indians, Koreans, Vietnamese, Hawaiians, Samoans, and Guamanians. There were 3,500,430 Asians in the United States in 1980. More than 56,000 lived in Michigan. Within Michigan, 92 percent resided in the state's twelve SMSAs. The Asian population ranged from 289 in metropolitan Bay City to 33,257 in metropolitan Detroit (U.S. Bureau of the Census, 1981).

Asians (compared to blacks, Hispanics and American Indians) are closer to the white majority population in terms of income, education, and occupation. In some Michigan SMSAs, Asians are either equal to or above the white population in socioeconomic status. Based on ecological theory, Asians should be the least residentially segregated from the white population and the most suburbanized racial/ethnic minority group.

Table 7.7
Rank Order of Minority Group Suburbanization and Minority Group Residential Segregation, Metropolitan Areas of Michigan, 1980

Rank Order	Minority	Percent Suburban	Rank Order	Minority	Level of Metropolitan Segregation
1	Asian	71.4	1	Black	66.8
2	Indian	65.5	2	Hispanic	36.9
3	Hispanic	58.0	3	Indian	34.8
4	Black	34.3	4	Asian	27.0

Source: Computed by the author based on data from U.S. Bureau
    of the Census (1981).

As expected, Asians are on the average less residentially segregated from the white majority population than are blacks, Hispanics, and American Indians. The mean index of dissimilarity for Asians is only 27 percent compared to 66.8 percent for blacks, 36.9 percent for Hispanics, and 34.8 percent for American Indians (Table 7.3).

Asians are also the most suburbanized racial/ethnic minority group with 71.4 percent of its metropolitan population living in the suburbs where the housing is newer and of higher value. The level of minority group suburbanization appears to be inversely related to the level of minority group residential segregation in metropolitan areas (Table 7.7).

Housing Cost as a Factor in Asian American Residential Segregation

Is the spatial distribution of Asians associated with housing cost? The correlation analysis indicates that the relationship between the spatial distribution of Asians and housing cost was weaker than that for blacks, Hispanics, and American Indians. Furthermore, Asians were the only minority group where the relationship was generally positive, that is, as housing cost increased, so did the percentage of Asians. Unlike the other racial/ethnic minority groups, Asians are more likely to live in the areas of higher valued, and higher rent housing (Table 7.8). The cost of housing, therefore, clearly does not restrict Asian accessibility to nonsegregated housing.

Table 7.8

Correlation Coefficient *(r)* between Percent Asian and Median Housing Value and between Percent Asian and Median Rent in Michigan's SMSAs, 1980

	Median Value		Median Rent	
SMSA	r	N	r	N
Ann Arbor	+.19	83	-.00	84
Battle Creek	+.11	62	+.08	62
Bay City	+.13	34	+.13	34
Benton Harbor	+.27	66	+.03	67
Detroit	+.32*	903	+.24*	910
Flint	+.46*	127	+.41*	126
Grand Rapids	-.13*	149	-.04	150
Jackson	+.57*	43	+.59*	43
Kalamazoo	+.33**	94	+.09	95
Lansing	-.04	134	+.01	138
Muskegon	-.06	65	-.08	65
Saginaw	+.45*	56	+.43*	56

* and ** significant at 0.01 and 0.05 levels, respectively.

N: Number of census tracts on which the analysis is based.

Summary and Conclusions

This chapter has revealed that blacks, Hispanics, American Indians, and Asian Americans have differential accessibility to nonsegregated housing. Asians have the greatest accessibility and blacks have the least. The differential degree of accessibility is manifest in the differential levels of residential segregation. Asians are the least segregated racial/ethnic minority group and blacks are the most segregated. Asians are also the most suburbanized minority group and blacks are the least. Suburbanization then is linked to housing accessibility which in turn is linked to a reduction in metropolitan segregation.

Although the strength of the relationship between housing cost and the spatial distribution of each minority group varies, housing cost generally is not a primary factor which prohibits access to nonsegregated housing for either blacks, Hispanics, American Indians, or Asian Americans. Factors other than housing cost are responsible for the denial of equal accessibility to nonsegregated housing for minority groups. It may be concluded that if American metropolitan areas are to become desegregated, the explanation must be among factors other than housing cost.

References

Alonso, William. 1960. A Theory of the Urban Land Market. *Papers and Proceedings of the Regional Science Association* 6: 149–58.

Bleda, S. E. 1975. Bases of Ethnic Residential Segregation: Recent Patterns in American Metropolitan Areas. Paper presented at the American Sociological Association Annual Meeting in San Francisco.

Burgess, Ernest W. 1923. The Growth of the City: An Introduction to a Research Project. *Proceedings of the American Sociological Society* 18: 57–85.

Citizens Commission on Civil Rights. 1983. *A Decent Home*. A Report on the Continuing Failure of the Federal Government to Provide Equal Housing Opportunity. Washington, D.C.: Center for National Policy Review, Catholic University Law School.

Darden, Joe T. 1973. *Afro-Americans in Pittsburgh: The Residential Segregation of a People*. Lexington, Mass.: D. C. Heath and Company.

———. 1983. Demographic Changes 1970–1980: Implications for Federal Fair Housing Policy. In *A Shelter Crisis: The State of Fair Housing in the Eighties*, 7–30. Washington, D.C.: U.S. Commission on Civil Rights.

———. 1984a. Demographic Patterns in Housing: Changes in Chicago and the Nation Since 1950. In *Civil Rights in the Eighties: A Thirty Year Perspective*, 167–90. Chicago: Chicago Urban League.

———. 1984b. The Residential Segregation of American Indians in Metropolitan Areas of Michigan. *Journal of Urban Affairs* 6 (Winter): 29–38.

———. 1985a. The Housing Situation of Blacks in Metropolitan Areas of Michigan. In *The State of Black Michigan 1985*, 11–21. East Lansing: Urban Affairs Programs, Michigan State University.

———. 1985b. Asians in Metropolitan Areas of Michigan: A Retest of the Social and Spatial Distance Hypothesis. Paper presented at the Annual Meeting of the Association of American Geographers, Detroit, April 1985.

Darden, Joe T., and J. B. Haney. 1978. Measuring Adaptation: Migration Status and Residential Segregation Among Anglos, Blacks, and Chicanos. *The East Lake Geographers* 13 (June): 20–33.

Darden, Joe T., and A. Tabachneck. 1980. Algorithm 8: Graphic and Mathematical Description of Inequality, Dissimilarity, Segregation, or Concentration. *Environment and Planning* 12: 227–34.

Farley, John. 1983. *Segregated City, Segregated Suburbs: Are They Products of Black-White Socioeconomic Differentials?* CUERS Report No. 19. Edwardsville, Ill.: Southern Illinois University.

Farley, Reynolds. 1977. Residential Segregation in Urbanized Areas of the United States in 1970: An Analysis of Social Class and Racial Differences. *Demography* 14 (November): 497–518.

Gold, Neil. 1972. The Mismatch of Jobs and Low-Income People in Metropolitan

Areas and Its Implications for the Central City Poor. In Report of the Commission on Population Growth and the American Future, 443–86. Washington, D.C.: GPO.

Guest, Avery, and James Weed. 1976. Ethnic Residential Segregation: Patterns of Change. *American Journal of Sociology* 81: 1088–1111.

Hawley, Amos H. 1950. *Human Ecology*. New York: The Ronald Press Company.

Jackman, Mary R., and Robert W. Jackman. 1980. Racial Inequalities in Home Ownership. *Social Forces* 58 (June): 1221–34.

Kain, John F., and John M. Quigley. 1975. *Housing Markets and Racial Discrimination: A Micro-Economic Analysis*. New York: National Bureau of Economic Research.

Kiang, Y. C. 1968. The Distribution of Ethnic Groups in Chicago, 1960. *American Journal of Sociology* 74: 292–95.

Lopez, Manuel M. 1981. Patterns of Interethnic Residential Segregation in the Urban Southwest. *Social Science Quarterly* 62: 50–63.

Marshall, Harvey, and Robert Jiobu. 1975. Residential Segregation in United States Cities: A Causal Analysis. *Social Forces* 53 (March): 449–60.

Marston, Wilfred and Thomas L. Van Valey. 1979. The Role of Residential Segregation in Assimilation Process. *Annals of the American Academy of Political and Social Science* 441 (January): 13–25.

Massey, D. S. 1979. Effects of Socioeconomic Factors on the Residential Segregation of Blacks and Spanish Americans in U.S. Urbanized Areas. *American Sociological Review* 44 (December): 1015–22.

————. 1981. Hispanic Residential Segregation: A Comparison of Mexicans, Cubans, and Puerto Ricans. *Sociology and Social Research* 44 (April): 311–22.

Massey, Douglas and Brendan P. Mullan. 1984. Processes of Hispanic and Black Spatial Assimilation. *American Journal of Sociology* 89 (January): 836–73.

Park, Robert. 1926. The Urban Community as a Spatial Pattern and Moral Order. In *The Urban Community*, edited by E. W. Burgess, 3–28. Chicago: University of Chicago Press.

Sorenson, Annemette, Karl Taeuber, and Leslie Hollingsworth, Jr. 1975. Indexes of Racial Residential Segregation for 109 Cities in the United States, 1940–1970. *Sociological Focus* 8 (April): 125–42.

Steger, Wilbur. 1973. Economic and Social Costs of Residential Segregation. In *Modernizing Urban Land Policy*, edited by Marion Clawson. Baltimore: Johns Hopkins University Press.

U.S. Bureau of the Census. 1981. *1980 Census of Population and Housing: Advance Reports, Michigan*. PHC80-V–24.

————. 1982. *Population and Housing Summary Tape Files 1-A*. Michigan. Washington, D.C.: USBC, Data User Services.

————. 1983. *Census of Population and Housing, 1980: Summary Tape File 4*. Michigan. Washington, D.C.: USBC, Data User Services.

Villemez, Wayne J. 1980. Race, Class, and Neighborhood: Differences in the Residential Return on Individual Resources. *Social Forces* 59: 414–30.

8

Su casa no es mi casa: Hispanic Housing Conditions in Contemporary America, 1949– 1980

Manuel Mariano Lopez

The period of general prosperity following the close of World War II, aided in large part by the Housing Act of 1949, the Federal Housing Administration's loan program, and the GI benefits packages—including the Veterans Administration's loan program—led to improvements in housing for all Americans. Overall, improvements in housing from 1949 through 1980 were substantial.

Yet contradictions persist. While great improvements have occurred, continuing gaps remain in both the qualitative and quantitative aspects of units occupied by the dominant whites and various minority groups. That housing for Hispanic Americans is better in 1980 than it was in 1970, and presumably in the 1950s and the 1960s, is to miss the essence of the issue at hand.[1]

As Myrdal (1944: 375) noted, housing is much more than mere shelter; it provides a setting for one's entire social existence. Differential access to housing provides "the base structure for other forms of segregation" (Johnson, 1944; Hershberg et al., 1979: 57). Being "ill-housed" can mean deprivation along several dimensions such as health, safety, and transportation. Such relative deprivations then lead to differential disadvantages in employment, educational opportunities, and most importantly economic stability.

For the non-Hispanic white population, as families' ability to pay for housing increase so do their options relative to housing: desirability of location, suitability of dwelling for family needs at different life-cycle stages, personal taste, and proximity to employment and other services (Feagin and Feagin, 1978: 85). The issue, then, is the extent to which Hispanic households have the option in choosing quality housing comparable to those of non-Hispanic white population.[2]

Five widely accepted characteristics have generally been used to indicate the relative quality of a minority group's housing: (1) location; (2) home ownership; (3) degree of overcrowding; (4) completeness; and, (5) relative costs (DeFleur, 1983: 187). The data to be presented for each of these measures clearly demonstrates that Hispanic housing at the national level falls short of the non-Hispanic white group's standards by a relatively wide margin.

Location

The most visible effect of discrimination in the housing market is the segregation and concentration of minorities in well-defined residential enclaves within the central city. Generally speaking, this has resulted in suburban tracts—defined as the noncentral city component of any SMSA—that are populated by dominant group households, as compared to the inner-city areas dominated by minorities.

Subsidy-based policies designed to encourage home ownership fostered suburban growth and, for the white population, the migration of the middle class population out of the central city. But the failure of government policies to provide the same opportunity to minorities during the post-World War II building boom is reflected in the segregation patterns of the 1960s and 1970s. Pervasive residential segregation continues to constrain housing choices (Struyk et al., 1978: 6) for Hispanics and other minorities into the 1980s (Hwang and Murdock, 1982; Bohland, 1982). With its relatively large Hispanic population, Texas may reflect a "typical" example of Hispanic segregation. The decline in the value of Hispanic/non-Hispanic white segregation, measured by index of dissimilarity, which first became evident in 1970 (Lopez, 1981), dropped from 0.59 in 1970 to 0.49 in 1980. Although the 0.49 value may be regarded as "moderate," an index of dissimilarity of 0.38 persisted when segregation was measured at the tract level (Hwang and Murdock, 1982).

The present situation for Hispanics in the housing arena cannot be fully understood without recognizing that it was produced and maintained in large part by forces of discrimination outside the housing market. Because housing types and quality tend not to be randomly distributed across urban areas, issues of segregation and supply/quality are interrelated. The structural constraints of the past continue to loom large. While more indirect than in days-gone-by they can nonetheless function just as effectively to prevent minority group advancement at the present. The broad focus chosen for this paper does not permit greater elaboration on this important dimension. But, the literature on residential segregation is bountiful and several quality analyses of the topic exist (Moore and Mittelbach, 1966; Kantrowitz, 1969; Massey, 1979; Lopez, 1981, 1982; Hwang and Murdock, 1982).

The dispersion of a minority group within a metropolitan area can be used as an *indirect* measure of the choice/opportunity structure available to the group. The concentration of minority households in the central city and their conspicuous absence from the suburban scene has been used as a measure of limited choice (U.S. Commission on Civil Rights, 1978: 69; Feagin and Feagin, 1978: 85, 112).

Hispanic households (88.2 percent) are more likely than non-Hispanic white households (73.4 percent) to reside in metropolitan areas, with a significantly greater proportion in the central city component—53 percent of Hispanics, as compared to only 27 percent whites (U.S. Bureau of the Census, 1983a). Intercensal changes in this indicator for Hispanics are minimal, which reflect stability. Nearly 45 percent of the Hispanic central city population over the age of five resided in the same house in 1975 and 1980, with another 34.3 percent having moved from one house to another within the same county. Parallel figures for non-Hispanic whites were 52.0 percent and 26.6 percent, respectively (U.S. Bureau of the Census, 1983a).

A significant volume of the literature on housing differentials assumes that the principal nonracial determinants of residential differences are due to individual differences in economic resources (Darroch and Marston, 1969, 1971; Farley, 1970). Some evidence exists suggesting that while income differentials may explain some location differences they fail to account for significant disparities in group distribution. One analysis of 1970 data found that the residential segregation of Mexican Americans from non-Hispanic whites persisted at comparable levels of housing value or rent, albeit at levels significantly lower than interracial segregation (Lopez, 1982). Controlling for household income, we see that Hispanics are more likely to be found in central cities than in the suburban fringe, or the noncentral city metropolitan areas, at all levels of household income (Table 8.1).

Home Ownership

There exists a strongly held, longstanding norm in American society favoring home ownership over renting (Dillman, Tremblay, and Dillman, 1979: 5). Home ownership has been viewed as a "stabilizing and positive influence in the United States" (U.S. Commission on Civil Rights, 1978: 74). While home ownership confers both economic and psychological benefits (Rosow, 1948), its greatest impact for the middle and lower classes is as a major form of saving and capital investment (Lake, 1979: 143). Additional economic benefits of home ownership occur because interest payments on mortgages and property taxes have special status in the tax law— they are tax deductible items. Renters cannot avail themselves of these commonly accepted loopholes in the tax laws designed to promote home ownership.

Home ownership in the United States is widespread. However, it is sig-

Table 8.1
Percent Distribution[a] of Hispanic and White Home Ownership across
Metropolitan and Nonmetropolitan Areas by 1979 Household Income

	Hispanic			Non-Hispanic White		
Income in $	Cen Cty	NonCC	NonMet	Cen Cty	NonCC	NonMet
Less than 5,000	61.4	24.9	13.7	30.7	34.3	35.0
5,000 - 9,999	56.3	29.9	13.9	29.0	38.1	32.9
10,000 - 12,499	54.0	33.2	12.8	28.2	41.0	30.8
12,500 - 14,999	53.0	34.8	12.2	27.4	42.6	30.0
15,000 - 19,999	51.0	37.3	11.7	26.3	45.6	28.1
20,000 - 24,999	47.9	41.7	10.4	24.7	50.1	25.2
25,000 - 34,999	45.2	46.0	8.8	23.9	55.1	21.0
35,000 - 49,999	41.4	51.4	7.2	24.0	59.9	16.1
50,000 or more	38.3	54.2	7.5	26.0	59.7	14.3

a: Percentages sum across areal designations within ethnic
   categories.

Source: Computed based on data from U.S. Bureau of the Census
   (1983a).

nificantly less common among Hispanics than among non-Hispanic whites.
As the data in Table 8.2 show, 43.3 percent of Hispanics in 1980, as
compared to 68.5 percent non-Hispanic whites, were home owners. While
the data in Table 8.2 indicate that differentials in income have some bearing
on the intraethnic distributions in home ownership, interethnic disparities
persist across all metropolitan types and income levels.[3]

Over the course of the decade, Hispanics have either lost slightly, or have
maintained their ground in the pursuit of home ownership; they have not
improved their condition. Overall, Hispanic home ownership dropped from
46.2 percent in 1970 to 43.3 percent in 1980. The decline occurs for metropolitan areas—central cities and the suburban fringe—while the nonmetropolitan households exhibit a slight improvement.[4] Parallel data for
the non-Hispanic white population illustrate increased home ownership
across all areas.[5]

A greater proportion of non-Hispanic white than Hispanic households
have been able to afford the expenses of home ownership. This is not
unexpected as the average cost of new housing increased by 134.1 percent,
and that for the existing units by 133.0 percent between 1972 and 1982,

Table 8.2
Percent Distribution[a] of Hispanic and White Home Ownership within Metropolitan and Nonmetropolitan Areas by 1979 Household Income

Income in $	Hispanic			Non-Hispanic White		
	Cen Cty	NonCC	NonMet	Cen Cty	NonCC	NonMet
Less than 5,000	15.0	29.9	48.4	31.2	51.9	60.6
5,000 - 9,999	20.5	32.9	50.0	39.0	57.1	66.3
10,000 - 12,499	26.1	37.2	55.8	40.9	57.5	68.4
12,500 - 14,999	31.3	43.1	60.0	46.3	61.5	72.2
15,000 - 19,999	39.2	51.6	66.6	53.3	67.8	77.4
20,000 - 24,999	50.7	63.3	74.6	64.0	76.9	83.3
25,000 - 34,999	61.4	74.4	80.5	73.6	84.8	88.2
35,000 - 49,999	71.0	82.7	82.5	80.6	90.3	91.2
50,000 or more	73.2	86.3	80.8	83.3	92.8	91.8
Components	33.5	52.3	60.0	54.5	72.4	73.1
Total		43.3			68.5	

a: Percentages sum across areal designations within ethnic categories.

Source: Computed based on data from U.S. Bureau of the Census (1983a).

while Hispanic household income rose by only 77.8 percent, as against an increase of 83.7 percent for whites (U.S. Bureau of the Census, 1984b: 442, 729). What is interesting is that recent (1977–1981) Hispanic buyers demonstrate significantly higher price/income ratios, especially when the ratio exceeds 3.0. About 26 percent of all Hispanic buyers compared to only 16.2 percent of white buyers[6] had purchased homes priced three or more times greater than their annual income (Table 8.3). This means that either Hispanics are buying significantly larger homes or they are being forced to pay more for housing units of comparable worth. The generally high proportion of renters among Hispanics at all income levels (Table 8.2) offers additional indirect evidence of higher home ownership costs for Hispanics. Unfortunately, the available empirical data do not permit a clear resolution of this issue.

For minorities the mortgage finance system is an impediment. That minorities face discrimination in obtaining loans has been documented repeatedly (U.S. Commission on Civil Rights, 1978: 74). In applying "sound business principles" revolving around the protection of profitable invest-

Table 8.3
Percent Distribution of Hispanic and White Purchase Price/Income Ratios for
Home Acquisition 1977–1981, by Mortgage Type

Price/	Hispanic				Non-Hispanic White			
Income Ratio	Total	FHA	VA	Conv	Total	FHA	VA	Conv
Less than 1.0	10.9	8.0	5.1	13.0	11.8	10.4	7.9	11.5
1.0 to 1.9	35.5	26.5	64.4	33.0	45.6	48.2	49.3	47.4
2.0 to 2.9	27.9	32.7	25.4	27.8	26.4	28.6	29.0	26.1
3.0 to 3.9	11.1	18.6	5.1	10.4	9.0	7.1	7.5	9.0
4 or more	14.6	14.2	0.0	15.9	7.2	5.7	6.3	6.0

Source: Computed based on data from U.S. Bureau of the Census
(1983b: 333, 361).

ments, lending organizations establish requirements that operate against minority applicants. Mortgages in ghetto/barrio areas are of shorter duration and higher interest rates (Feagin and Feagin, 1978: 98, 104).

The shortage of housing for the poor and/or minority families is due to a persistent shortfall of mortgage credit. Funds available through private savings institutions have not been enough to guarantee construction of housing aimed at low income groups (Schussheim, 1970: 19). At the national level, the Federal Housing Administration (FHA) has been one of the most influential agencies in shaping the nation's housing and residential patterns. Presumably, federal housing policy has been aimed at providing an opportunity for "a decent home and suitable living environment" for all Americans by filling the void left by private savings institutions. Through a program of decreasing the risk to a lender, mortgages were made available at lower interest rates, for longer periods of time, with lower monthly payments by the borrower (Feagin and Feagin, 1978: 105). An indirect assessment of the FHA's impact (U.S. Bureau of the Census, 1983b) in the case of Hispanic housing indicates that while the median length of FHA loans to Hispanics is about equal to that of whites—30.1 v. 30.2 years—the interest rates and timeframe of such loans leave some issues unresolved. For instance, as it may be noted from data in Table 8.4, a greater proportion of Hispanic recipients of FHA loans are paying higher (over 8.0 percent) or significantly higher (over 12.0 percent) interest rates than are whites.

Data in Table 8.5 reveal that white assumptions are more recent and exhibit a generally lower proportion of high-interest loans. A much greater proportion of Hispanic FHA loans are secured through federal entities—64.8 percent Hispanics compared to 40.6 percent whites (U.S. Bureau of

Table 8.4
Percent Distribution of Hispanic and White First Mortgage Interest Rates by Mortgage Type, 1981.

	Hispanic			Non-Hispanic White		
Interest Rates (%)	FHA	VA	Conv	FHA	VA	Conv
Less than 6.0	15.2	21.5	3.6	34.4	25.8	6.7
6.0 t0 7.9	26.8	19.2	18.9	21.4	21.5	24.1
8.0 to 9.9	39.3	52.3	50.6	28.2	38.0	46.4
10.0 to 11.9	11.7	5.2	18.0	11.8	10.8	14.0
12 or more	7.0	1.7	8.9	4.2	3.9	8.8

Source: Computed based on data from U.S. Bureau of the Census
   (1983b: 336, 364).

the Census, 1983b). The greater probability of higher interest rates for Hispanics would be understandable if Hispanics demonstrated a greater recency of purchases or mortgage assumptions. But intercensal comparisons earlier in this chapter indicated that Hispanic purchases have not kept up with non-Hispanic white buyers. Given that white mortgages with the FHA program are more recent, an assumption that whites should exhibit higher interest rates seems in order. Yet the data in Table 8.4 indicate a lower proportion of high-interest loans for whites. While FHA loans have undoubtedly helped Hispanics acquire their own homes (25.4 percent of home owners have FHA first trust mortgage) they have not been as prevalent in the most recent past and they have had a "cost" associated with them in the form of somewhat higher interest rates—a median interest rate of 8.6 percent for Hispanic as compared to 7.0 percent for whites.

The Veterans Administration (VA) loan program has accounted for 17.0 percent of all first trust mortgages on Hispanic homes. Once again, there is no difference in the life of the loan (median of 30.2 years for both) and explainable differences in interest rates. The VA program seems to have operated to the greatest advantage of Hispanics in the immediate World War II and Viet Nam periods (Table 8.5). Whites were more likely to have been recipients in the most recent past. This pattern of loans is reflected in VA interest payments where the "early" Hispanic loans translated into low rates; and "late" white loans translated into high interest rates. Federal entities secure roughly equal proportions (37.8 and 39.2 percent, respectively) of Hispanic and white loans (U.S. Bureau of the Census, 1983b).

Table 8.5
Percent Distribution of Year First Mortgage Assumed by Hispanics and Whites,
and Mortgage Type, 1981

Year Assumed	Hispanic			Non-Hispanic White		
	FHA	VA	Conv	FHA	VA	Conv
1975–1981	44.0	54.1	63.8	55.5	61.1	68.3
1970–1974	19.3	16.2	19.4	27.0	11.6	20.2
1965–1969	16.3	11.0	10.2	7.4	14.0	7.2
1960–1964	14.2	10.8	5.7	5.5	9.3	3.1
1959 or earlier	6.2	7.9	0.8	4.7	4.1	1.2

Source: Computed based on data from U.S. Bureau of the Census
    (1983b: 335, 363).

Thus, the VA program appears, in aggregate, to have been more evenhanded than the FHA program in its treatment of Hispanics.

Conventional loans by private institutions represent the weak link in the Hispanic home purchasing system; while representing the majority of all loans (56.6 percent of all first trust mortgages), it compares very unfavorably with the mortgage patterns for whites. In contrast to Hispanics, 73.1 percent of all first trust mortgages of homes owned by whites are financed by private institutions. In the private loan arena the federal program loan patterns are repeated; Hispanics are more likely to pay high (over 8.0 percent) and significantly high (over 12.0 percent) interest rates despite being less likely to be recent borrowers. While the students of black housing have numerous works to corroborate discriminatory practices by the financial institutions, no such studies appear to exist for Hispanics. Nonetheless, these patterns raise questions concerning mortgage policies as they impact on Hispanic housing conditions.

Overcrowding

Contemporary treatments of overcrowding focus not on its dangerous physical effects, but rather on questions of comfort and equality (U.S. Commission on Civil Rights, 1978: 75). The number of persons per room is a commonly used measure of comfort/privacy. Here, the widely accepted definition of "overcrowded" as more than one person per room is used to analyze overcrowding in owner-occupied and rental units.

In 1980, roughly 16 percent of all Hispanic owner-occupied and 24 per-

Table 8.6
Percent Overcrowded Hispanic and White Owner- and Renter-Occupied Housing Units by Place of Residence, 1980

Place of Residence by No. of Persons Per Room	Hispanic		Non-Hispanic White	
	Owner	Renter	Owner	Renter
Metropolitan Area Central City	15.9	24.1	1.5	2.7
1.01 to 1.50	10.4	12.7	1.3	2.0
1.51 or more	5.5	11.4	0.2	0.7
Noncentral City				
1.01 to 1.50	10.0	12.9	1.4	2.2
1.51 or more	5.8	12.8	0.2	0.6
Nonmetropolitan				
1.01 to 1.50	15.9	23.8	2.5	4.2
1.51 or more	4.9	10.0	0.4	0.9

Source: Computed based on data from U.S. Bureau of the Census (1983a).

cent of the rental units in the United States were overcrowded. For both owners and renters this represents a likelihood of overcrowding eight times greater than that of comparable non-Hispanic whites. This compares with the 1970 probabilities of 4.7 times for non-Hispanic white owner-occupied (5 percent overcrowded) units and 4.2 times for renter-occupied (6.5 percent overcrowded) units (U.S. Bureau of the Census, 1977, 1973b). In other words, while Hispanic households have reduced the degree of overcrowding by 32.1 percent among owners, and by 11.7 percent among renters, they have lost ground relative to non-Hispanic white households which reduced overcrowding by 64.0 percent among owners and 55.4 percent among renters during the same period.

Hispanic homeowners and renters are disproportionately situated in crowded conditions across geographic areas. The relative disparities as manifested in Table 8.6 are more pronounced for metropolitan residents. In 1980, "severe overcrowding"—defined as 1.51 or more persons per room—across all geographic designations was much more pronounced among Hispanic householders than among non-Hispanic whites, continuing a pattern already evident in 1970 (U.S. Bureau of the Census, 1982).

While less pronounced at the upper income categories, Hispanic/non-

Table 8.7
Percent Overcrowded Hispanic and White Owner-Occupied Housing Units by
1979 Household Income and Metropolitan/Nonmetropolitan Location

Income in $	Hispanic			Non-Hispanic White		
	Cen Cty	Non-CC	Non-Met	Cen Cty	Non-CC	Non-Met
Less than 5,000	11.3	14.5	9.9	0.5	0.9	1.4
5,000 - 9,999	14.7	9.0	16.5	0.7	1.1	2.1
10,000 - 12,499	17.6	20.0	20.0	1.0	1.6	2.9
12,500 - 14,999	18.0	19.3	19.1	1.2	1.8	2.9
15,000 - 19,999	17.4	18.1	18.2	1.5	2.0	3.0
20,000 - 24,999	16.3	15.8	15.5	1.6	1.9	2.7
25,000 - 34,999	15.8	13.8	15.9	1.6	1.7	2.5
35,000 - 49,999	16.4	13.3	16.5	1.7	1.6	2.6
50,000 or more	15.3	12.6	12.4	1.4	1.4	2.1

Source: Computed based on data from U.S. Bureau of the Census
(1983a).

Hispanic white differentials in overcrowding for owner- and renter-occupied units exist across all income levels (Tables 8.7 and 8.8). Once again, the interethnic differentials are more pronounced among home owners than renters. The results, even when differentials in income are "controlled," indicate that the disparity is not solely economic; ethnic factors apparently continue to affect access to adequate housing. While the acknowledged difference in the average family and/or household size between Hispanics and non-Hispanic whites cannot logically account for the remaining differences, it may still account for some of the disparity after controlling for income. The available data do not permit further elaboration of this point, however.

Hispanics appear to get less space/privacy for their housing dollar when measured in terms of the value of the home or the amount of rent. In 1980, Hispanic home owners experienced greater overcrowding at all levels of home value across all locations. For each value category the greatest differential existed for central city locations and the least for nonmetropolitan areas. Nonetheless, overcrowding among Hispanics was found to be 5.0 times greater than that among non-Hispanic whites in housing units in nonmetropolitan areas valued at less than $10,000; it was nearly 18 times greater in housing units valued at $60,000–79,999 located in the central cities. Differentials in overcrowding by gross rent were less severe—3.8 times

Table 8.8
Percent Overcrowded Hispanic and White Renter-Occupied Housing Units by
1979 Household Income and Metropolitan/Nonmetropolitan Location

Income in $	Hispanic			Non-Hispanic White		
	Cen Cty	NonCC	NonMet	Cen Cty	NonCC	NonMet
Less than 5,000	15.7	20.7	19.3	1.6	2.0	2.7
5,000 - 9,999	24.5	26.7	25.5	2.4	2.8	4.3
10,000 - 12,499	26.0	26.9	24.2	2.5	2.9	4.7
12,500 - 14,999	26.7	28.0	26.3	2.6	3.0	4.5
15,000 - 19,999	26.6	26.9	25.2	2.7	2.9	4.7
20,000 - 24,999	27.1	25.4	26.2	3.0	3.0	4.8
25,000 - 34,999	29.0	26.2	26.3	3.4	3.1	4.9
35,000 - 49,999	33.1	29.8	28.3	3.8	3.4	5.6
50,000 or more	30.9	29.6	28.4	3.5	3.3	5.8

Source: Computed based on data from U.S. Bureau of the Census
    (1983a).

at the $500 and over rent level in nonmetropolitan areas, and 13.9 times for the less than $100 rent level in the suburban fringe—but nonetheless exhibit a pattern parallel to that of home owners.

Completeness and Quality of Housing

Housing quality is difficult to assess. Analysts lack an agreed-upon definition of what constitutes substandard housing and the most recent censuses lack objective measures which might define less-than-desirable conditions. Census data on housing quality are astonishingly sparse. When dealing with the issue of quality we are reduced to indirect assessment dictated by the nature of the available data.

Housing "completeness," the traditional measure of quality, is measured by simply noting the presence or absence of a specified facility. Given the 1980 census schedule, only "complete plumbing for exclusive use" seems a usable measure. The presence of heating units is not as crucial in southern California or Texas as is in Maine or Vermont; neither is air conditioning as crucial in New Hampshire as is in Texas. In the absence of a clear standard, the percentage of units with "complete" plumbing facilities for "exclusive use" will be taken as the measure of housing "completeness."

More than 95 percent of all contemporary American households have complete plumbing facilities for exclusive use. In the United States as a whole, based on the 1980 census data, 97.9 percent Hispanic owners, as compared to 99.0 percent non-Hispanic whites, and 95.5 percent Hispanic renters, as compared to 97.4 percent non-Hispanic white households did have complete plumbing facilities. Depending on location (metropolitan, nonmetropolitan, central city, and noncentral city), 95.3 to 98.6 percent of Hispanic owners, and 92.8 to 96.2 percent Hispanic renters in 1980 did have complete plumbing facilities. The corresponding figures for non-Hispanic whites were 95.5 to 99.6 percent, and 95.2 to 98.1 percent respectively (U.S. Bureau of the Census, 1983a). The small disparity at the level of one percent range for owner-occupied housing and less than two and a half for renters at the national level indicates near "equality" with regard to completeness. Unfortunately, the census only tells us if the facilities are present, not if they work properly.

The Annual Housing Survey (U.S. Bureau of the Census, 1977, 1981) provides researchers with some additional information related to housing quality. Hispanic households are more likely than the population at large to live in units exhibiting less-than-adequate conditions.[7] As we may note from data in Table 8.9, while the difference relative to exposed wiring is minimal, differences related to leakages from the roof, cracks in the walls, broken plaster, and peeling paint are significant. The results would indicate little or no improvement for either Hispanic owners or renters with regard to several housing "quality" measures between 1975 and 1981. Limited data on the central city (U.S. Bureau of the Census, 1981) indicate that these conditions exist across metropolitan subcomponents. In short, Hispanic housing appears to be of inferior overall quality.

Despite problems in equating age of structure with "quality," age of housing unit does serve as another indirect measure of quality (Feagin and Feagin, 1978: 85, 112). An old housing unit presents an "image" problem even if the roof does not leak and the wind does not rustle through the cracks. Owner-occupied housing shows few national differences, due partially to differences in regional population concentrations and structural differences. But, Hispanic rental housing is older than that for non-Hispanic whites even when regional differences remain uncontrolled.

An examination of recently acquired (1975–1980) owner-occupied housing shed light on the existing market conditions. For all location designations Hispanics are purchasing older structures, except apparently in the oldest (pre–1939) category (Table 8.10). While a "gentrification" explanation for this exception would appear to be more plausible for non-Hispanic whites than Hispanics, it actually reflects concurrent regional variations in availability of old housing and the distribution of the Hispanic population. In three of the four major census regions "new" Hispanic home owners represent a greater relative proportion of purchasers of pre–1939 structures than do non-Hispanic whites. Only in the South do non-Hispanic whites

Table 8.9

Percent Hispanic and White Owner- and Renter-Occupied Housing Units with Specified Deficiency Conditions, 1975 and 1981

Deficiency/ Characteristic	Spanish Origin				Total Population			
	Owner		Renter		Owner		Renter	
	1975	1981	1975	1981	1975	1981	1975	1981
Conditions								
Exposed Wiring	1.7	2.3	3.0	4.6	1.4	2.2	2.6	4.1
Roof Leak (Signs)	5.2	6.6	8.4	9.7	4.9	4.9	8.6	7.8
Cracks in walls	4.1	5.2	15.7	15.5	2.7	2.9	10.1	10.6
Broken Plaster	3.7	3.2	9.5	10.3	1.9	1.9	6.3	6.4
Peeling Paint	3.5	3.6	12.0	11.6	2.2	2.1	7.6	7.6
Crime	17.6	21.1	24.5	25.6	16.2	19.9	22.4	26.2
Services								
No Pub. Transit	33.2	33.5	18.6	18.6	1.4	4.8	1.9	28.7
Evaluation								
Like to move	4.4	12.2	7.4	18.0	3.8	6.9	6.2	14.1
Overall Evaluation								
Excellent	31.8	34.8	13.5	15.0	42.3	46.5	19.8	24.3
Poor	1.1	1.4	9.5	8.8	0.9	0.8	6.1	5.1

Source: Computed based on data from U.S. Bureau of the Census
(1977: 41-44, 279-282; 1981: 4-11, 34-41).

represent a greater relative proportion of the purchasers of pre–1939 structures.

For the central cities, 52.5 percent of "new" Hispanic owners purchased housing units that were over 16 years old as opposed to 47.7 percent of the "new" non-Hispanic white owners. This pattern is paralleled for renters (Table 8.10). A "filtering down" process appears to be at work; Hispanics are "inheriting" older units which other groups are leaving for newer/better housing. This process appears to be corroborated by data on residential finance indicating that a greater proportion of whites financed new purchases through the sale of a previous home (U.S. Bureau of the Census, 1983b). U.S. Bureau of the Census (1981) data indicate that a greater pro-

Table 8.10
Percent Recently Acquired Hispanic and White Owner- and Renter-Occupied
Housing Units by Age of Structure and Metropolitan Location, 1980

Year Structure Built	Hispanic			Non-Hispanic White		
	Cent Cty	NonCC	Non-Met	Cent Cty	NonCC	NonMet
Owner-Occupied						
1975–1980	20.0	34.2	40.0	23.4	40.4	41.5
1970–1974	10.3	13.5	14.3	11.6	16.1	15.0
1960–1969	17.2	18.5	14.3	17.2	16.6	12.8
1940–1959	32.5	26.1	20.4	26.0	17.4	14.0
1939 or earlier	20.0	7.7	11.0	21.7	9.6	16.8
Renter-Occupied						
1975–1980	7.5	11.7	13.0	12.9	16.3	14.8
1970–1974	8.8	14.6	12.6	14.4	19.8	13.3
1960–1969	16.3	24.6	18.1	19.8	24.5	16.0
1940–1959	35.5	34.6	35.7	25.3	22.8	25.6
1939 or earlier	32.0	14.5	20.7	27.7	16.7	30.4

Source: Computed based on data from U.S. Bureau of the Census
 (1983a).

portion of recent (1977–1981) Hispanic owners were first-time owners—
62.9 percent v. 41.5 percent for all races.

But "decent housing" cannot be defined in purely structural terms. Inequities in delivery of municipal services and other "intangibles" also affect
the quality of housing. Annual Housing Survey data (U.S. Bureau of the
Census, 1977, 1981) indicate that Hispanics are much more likely to live
in areas which are not served by public transit, are less likely to be rated
as "excellent" and more likely to be rated as "poor" (Table 8.9), and more
likely to express a desire to move as a result of neighborhood conditions.
As expected, renters exhibit less positive attitudes toward their neighborhoods and a greater desire to move. If the Hispanic householders' "desire"
to move is unmatched by an ability to move as might be reasoned by the
dramatic increments in "willingness" between 1975 and 1981, they will
find themselves "trapped" in housing whose condition will deteriorate. As
it has been so aptly written: "From the perspective of the real estate investor,
the rent-paying ability of poor families simply does not promise a rate of

return sufficient to justify large expenditures on upkeep and services, not to mention major renovations and improvements" (Solomon, 1974: 5).

Relative Housing Costs

Housing costs cannot generally be deferred or reduced from month to month; they are crucial components of the household budget. One of the operating assumptions of federal programs was to limit housing expenses to roughly 25 percent of the household's income (U.S. Commission on Civil Rights, 1978: 84; LaGory and Pipkin, 1981: 266). Measuring relative housing costs as the percentage of income spent on housing serves to adjust for regional differentials in levels of living. The available data, as shown in Tables 8.11 and 8.12, indicate that Hispanic households, especially home owners with mortgages, are more likely to exceed the 25 percent guideline than those of non-Hispanic whites. Hispanics must pay a higher proportion of their income to acquire and maintain housing; this is true across all geographic designations. Among mortgage holders Hispanics manifest a significantly higher proportion of "high cost"—that is, costs in excess of 35 percent of the household income. Over 17 percent of all Hispanic households, as compared to roughly 13 percent of non-Hispanic white households spent more than 35 percent of their income for housing. This finding is consistent with the earlier observation that recent (1975–1980) Hispanic buyers had significantly higher price/income ratios than whites. The data in Table 8.12 show that Hispanics spending 35 percent or more of their income for rent is substantially greater than the corresponding figure for whites.

Conclusion

Housing continues to be one of the most persistent problems in the American society. While discrimination is illegal and segregation has been on the decline, the basic mechanisms of our private enterprise system—that is, loan policies of government agencies and private financial institutions—have reinforced existing trends which emerged in a discriminatory past. Consequently, Hispanics continue to be segregated from non-Hispanic whites and are more likely to be concentrated in central city housing with its presumably inferior older structures and services; and, they are less likely to own their homes; more likely to live under crowded conditions; more likely to live in aged housing units or units having structural deficiencies; and, more likely to pay a greater price/rent for comparable housing, resulting in deprivation of the attendant economic and psychic benefits associated with better housing enjoyed by the non-Hispanic whites.

While the 1970s witnessed some gains for Hispanics in the housing arena, there were also losses. Even in areas where Hispanics made absolute gains

Table 8.11

Percent Distribution of Selected Monthly Hispanic and White Owner Costs as a Percent of 1979 Household Income by Location and Type of Mortgage

Percent Income	Hispanic			Non-Hispanic White		
	Cent Cty	NonCC	NonMet	Cent Cty	NonCC	NonMet
			Mortgaged Units			
Less than 15%	33.3	29.1	30.9	36.4	32.5	31.0
15 to 19 %	18.7	18.4	19.4	20.2	21.3	21.5
20 to 24 %	14.5	15.5	15.2	15.0	16.5	16.4
25 to 29 %	10.0	11.3	10.6	9.6	10.6	10.5
30 to 34 %	6.5	7.6	6.4	5.7	6.2	6.1
35 % or more	17.1	18.1	17.4	13.2	12.9	14.4
Median	18.6	20.7	18.9	17.7	18.3	18.5
			Not Mortgaged Units			
Less than 10%	54.3	56.0	45.4	45.8	45.6	42.6
10 to 14 %	18.1	17.9	19.0	20.2	20.8	20.3
15 to 19 %	9.0	8.7	10.8	11.4	11.3	11.9
20 to 24 %	5.4	5.2	7.0	6.9	6.7	7.6
25 to 29 %	3.5	3.1	4.6	4.4	4.3	4.9
30 to 34 %	2.2	2.2	3.1	3.0	2.9	3.3
35 % or more	7.4	6.8	10.2	8.4	8.5	9.3
Median	10.0	10.0	11.0	10.8	10.9	11.5

Source: Computed based on data from U.S. Bureau of the Census (1983a).

there were often relative losses, as in the case of overcrowding where the decline in overcrowding among non-Hispanic whites was twice as large as that for Hispanics.

We can summarize the contemporary situation of Hispanic housing quite simply by altering a traditional Spanish extension of courtesy from "mi casa es su casa" to "su casa no es mi casa." Even in 1980, "your house is not my house!"

Table 8.12
Percent Distribution of Hispanic and White Gross Rent as a Percent of 1979
Household Income for Renter-Occupied Units by Location

Percent Income	Hispanic			Non-Hispanic White		
	Cnt Cty	NonCC	NonMet	Cent Cty	NonCC	NonMet
Less than 15 %	18.3	17.8	16.6	18.6	18.2	16.2
15 to 19 %	15.3	16.1	11.2	16.4	17.7	12.6
20 to 24 %	13.2	14.4	9.7	15.0	15.9	11.2
25 to 29 %	10.0	10.9	7.2	11.2	11.7	8.3
30 to 34 %	7.2	7.9	5.1	7.8	8.0	5.6
35 to 49 %	12.7	13.4	8.7	13.2	12.7	9.6
50 % or more	23.3	19.4	13.5	17.8	15.9	12.5
Median	26.3	25.6	35.3	25.0	23.6	31.2

Source: Computed based on data from U.S. Bureau of the Census
(1983a).

Notes

1. The term "Hispanic" refers to all those who identified themselves as belonging to one of the Spanish origin categories listed in the 1980 census questionnaire number 7 (U.S. Bureau of the Census, 1975: 2).

2. Non-Hispanic white population is calculated by subtracting Hispanics, blacks, Asians, Pacific Islanders, American Indians, Aleuts and Eskimos from the *total* population (U.S. Bureau of the Census, 1979).

3. For households with incomes between $15,000 and 19,999 Hispanics were 1.4 to 2.6 times (depending on location), and non-Hispanic whites 1.3 to 1.7 times as likely to own their homes as their fellow ethnics with earnings less than $5,000.

4. In addition to the definitional problems in intercensal Hispanic comparisons, the use of different data sources also presents inconsistencies based on sampling variability (U.S. Bureau of the Census, 1982, 1973a, 1983a, 1984a).

5. Using a source allowing calculations of a non-Hispanic white category (U.S. Bureau of the Census, 1973a), the increase is from 61.8 to 68.5 percent overall, 46.7 to 54.4 percent for central cities, and 69.1 to 72.4 percent for suburban fringe.

6. In this case only the total "white" population is available for comparison. Therefore, all data presented should be viewed as conservative estimates of differentials for some Hispanic data are incorporated in the white category.

7. The weakness of the Annual Housing Survey is the absence of racial categories, allowing the calculation of a non-Hispanic white category. Consequently, the total (all races) population is used in these comparisons.

References

Bohland, James R. 1982. Indian Residential Segregation in the Urban Southeast: 1970 and 1980. *Social Science Quarterly* 63: 749–61.

Darroch, A. G., and W. G. Marston. 1969. Ethnic Differentiation: Ecological Aspects of a Multidimensional Concept. *International Migration Review* 4: 71–95.

———. 1971. The Social Class Basis of Ethnic Residential Segregation: The Canadian Case. *American Journal of Sociology* 77: 491–510.

DeFleur, Melvin L. 1983. *Social Problems in American Society*. Boston: Houghton Mifflin Company.

Dillman, Don A., Kenneth R. Tremblay, Jr., and Joyce J. Dillman. 1979. Influence of Housing Norms and Personal Characteristics on Stated Housing Preferences. *Housing and Society* 6: 2–19.

Farley, Reynolds. 1970. The Changing Distribution of Negroes within Metropolitan Areas: The Emergence of Black Suburbs. *American Journal of Sociology* 75: 512–29.

Feagin, Joe R., and C. Booher Feagin. 1978. *Discrimination American Style. Institutional Racism and Sexism*. Englewood Cliffs, N.J.: Prentice-Hall, Inc.

Hershberg, Theodore, et al. 1979. A Tale of Three Cities: Blacks and Immigrants in Philadelphia, 1850–1880, 1930, and 1970. *The Annals of the American Academy of Political and Social Science* 441: 55–81.

Hwang, Sean-Shong, and Steve H. Murdock. 1982. Residential Segregation in Texas in 1980. *Social Science Quarterly* 63: 737–48.

Johnson, Charles S. 1944. *Patterns of Negro Segregation*. New York: Harper and Brothers.

Kantrowitz, Nathan. 1969. Racial and Ethnic Segregation in the New York Metropolis, 1960. *American Journal of Sociology* 74: 685–95.

LaGory, Mark, and John Pipkin. 1981. *Urban Social Space*. Belmont, Calif.: Wadsworth Publishing Company.

Lake, Robert W. 1979. Racial Transition and Black Homeownership in American Suburbs. *The Annals of the American Academy of Political and Social Science* 441: 142–56.

Lopez, Manuel M. 1981. Patterns of Interethnic Residential Segregation in the Urban Southeast, 1960 and 1970. *Social Science Quarterly* 62: 50–63.

———. 1982. Housing Characteristics and Residential Segregation: Mexican Americans in the Urban Southeast. *Housing and Society* 9: 16–28.

Massey, Douglas S. 1979. Residential Segregation of Spanish Americans in United States Urbanized Areas. *Demography* 16: 553–63.

Moore, Joan W., and Frank G. Mittelbach. 1966. *Residential Segregation in the Urban Southwest: A Comparative Study*. Mexican American Study Project, Advance Report 4. Los Angeles: University of California Press.

Myrdal, Gunnar. 1944. *American Dilemma: The Negro Problem and Modern Democracy*. New York: Harper & Brothers Publishers.

Rosow, Irving. 1948. Home Ownership Motives. *American Sociological Review* 13: 751–56.

Schussheim, Morton J. 1970. Housing in Perspective. *The Public Interest* 19: 18–30.

Solomon, Arthur P. 1974. *Housing the Urban Poor: A Critical Evaluation of Federal Housing Policy.* Cambridge, Mass.: The MIT Press.

Struyk, Raymond J., et al. 1978. *Housing Policies for the Urban Poor: A Case for Local Diversity in Federal Programs.* Washington, D.C.: The Urban Institute.

U.S. Bureau of the Census. 1973a. *Census of Housing: 1970. Housing Characteristics by Household Composition.* Washington, D.C.: GPO.

————. 1973b. *Housing of Selected Racial Groups. Census of Housing: 1970.* Subject Reports. Final Report HC(7)–9. Washington, D.C.: GPO.

————. 1975. *Data on the Spanish Ancestry Population Available from the 1970 Census of Population and Housing.* Data Access Description No. 41. Washington, D.C.: GPO.

————. 1977. *Financial Characteristics by Indicators of Neighborhood Quality for the United States and Regions: 1975.* Current Housing Reports. Annual Housing Survey 1975, Part F. Washington, D.C.: GPO.

————. 1979. *Questionnaire Reference Book, 20th Decennial Census, 1980.* Washington, D.C.: GPO.

————. 1981. *Indicators of Housing and Neighborhood Quality by Financial Characteristics for the United States Regions: 1981.* Current Housing Reports, Annual Housing Survey: 1981, Part B. Washington, D.C.: GPO.

————. 1982. *General Housing Characteristics for the United States and Regions: 1980.* Current Housing Reports, Annual Housing Survey: 1980, Part A. Washington, D.C.: GPO.

————. 1983a. *Metropolitan Housing Characteristics.* 1980 Census of Housing. Volume 2. Washington, D.C.: GPO.

————. 1983b. *Residential Finance.* 1980 Census of Housing. Volume 5. Washington, D.C.: GPO.

————. 1984a. *Residence in 1975 for States by Age, Sex, Race, and Spanish Origin.* Supplementary Report. Washington, D.C.: GPO.

————. 1984b. *Statistical Abstracts of the United States: 1985.* Washington, D.C.: GPO.

U.S. Commission on Civil Rights. 1978. *Social Indicators of Equality for Minorities and Women.* Washington, D.C.: U.S. Commission on Civil Rights.

9

American Indian Housing: An Overview of Conditions and Public Policy

C. Matthew Snipp and Alan L. Sorkin

Introduction

Compared to other racial and ethnic groups in the United States, American Indians are relatively small in number. According to the 1980 Census, 1,423,045 persons reported their race as American Indian, Eskimo, or Aleut.[1] Slightly under half (49 percent) of these individuals reside in metropolitan localities while the balance live outside of Standard Metropolitan Statistical Areas (SMSAs).[2] About one-fourth live on 278 reservations or in 209 Alaska Native villages. Overall, American Indians and Alaska Natives make up about 0.6 percent of the total U.S. population (U.S. Bureau of the Census, 1984a).

Despite this small size, the housing of American Indians merits significant attention for other than intrinsic reasons. One is that unlike any other racial or ethnic group in America, American Indians have a special relationship with the federal government. Through treaties, leases, and other kinds of agreements, insuring adequate shelter has been a foremost responsibility of government authorities, although not necessarily well handled (Utley, 1984). Another reason is that American Indians, as a group, form an important baseline for measuring the well-being of American society. Traditionally, American Indians have been one of the most economically disadvantaged groups in the United States, and observers have repeatedly commented on the dire housing conditions under which Indians live (Brophy and Aberle, 1966; Levitan and Hetrick, 1971; Sorkin, 1971, 1978; AIPRC, 1977). In this regard, the housing of American Indians stands as a benchmark for judging how well the lowest economic strata of Americans are sheltered.

This chapter has two distinct thrusts. First, it presents empirical data about Indian housing based on the 1980 U.S. Census of housing. Second, it focuses on housing programs designed to upgrade Indian housing on the reservations and in the Alaska Native villages. These activities are carried out more or less jointly by the Bureau of Indian Affairs (BIA) and the Department of Housing and Urban Development (HUD).

Characteristics of Indian Housing

Indian housing characteristics may be viewed from several different perspectives: the kinds of housing available and occupied by American Indians; and, the quality and the cost of housing. These vantage points provide a framework for describing Indian housing by raising three basic questions: In what kind of dwellings do Indians reside? How good are these structures? And, what do they cost? Each of these questions will be dealt with in this chapter.

In this chapter, Indian housing is defined in three ways. Data published by the U.S. Bureau of the Census impose a definition which identifies Indian housing as dwellings occupied by an Indian householder.[3] This is a highly restricted definition that excludes housing occupied by the Indian spouses of non-Indian householders, the adopted children of non-Indian parents, and many other types of living arrangements in which Indians reside with non-Indian householders. Whenever using published data, we must adhere to the definition given by the U.S. Bureau of the Census.

A less restrictive definition identifies Indian housing as dwellings occupied by one or more persons reporting their race as American Indian. It is possible to apply this definition to machine readable microdata also distributed by the Census Bureau. An especially desirable feature of this definition is that it does not exclude Indian-occupied housing owned or rented-out by non-Indian householders.

When we discuss Indian housing in the context of public policy, a third definition is used, which refers to all owner- or renter-occupied units by those who are recognized by the BIA as the members of an Indian tribe, and are located within a BIA service area, typically a reservation or an Alaska Native village. This is a fine and very important distinction, because not all persons who report their race as Indian on their Census form are legally recognized as Indian by the BIA. It also means that most Indians living in urban areas are ineligible for assistance.

From the outset, it is also important to point out the structural design of housing units inhabited by most American Indians is not unique. Except for occasional ornamental embellishments, the quarters in which American Indians reside resemble the dwellings of other segments of the American society, especially low income groups. Most of these dwellings are constructed using conventional materials such as bricks, wood frames, and stucco. The point is that most American Indians no longer live in *wigwams*, *longhouse, tipis,* or *hogans.* However, traditional Navajos have consistently refused to give up their *hogans.* Otherwise, most traditional forms of Indian dwelling units, such as the *tipis* at pow-wows, are mainly built for ceremonial purposes, and are seldom used for year-round residence.

American Indian acceptance of European housing design was, in some cases, gradual and voluntary. For example, some southeastern tribes such as the Cherokees were living in log cabins at the turn of the nineteenth century. In other cases, European tastes in housing were abruptly forced on the tribes after they settled on reservations. In describing the confrontations between the Sioux and Federal authorities in the late 1800s, Utley (1984: 230) noted that "at first the... Indians lived in their traditional dwellings but later, responding to official pressures to adopt white ways, moved into dark, unhealthful cabins." The Sioux holy man, Black Elk, sadly observed that " 'all our people now were settling down in square gray houses, scattered here and there across this hungry land' " (Utley, 1984: 230).

The urbanization of America and particularly technological developments such as large scale waste disposal systems, electrification, indoor plumbing, and heating and cooling systems, as well as the implementation of building codes were responsible for quantal improvements in the housing of most Americans. However, for Indians outside of the urban American mainstream and too poor for luxuries such as pressurized water systems, housing conditions improved very little during the first half of this century. This prompted the observers to comment on the dismal housing conditions endured by American Indians. For instance, as pointed out by Brophy and Aberle (1966: 165), in 1959 a medical team visiting Cherokee homes in eastern Oklahoma observed that:

The houses were made of unpainted irregular slabs, sometimes partially covered with tarpaper. Almost all homes had kitchens and sinks although some depended on hand pumps for water. Where there was no well, water was often brought in buckets from a nearby brook or spring and stored by the kitchen sink.... A typical Cherokee family consisted of one or more young women in their twenties, perhaps an elderly woman, many children and infants, and the husbands of the young women.

These arrangements were considered relatively good compared to conditions on reservations elsewhere.

The 1970–1980 decade was an especially crucial period because of federal efforts to upgrade the housing of Indians. It is impossible to say with certainty that the improvements during the decade were the results of governmental housing assistance, but it is not unreasonable to assume that these programs played important roles. The comparisons that can be made between 1970 and 1980 are limited for two reasons, however. First, in 1970 very little data are available about Indian housing; second, the data published from the 1970 Census are not always comparable with the 1980 figures. The most serious limitation is that the 1970 data were based only on the states with an Indian population of 10,000 or more, while the 1980 data were based on all the 50 states, irrespective of the size of their Indian population.

Home Ownership

Home ownership is a basic dimension of the American housing supply. Owner-occupied housing, a measure of the number of housing units belonging to the Indian population, represents a major source of economic collateral. In contrast, renter-occupied units reflect the degree to which Indian households must rely on housing belonging to others, and the degree of exposure to the uncertainty of rental housing markets. Needless to say renters face greater risks in escalating rents, eviction actions, and the inability to find adequate housing.

The following figures[4] show percent changes in owner-occupied housing units between 1970 and 1980 for American Indians, blacks and whites (U.S. Bureau of the Census, 1973, 1983a, 1983b).

Race	1970	1980
American Indian	49.8	53.2
Black	41.6	44.4
White	65.4	67.8

As the above data indicate, between 1970 and 1980, the proportion of owner-occupied units increased in all three groups. This is not surprising. Housing programs during the 1970s assisted the low-to-moderate income families to become home owners; also, inflation was perhaps an even greater influence than most people may believe. Inflation during the 1970s increased the costs of housing significantly, and thus, made home ownership highly attractive as a hedge against inflation and shelter costs, and as means of personal investment with best returns. Despite these benefits of home ownership, however, it may be noted that increases were relatively small, and the relative differentials in home ownership by race remained relatively the same.

Table 9.1 displays the geographic distribution of the American Indian owner-occupied housing units. Generally speaking, these data reveal that the rate of home ownership is higher in the nonmetropolitan areas of all nine geographic divisions of the nation. Home ownership in the nonmetropolitan component ranged from a low of 56.6 percent in the E.S. Central division to a high of 67.9 percent in the West South Central division. In the metropolitan areas, it ranged between a low of 41.0 percent in the Middle Atlantic to a high of 62.0 percent in the West South Central division.

Regarding on or off reservation place of residence, the data in Table 9.1

show a higher rate of home ownership on or near reservation than off reservation. The proportion of home ownership off reservation ranged between a low of 38.6 percent in the Middle Atlantic to a high of 63.1 percent in the West South Central division. The corresponding figures for those residing on or near reservation were between a low of 44.7 in East South Central to a high of 65.8 percent in the West South Central division. The lowest rates of home ownership among American Indians are found in the highly urbanized areas of metropolitan New England and Middle Atlantic divisions. These geographic divisions include the states of Maine, New Hampshire, Vermont, Massachusetts, Rhode Island, Connecticut, New York, New Jersey, and Pennsylvania.

It should be remembered that relatively speaking fewer Indians live in these divisions; among those who do, home ownership is more common in the nonmetropolitan areas. Also, the data indicate that proximity to or residence on reservation lands increases the likelihood of home ownership. There are relatively few reservations in the New England and the Middle Atlantic divisions. Several of the reservations that exist in these divisions are located in rural upstate New York. In contrast, American Indian home ownership is highest in the West South Central division, which includes the states of Arkansas, Louisiana, Oklahoma, and Texas.

The largest number of Indians and Indian reservations are located in the Pacific and Mountain states: Montana, Idaho, Wyoming, Colorado, New Mexico, Arizona, Utah, Nevada, Washington, Oregon, California, Alaska, and Hawaii. In these two divisions, except for the metropolitan and off reservation areas of the Pacific states, the majority of American Indians own their homes. Overall, Indians on reservations and in nonmetropolitan areas are more likely to be home owners than nonreservation Indians, particularly in the Western states.

Reservation Housing

One of the major innovations of the public housing programs for reservations during the 1960s and 1970s was the creation of housing authorities operated by the tribes, the BIA, or both. Tribal/BIA housing authorities supervised the construction of public housing for low income families and once constructed, these authorities managed and maintained often extensive systems of rental housing. As we will explain shortly, tribal leaders are chagrined that public housing programs do not encourage home ownership. The impact of these programs is evident in the figures presented in Table 9.2. Between 1970 and 1980, in ten of the sixteen largest reservations housing units increased, while the number of owner-occupied units remained the same, resulting in a proportional reduction of home owners on these reservations.

In some instances, the decline was dramatic. For instance, in 1970 the

Table 9.1
Percent American Indian and Alaska Native Owner-Occupied Housing Units by
Geographic Division and Place of Residence[a]

	Place of Residence			
Geographic Division	Metro- politan	Nonmetro- politan	Off Reser- vation	On or Near Reservation
New England	44.6	56.9	45.0	50.5
Mid Atlantic	41.0	63.9	38.6	64.7
E.N. Central	52.1	58.2	52.9	56.3
W.N. Central	50.7	50.7	51.5	49.7
S. Atlantic	52.2	62.8	55.8	60.7
E.S. Central	52.2	56.6	54.1	44.7
W.S. Central	62.0	67.2	63.1	65.8
Mountain	53.6	64.5	51.5	61.6
Pacific	48.2	60.6	46.9	56.2

a: Estimates are based on housing units with at least
   one American Indian or Alaska Native Resident.

Source: Public Use Micro Sample, 5 percent A File.

Zuni Pueblo owned 546 (92.5 percent) of a total of 590 Indian occupied
units. By 1980, there were 1077 Indian occupied units, of which 739 (68.6
percent) were owner-occupied. During the 1970s, housing units increased
on the Zuni Pueblo reservation by 83 percent, while owner-occupied homes
grew by 35 percent. The net result is that the proportion of the owner-
occupied units declined from 92.5 in 1970 to about 69 percent in 1980.
Overall, between 1970 and 1980, two-thirds of the sixteen largest reservations experienced a relative decline in owner-occupied housing, but the
gain in new units meant larger housing units as the median number of rooms
per unit (Table 9.2) increased during this period. In 1970, the median
number of rooms between reservations ranged from a low of 2.0 on the
Navajo reservation to a high of 4.8 rooms on the Yakima reservation. In
contrast, by 1980, the median number of rooms ranged between a low of
2.7 on the Navajo and a high of 5.2 rooms on the Osage reservation.

Table 9.2
Percent of Owner-Occupied Housing Units and Median Number of Rooms per
Unit on 16 Largest American Indian Reservations, 1980

Reservation	Percent Owner Occupied Units		Median No. of Rooms	
	1970	1980	1970	1980
Navajo [a] (AZ, NM, UT)	61.5	67.7	2.0	2.7
Pine Ridge (SD)	62.2	44.8	3.3	4.3
Gila River (AZ)	78.1	65.7	2.8	3.9
Papago (AZ)	87.9	72.9	2.5	3.5
Fort Apache (AZ)	79.1	68.5	3.0	4.3
Hopi [a] (AZ)	82.5	77.3	2.7	2.8
Zuni Pueblo (NM)	92.5	68.6	4.5	5.1
San Carlos (AZ)	88.0	74.9	2.8	3.8
Rosebud (SD)	68.2	52.2	3.9	4.4
Blackfeet (SD)	60.3	61.1	4.1	4.8
Yakima (WA)	53.8	60.0	4.8	4.8
Eastern Cherokee (NC)	80.6	83.8	4.2	5.0
Standing Rock (ND,SD)	61.2	35.8	3.3	4.5
Osage (OK)	NA	72.5	NA	5.2
Fort Peck (MT)	42.2	54.4	4.1	4.9
Wind River (WY)	75.3	67.4	4.0	4.8

a: Navajo and Hopi reservation data are not strictly comparable
   because of administrative changes in the Navajo-Hopi joint
   use area during the 1970s. NA: Data not available.

Source: U. S. Bureau of the Census (1973, 1983a).

Single Family Homes

The difference in black and Indian home ownership, and the advantages of the white dominant population, are reflected in their occupancy of single family dwellings. Single family homes are an especially symbolic measure of racial differentials in social status. Owning a single family, detached dwelling unit is an aspiration for many American Indians, no less than for any other segment of the American population. Ownership of single family dwellings also comprises the most important component of nonrental housing units among Indians, because few Indian home owners reside in multiunit buildings. Only about 0.8 percent of all Indian owned units are condominiums. The following figures show the rate of occupancy of single family units among American Indians as compared to blacks and whites (U.S. Bureau of the Census, 1970, 1983a).

Race	1970	1980	Percent in Mobile Homes
American Indian	77.6	77.6	8.6
Black	59.8	64.3	2.2
White	72.6	79.3	5.2

As the above figures show, in 1970, over three-fourths of all American Indian householders occupied single family units. This figure exceeded the proportion for both blacks and whites living in single family, detached units in 1970. However, between 1970 and 1980 the proportion of black and white occupants in single family, detached units grew significantly, while it remained unchanged for American Indians. By 1980, more whites than Indians resided in such units.

An especially unique characteristic of Indian housing is the relatively extensive use of temporary shelters in the form of mobile homes. A significantly higher proportion of Indians than either blacks or whites reside in mobile homes. As the above data indicate, 8.6 percent of Indian households, as compared to 2.2 percent blacks and 5.2 percent whites reside in mobile homes. Due to the lack of data for 1970, we are unable to examine trends in Indian occupancy of mobile homes. However, the growing commercial availability of this type of shelter, and the subsidies for the purchase of mobile homes by the government and tribal programs in recent years may explain the higher incidence of mobile home occupancy by American Indians.

Number of Rooms

Home ownership and occupancy in single family dwellings are important measures of housing quality and standards of living. But they reveal very little about the actual living space available to the household and/or the family. In this regard, the number of rooms in a housing unit are used as a measure of space available. The median number of rooms or the proportion of units with three or less rooms may be used to measure the differentials in living space by race. The following data show the percentage of dwelling units with three or less rooms and the median number of rooms in units occupied by the American Indians, blacks, and whites in 1970 and 1980.

Characteristics	White	Black	American Indian
Percent with 3 or less rooms, 1970	15.0	23.0	33.0
Percent with 3 or less rooms, 1980	11.5	20.8	24.1
Median number of rooms, 1970	4.8	4.6	4.2
Median number of rooms, 1980	5.3	4.8	4.6

Between 1970 and 1980, the proportion of American Indian housing units with 3 or less rooms declined from 33.0 to 24.1 percent; for blacks it declined from 23.0 to 20.8 percent; for whites it declined from 15.0 to 11.5 percent. This clearly demonstrates an increase in the housing space for the American Indians during the 1970–1980 decade. This is also reflected in the median number of rooms, which rose from 4.2 to 4.6 between 1970 and 1980. In relative terms, Indians lag behind blacks, and significantly behind whites, in this measure, but the gap has narrowed between 1970 and 1980. Two plausible explanations for this improvement include federal Indian housing programs which built new units, and declining numbers of Indian householders living in traditional Indian housing units such as one-room Navajo *hogans*.

Crowding: An Indicator of Housing Quality

Although difficult to measure for its direct relationship to the level of comfort and well-being, the quality of housing is an important variable. Crowding, as measured by the number of persons per room, is often used as an indicator of quality. Crowded dwellings offer less privacy and less comfort than less crowded homes. According to this measure, a significant segment of the American Indian and Alaska Native population is not well housed. Evidence for this problem is displayed in Table 9.3.

As a rule of thumb, crowded housing conditions exist when there are more occupants than rooms in a dwelling. For example, a family of four occupying a small two bedroom apartment. Units with 1.01 or more persons per room are generally regarded as *crowded*, and those with 1.51 or more persons per room as *overcrowded*. In 1970 and 1980, the level of crowding was substantially higher among American Indians than either blacks or whites. Crowding lessened among all three groups during the decade. But even in 1980, a significant gap remained between Indians and the other two groups. Ironically, this was true despite the fact that Indians are considerably

Table 9.3
Percent Persons per Room in Occupied Housing Units by Year and Race

	Number of Persons per Room			
Year/Race	1.00 or less	1.01 to 1.51	1.51 or more	1.01 or more
1970				
Amer. Indian	68.8	13.8	17.4	31.2
Black	80.1	12.4	7.5	19.9
White	93.1	5.3	1.6	6.9
1980				
Amer. Indian	82.4	9.2	8.4	17.6
Black	88.8	7.8	3.4	11.2
White	97.1	2.2	0.7	2.9

Source: U.S. Bureau of the Census (1970, 1973, 1983a).

more likely to own their homes and live in the single family, detached units than blacks in 1980.

In 1970, more than 31 percent of Indian-occupied units, as compared to 19.9 percent black-occupied units and 6.9 percent white occupied units, were classified as *crowded*. More than 17 percent of the Indian housing units in 1970, as compared to 7.5 percent of black housing units and only 1.6 percent of white units were classified as *overcrowded*. Changes during the decade meant that all three groups resided in less crowded housing; yet 17.6 percent of Indian housing, as compared to 11.2 percent of black housing and only 0.7 percent of white units, were crowded in 1980. Nonetheless, in 1980, the relative incidence of crowded housing among American Indians was about 2.5 times greater than that among blacks and 12 times greater than that among whites.

Age of Indian Housing

The age of a house is usually used as another indicator of housing quality, because aging leads to decay and dilapidated conditions. BIA housing surveys indicate that the housing units occupied by many American Indians are in need of renovation, or are dilapidated beyond repair. Table 9.4 shows

Table 9.4
Percent Occupied Housing Units by Year, Race, and Age of Structure

Year/Race	Age of Structure in Years			
	Under 10	10-20	21-30	Over 30 Yrs.
1970				
Amer. Indian	25.2	19.2	14.9	40.7
Black	15.8	17.5	18.1	48.6
White	26.0	21.8	12.5	39.7
1980				
Amer. Indian	32.3	20.6	15.5	31.6
Black	17.9	19.3	18.6	44.2
White	26.1	19.8	17.1	37.0

Source: U.S. Bureau of the Census (1970, 1973, 1983a).

occupied housing units by race and age of structure for 1970 and 1980. According to these data a greater proportion of blacks than either whites or American Indians live in structures over thirty years old. In 1970, 48.6 percent of black-occupied units, as against 39.7 percent of white-occupied units and 40.7 percent of American Indian-occupied units were over 30 years old. The parallel figures for 1980 were: 44.2 percent of the black-occupied units, 37.0 percent of the white-occupied units, and only 31.6 percent of the American Indian-occupied units were over thirty years old. While economic affluence may explain the lower rate for whites, governmental intervention may be responsible for the lower rate of occupancy of older housing units among American Indians. If we define buildings less than ten years old as "new," about one out of every three American Indian housing units, one out of every four white-occupied units, and one out of every six black-occupied units could be classified as new housing. Public housing programs were undoubtedly important for changes after 1970 as a large number of new units were made available for Indian occupancy.

The evidence bearing on the quality of Indian housing is at best contradictory in several respects. Newer housing should be better and more comfortable than older units; modern dwellings are more available in areas such as reservations where the Indian population has been the target of public housing programs. Paradoxically, the areas with the largest concentrations

Table 9.5
Percent Housing Units Occupied by America Indians and Alaska Natives, by
Selected Structural Characteristics and Place of Residence[a]

	Place of Residence			
Structural Characteristics	Metro-politan	Nonmetro-politan	Off Reser-vation	On or Near Reservarion
Complete Bathroom	96.0	83.0	95.9	84.8
Public Water	87.1	67.1	82.7	84.8
Public Sewer	77.4	50.0	73.3	60.4
Air Conditioning	47.7	32.1	50.1	29.9
Central Heating	46.5	33.9	44.9	38.1
Complete Kitchen	97.0	84.8	97.0	86.3
Telephone	84.2	64.5	84.8	67.8

a: Estimates are based on housing units with at least one
   American Indian or Alaska Native Resident.

Source: Public Use Microdata Sample, 5 Percent A File.

of modern units are areas with the most heavily occupied, if not most overcrowded housing.

The data for housing equipment provide further insights into housing quality. Differences in housing amenities are shown in Table 9.5. The figures in Table 9.5 indicate that housing quality in nonmetropolitan and reservation areas is lower, insofar as units in these areas are more poorly equipped than those in nonreservation and metropolitan locations. However, differences in the utilization of public water and sewer are as much evidence of rural isolation as they are of low quality housing. On many reservations, community sewer and piped water systems developed in the 1960s and 1970s have narrowed the gap between reservation and nonreservation areas. The result is that the largest differences in these amenities exist between metropolitan and nonmetropolitan areas. Other kinds of amenities such as complete plumbing and kitchen facilities are less dependent on location. Public water and kitchen facilities are, by most standards, considered essential. Approximately 15 percent of housing units on or near reservation land in 1980 did not have these facilities, as compared to 4 percent in the nonreservation areas. Similarly, slightly smaller differences exist between metropolitan and nonmetropolitan areas. Telephone, air conditioning, and central heating systems are discretionary items for which there are especially large differences by location. About 30 percent of dwellings on or near reservation lands have some type of air conditioning as compared to 50 percent in nonreservation areas.

Table 9.6 presents selected measures of housing quality for the sixteen largest reservations for 1970 and 1980. Compared to other American households, there should be no question that housing units on these reservations are crowded. In 1970, the relative proportion of units with 1.01 or more persons per room was extremely high—it ranged between a low of 36.9 percent of the units in the Fort Peck reservation to a high of 75.8 percent of all units among Navajos. During the 1970–1980 decade, the degree of crowding on these reservations eased considerably. In 1980 the incidence of crowded units was lowest in the Osage and Eastern Cherokee reservations—5.6 percent of units in Osage and 12.4 percent of units in the Eastern Cherokee reservations were categorized as crowded. Despite this, however, in 1980 some reservation units were highly crowded. In the remaining fourteen reservations, the percent of dwellings with more than one person per room ranged between a low of 23 (in Yakima reservation) to a high of 65 percent (in Navajo reservation). As mentioned earlier, this is despite the fact that between 1970 and 1980 every reservation listed in Table 9.6 experienced a substantial decline in crowding. The Zuni Pueblo in New Mexico, and the Eastern Cherokee in North Carolina registered the largest decreases of the decade—declines in the magnitude of 28 and 26 percent, respectively. In contrast, the Navajo and Hopi reservations had the smallest reduction in crowding.

The structural age data presented in Table 9.6 are not strictly comparable between 1970 and 1980; the former is based on units with Indian householders, but the latter is based on all year-round housing units on the reservation, whether or not inhabited by an Indian householder. Yet, this information provides a general, if somewhat imprecise, view of changes between 1970 and 1980. The Rosebud Sioux reservation is particularly interesting, because in 1970 it had the largest percent (69.5) of new housing units. It achieved this status with a building boom that increased the number of new units built from 67 for the 1960–1964 period to 569 units built between 1965 and 1968 (U.S. Bureau of the Census, 1973). Between 1969 and 1970, 92 units were built, which were more than the number of units built during the entire first half of the decade. The Rosebud reservation also is one of the few reservations for which 1970 and 1980 data are reasonably comparable. Table 9.6 shows that 29 percent of all dwellings on the Rosebud reservation have been built since 1970, but 434 (33 percent) of 1,311 dwellings occupied by Indian householders were constructed after 1970. This also means that 24 percent fewer new units were constructed on the Rosebud reservation in the 1970s as compared to the 1960s, lending some credence to the complaints

Table 9.6

Percent Housing Units with More than 1.00 Person per Room, and Percent Units 10 Years Old or Newer on 16 Largest American Indian Reservations, 1980

Reservation	1.01 Or More Persons/Room		Housing Units 10 Years Old or Newer	
	1970	1980	1970	1980
Navajo[a] (AZ, NM, UT)	75.8	64.9	54.0	47.1
Pine Ridge (SD)	63.8	49.0	27.0	43.6
Gila River (AZ)	62.9	42.2	27.4	48.3
Papago (AZ)	68.8	49.4	19.0	47.8
Fort Apache (AZ)	69.6	48.2	42.6	50.0
Hopi[a] (AZ)	65.8	58.0	9.2	33.1
Zuni Pueblo (NM)	70.5	42.2	28.8	42.8
San Carlos (AZ)	69.4	55.1	40.4	43.6
Rosebud (SD)	49.2	28.9	69.5	29.3
Blackfeet (SD)	49.6	25.9	38.0	28.2
Yakima (WA)	38.7	22.8	20.7	22.0
Eastern Cherokee (NC)	38.4	12.4	57.6	60.8
Standing Rock (ND,SD)	49.8	33.7	53.9	29.9
Osage (OK)	NA	5.6	NA	31.3
Fort Peck (MT)	36.9	24.0	32.6	27.7
Wind River (WY)	51.8	35.2	35.2	43.7

a: Navajo and Hopi reservation data are not strictly comparable because of administrative changes in the Navajo-Hopi joint use area during the 1970s. NA: Data not available.

Source: U. S. Bureau of the Census (1973, 1983a, 1983b).

Table 9.7
Median Rent, Value of Owner-Occupied Housing Units, and Mortgage Payments
by Year and Race (Figures in Constant 1980 Dollars)

Year, Rent/Value/Mortgage	Amer. Indians	Blacks	Whites
1970			
Contract Rent	127	124	164
Gross Rent	NA	155	206
Housing Value	19,347	22,786	36,651
Mortgage Payments	NA	NA	NA
1980			
Contract Rent	171	156	208
Gross Rent	224	208	251
Housing Value	34,400	27,200	48,600
Mortgage Payments[a]	319	307	371

a: Includes selected purchase related costs.

NA: Data not available.

Source: U.S. Bureau of the Census (1973, 1983a, 1983b).

that rapidly rising costs slowed Indian housing development in this period
(Stea, 1982). Nevertheless, from the standpoint of total year-round units,
most of the largest reservations had a higher percent of recently built units
in 1980 than in 1970.

Housing Costs: Mortgage and Rent

Space limitations prohibit more detailed examination of American Indian
housing costs. Costs such as rent and mortgage vary greatly by state and
location. These costs, to a large degree, reflect the match between family
resources and conditions in the local housing market; both may vary greatly
across areas. Table 9.7 shows figures for median rents, housing value, and
mortgage payments of owner-occupied housing units by year and race.
Contract rent is distinguished from gross rent in that the latter is the same
as the former plus the cost of fuel and utilities paid either by the renter or

the landlord. As these figures show, contract rent increased during the 1970s for all three groups. In 1970, the contract rent for American Indians and blacks were about the same. But for reasons which are not all together clear, the rents paid by Indians increased at a faster pace than the rents paid by both blacks and whites. In 1980, contract rents paid by American Indians were about 25 percent higher than that paid in 1970; for blacks it was 21 percent higher; and, for whites it was 22 percent higher in 1980 as against 1970. One possible explanation may be that more Indians moved into high rent urban areas during the 1970s; another possibility is that Indians may have experienced more economic progress than blacks in the 1970s, allowing them to rent more expensive units. The median household income of Indian renters exceeded the median household income of black renters by almost 20 percent in 1980—$9,875 for Indians as against $8,233 for blacks (U.S. Bureau of the Census, 1983b).

Value of Housing

In 1970, the average value of an Indian-owned unit was 53 percent of the value of an average unit owned by whites. The value of a black owned unit was 62 percent of a white owned unit. By 1980, the average value of an Indian owned unit had jumped to 71 percent of the value of white owned units, while the value of black owned units had declined from 62 percent in 1970 to 55 percent of the average value of white owned units in 1980. This may reflect greater improvements in American Indian housing than in black housing during the decade. The following data show the mean value (in thousands of dollars) of owner-occupied housing units in the U.S. metropolitan areas by race and location in 1980 (U.S. Bureau of the Census, 1984b).

Location	White	Black	American Indian
U.S. metropolitan areas	57.3	33.8	43.3
Inside SMSAs	62.7	36.4	53.8
Central cities of SMSAs	56.4	33.0	52.2

In the metropolitan United States in 1980, the mean value of an average black owned home was 59 percent of the average mean value owned by whites. The value of an American Indian owned unit was 75 percent of the average value of a white owned unit. Inside SMSAs, the Indian-black differential in values was higher. Based on the above data, the mean value of an average black-owned home had 58 percent of the value of a white-owned home, as against Indian owned units with a mean value equal to nearly 86 percent of the mean value of a white-owned home. In central cities of SMSAs, American Indians *almost* attained parity with whites. The mean value of an Indian owned unit was 91 percent of the value of an average white-owned structure, while those owned by blacks had an average value equiv-

Table 9.8
Selected Median Monthly Housing Costs for American Indians and Alaska Natives, by Place of Residence, 1980ᵃ (Figures in Constant 1980 Dollars)

	Place of Residence			
Selected Cost Items	Metro- politan	Nonmetro- politan	Off Reser- vation	On or Near Reservarion
Gross Rent	255	188	246	220
Mortgage Payments	270	182	253	236
Natural Gas	30	35	30	30
Other Fuel	21	21	21	21

a: Estimates are based on households with at least one American Indian or Alaska Native resident.

Source: Public Use Microdata Sample, 5 percent A File.

alent to less than 59 percent of the mean value of white-owned units. This significantly lower mean value of black-owned units in central cities may partly be attributed to the fact that black female householders constitute a significant segment of the central city black population.

Location and Costs

An indication of how housing costs depend on location is provided by the data in Table 9.8. Indian households living on or near reservations typically pay about the same amount for utilities as Indians in other locations. However, rents or mortgage payments appear to be more variable. They are lowest in nonmetropolitan areas. Median gross rents and mortgage payments were 36 and 48 percent higher inside of SMSAs.

In view of the above description of reservation housing, it may be surprising to know that reservation housing is more expensive than housing in nonmetropolitan areas. However, reservation and metropolitan areas are not always mutually exclusive. Some reservations are inside metropolitan areas. In some other instances, nonmetropolitan housing includes a sizable number of structures inside reservations. The mix of reservations inside and outside metropolitan areas has the net effect of reducing the gap in housing costs between Indian households living inside and outside reservations. This also implies that the nonmetropolitan location of reservation, rather than reservation status per se, is a major factor in the lower cost of housing in these areas.

Housing costs on the sixteen largest reservations are nevertheless lower. However, comparison of data shown in Table 9.8 with those shown in Table 9.7 may be misleading, because of definitional differences concerning reservation status and type of rent. The statistics in Table 9.9 show median contract rents and housing values for dwellings *strictly within* reservation boundaries. For the ten reservations with complete data for 1970 and 1980, most have experienced relatively small rent increases. Six of the ten experienced increases resulting in 17 to 34 percent higher rents in 1980 than in 1970. In contrast, four reservations (Pine Ridge, Blackfeet, Standing Rock, and Fort Peck) enjoyed decreases in contract rents ranging from 10 to 27 percent. Still others experienced only a minor increase. The reasons for these fluctuations in an inflationary period are not readily apparent. Public housing programs may have induced these declines but reporting errors may also be a factor.

With a single exception, housing values on all of the largest reservations increased during the 1970s. About one half of these reservations experienced relatively small gains. The Navajo reservation where the median value of housing was less than $7,000 in 1970, and did not exceed $10,000 in 1980 exemplifies a typical small increase. Because housing values less than $10,000 are not reported, ascertaining exact increases is not possible. On reservations with housing values greater than $10,000, most of the increases in housing values were substantial. The Wind River reservation in Wyoming experienced the largest increase in the 1970s and by 1980 reported the highest median value of $38,700—up 169 percent from $14,402 in 1970. The Rosebud in South Dakota is the only reservation where the median value of housing declined. The spate of new housing built on the Rosebud during the mid–1960s may partly account for the decline in the value of the older units resulting in a lower median value of all units combined. This is especially alarming because it may foretell a similar pattern of decline in reservations where new housing units were built in the 1970s.

American Indian Housing Programs

The foregoing data illustrating the characteristics of Indian housing provide evidence, albeit indirect, of the impact of Indian housing programs in

Table 9.9
Median Monthly Contract Rent and Value of Owner-Occupied Units on 16
Largest American Indian Reservations, 1980 (Figures in Constant 1980 Dollars)

Reservation	Contract Rent		Value of Housing Unit	
	1970	1980	1970	1980
Navajo (AZ, NM, UT)	82	96	6,664	a
Pine Ridge (SD)	108	98	6,449	a
Gila River (AZ)	a	54	6,664	a
Papago (AZ)	a	69	6,449	a
Fort Apache (AZ)	64	81	7,739	17,800
Hopi (AZ)	66	83	6,449	16,500
Zuni Pueblo (NM)	a	a	13,327	21,800
San Carlos (AZ)	a	a	6,449	16,500
Rosebud (SD)	82	103	14,832	a
Blackfeet (SD)	97	86	10,533	29,900
Yakima (WA)	88	118	20,636	31,000
Eastern Cherokee (NC)	a	92	13,972	34,900
Standing Rock (ND,SD)	92	79	13,972	34,900
Osage (OK)	NA	97	NA	26,200
Fort Peck (MT)	113	89	12,253	21,600
Wind River (WY)	78	99	14,402	38,700

a: Census publications do not show rents less than $ 50, and
   housing valued less than $10,000. NA: Data not available.

Source: U.S. Bureau of the Census (1973, 1983a).

general, and on reservation housing in particular. Although critics (Stea, 1982) point to the failure of these programs, and we do not dispute them, these programs have had significant impact on Indian housing. Because of this impact, it is extremely important to understand the nature of public housing for American Indians.

Reservation Indians have the poorest housing conditions of any racial or ethnic minority group in the United States. The most recent data available from the Bureau of Indian Affairs (1985) indicate that in 1984 there were 150,437 housing units located in the reservation areas. Of these, 54,314 (or 36.1 percent) were in substandard condition; another 30,778 (or 20.5 percent) needed extensive renovation and 23,536 units (15.6 percent) needed replacement (Table 9.10). Moreover, 35,235 families with no housing of their own are living in tents, cars, or with relatives (Treuer, 1982: 7). The number of houses that were substandard in 1984 is approximately the same as it was in 1966 (Sorkin, 1971: 176).

Low Rent Programs

Under the 1937 Housing Act, the Department of Housing and Urban Development (HUD) is authorized to make loans and annual contributions to local housing authorities to assist in developing housing projects for low income householders. Local housing authorities are corporate bodies authorized to function in a locality pursuant to state law for the purpose of developing, owning, and managing low income housing projects. When an Indian tribe has an established governing body, that organization can function as a local housing authority. Each Indian housing authority administers its own housing program. The two primary housing programs financed by HUD are *conventional* low rent and *mutual* help.

The *conventional* low rent program operates in the same manner in Indian and non-Indian communities. The local housing authority undertakes (with HUD's approval of plans, specifications, and costs) the development of housing by contracting with a private developer or, in some cases, an Indian housing development enterprise. In *conventional* low rent housing, the dwellings are rented to low income families with HUD's financial assistance payments being made over a forty-year period during which the development cost of the project is depreciated. Rents are based on family income. Thus, the higher the income, the larger the rental payment. If rents from tenants are not sufficient to pay the housing authority's operating expenses, operating subsidies are paid by HUD to ensure the low income character of the project. In 1983 HUD provided about $20 million in operating subsidies to make up the difference between the payments by the families and the operating costs (HUD, 1983).

Indian leaders indicate that tenants' dissatisfaction centers on two aspects of this program. First, some Indians prefer to stay in the units they themselves

Table 9.10
Structural Conditions of Consolidated Housing Inventory on 12 American Indian
Reservations, Fiscal Year 1984

Area/ Reservation	Total Existing Units	Units in Standard Condition	Units in Substandard Condition	Units Needing Renovation	Units Needing Replacement[a]	Families Needing Housing	Total New Units Required
Aberdeen	13,107	11,035	2,072	1,016	1,056	1,714	2,770
Albuquerque	11,360	7,508	3,852	2,745	1,107	2,772	3,879
Anadarko	6,306	3,838	2,468	1,438	1,030	2,215	3,245
Billings	6,506	4,914	1,142	406	736	1,868	2,604
Eastern	5,941	5,317	624	684	-60	829	769
Juneau	11,209	6,097	5,112	1,757	3,355	1,739	5,094
Minneapolis	9,456	6,280	3,176	2,044	1,132	2,292	3,424
Muskogee	21,943	17,545	4,398	2,362	2,036	5,013	7,049
Navajo	25,377	10,735	14,642	11,116	3,526	5,644	9,170
Phoenix	13,068	8,996	4,072	932	3,140	2,965	6,105
Portland	10,541	8,424	2,117	1,358	759	1,940	2,669
Sacramento	16,073	5,434	10,639	4,920	5,719	6,244	11,963
Total	150,437	96,123	54,314	30,778	23,536	35,235	58,771

a: Housing units needing replacement are estimated by subtracting housing units needing
renovation from housing units in substandard condition.

Source: HUD (1985).

own rather than moving into the subsidized rental units, even though the rental units are of better quality. Second, a number of low rental units are deteriorating because of the lack of proper maintenance by the inhabitants and the mediocre quality of the construction materials used. Perhaps, if the units were owned rather than rented, the residents would be more likely to maintain the unit at a level to be kept in the housing inventory for a longer period of time.

Mutual Help Program

The Mutual Help program presently constitutes about 60 percent of housing assistance on the Indian reservations. According to this program, each participating Indian family must make a contribution toward the cost of the dwelling (at least $1,500) in the form of land, labor, cash, or equipment. This is in effect the *downpayment*. After construction, the prospective home buyer occupies the unit under a lease-purchase agreement. He is obligated to maintain the unit, pay the utility bills, and make a required monthly payment (mortgage). Normally, the participating family will acquire ownership at the end of twenty-five years. However, if the family is able to make larger than expected monthly payments, the equity builds at a faster rate, thus shortening the debt period. In the Mutual Help program, HUD provides the Indian housing authorities with financial assistance for the cost of developing the project (excluding the mutual help contributions).

Before 1981, it took approximately four years to develop an Indian mutual help project. Currently it takes about eighteen to thirty months to develop such a project. Some projects have even started in fewer months. For example, the Choctaw Housing Authority was successful in getting one project started in four months (HUD, 1983). The main reason for the reduction in the length of the preconstruction phase of the project today is the faster processing through the HUD-Indian field offices.

Housing Costs

HUD has put considerable pressure on Indian housing authorities to reduce development costs. According to Meyers (1985), these costs fell by 26 percent between 1981 and 1984. The average cost of a new home was $54,270 in 1984. Reduction in costs enabled HUD to provide for 587 more units than originally budgeted. It is unclear, however, whether these cost reductions have been at the expense of quality or not, but the great emphasis on factory built or modular housing (because of lower costs) has proved unpopular among reservation families.

The Comprehensive Improvement Assistance Program (CIAP), established by the 1980 Housing and Community Development Act, authorizes HUD to provide financial assistance to public housing authorities. On the Indian

Table 9.11
Number of Indian Housing Units Provided through HUD's Public Housing
Program, 1962–1984

Year	Started Construction	Completed Construction
1962	50	0
1964	320	50
1965	564	250
1970	3,688	968
1975	2,336	4,156
1976	3,229	3,415
1977	3,763	2,048
1978	4,581	2,861
1979	4,599	4,363
1980	4,163	5,379
1981	4,337	4,084
1982	2,193	3,729
1983	3,248	3,062
1984	2,130	3,093

Source: HUD (1983); Meyers (1985).

reservations, the money has been used to improve the physical conditions of the existing units and to upgrade the management and operation of the low-rent and Mutual Help programs.

HUD Program Development

The HUD Indian Housing Programs grew rapidly between 1962 and 1981 (Table 9.11). Since 1980, activities have slowed down because of funding limitations. For fiscal year 1985, the HUD Appropriation Bill contained funds for 2,000 new units, or less than the number started in 1981. The budget for the 1986 fiscal year, submitted by President Reagan to the Congress on February 4, 1985, proposed a two-year moritorium for Indian housing programs. This policy is a part of the administration's deficit reduction efforts. This action will not affect the approximately 12,000 units already in the development pipeline. It is estimated that 2,800 units will be started and 3,300 units will be completed during the 1986 fiscal year as a result of pre–1985 program fundings. Indian housing programs are expected to be resumed in the 1988 fiscal year (Meyers, 1985), but continued high federal deficits make this resumption uncertain.

Given the extreme need for new and improved housing, it is very difficult to justify a moritorium on new home constructions on the Indian reservations. This policy will not only lead to more overcrowding in the existing housing units, but also will prolong the time period before many Indian families will be able to secure adequate housing.

Financial Problems

There are approximately 165 Indian housing authorities (IHAs) that manage more than 50,000 units occupied by families on the Indian reservations. At the end of 1983 there were 51 IHAs in financial difficulty. Financially troubled IHAs are identified on the basis of several criteria. For example, diversion of program funds for inappropriate uses, program operating reserves below established standards, and unacceptably low amount of accounts receivable are symptomatic of financial problems in IHA administration.

A problem for many IHAs, and a major cause of financial instability, is the failure of residents to make their mortgage and/or rent payments. This problem has been especially prevalent at IHAs which are in financial difficulty. The slowness with which payments are received sometimes results in IHAs utilizing resources other than general operating funds to support program operation. As of September 30, 1983, one-third of all Indian housing authorities averaged more than three months in arrears regarding rent or mortgage collection (HUD, 1983).

Approximately nine IHAs have implemented payroll deduction plans for tribal and IHA employees who are behind in their payments. This has resulted in a significant improvement in rent collection. While evictions can be a last resort for nonpayment of rent or mortgage, very few evictions are actually carried out. In many cases, tribal courts are reluctant to evict families, especially if there is no alternative housing available.

HUD has placed sanctions against some Indian housing authorities and tribal organizations because of reluctance to enforce stricter policies against those delinquent in their rent or mortgage payments. Some of these sanctions have included refusing to provide funding for new units, denying development funds, and limiting Comprehensive Improvement Assistance Program funds.

BIA and Housing Improvement

The Bureau of Indian Affairs funds a Housing Improvement Program (HIP) which provides assistance to needy Indians who are unable to obtain housing assistance from any other source (BIA, 1979). This is a grant program principally involving the repair or enlargement of existing housing units, and the construction of new homes. The program also provides funds to qualified Indian families for closing costs and making downpayments for the purchase of a house. Indians who wish to participate in the HIP program may do so by contacting their tribes, tribal housing authorities, or committees which may be involved in selecting qualified families for the program.

HIP started in 1964 as an outgrowth of the program that provided funding for disaster relief resulting from floods in Montana and California. The program was established with the understanding that those assisted would engage in self-help involving construction and renovation. Active participation in the construction process still occurs and families are encouraged to contribute resources such as land, labor, and materials.

From its inception, and to avoid overlapping HUD's programs, it was decided that HIP would serve the poorest of the reservation families and individuals. As HUD programs grew, the Bureau of Indian Affairs reduced its new home construction activities. Instead, it emphasized housing repair and renovation (BIA, 1984). Presently, 65 percent of HIP funding is allocated for repairs and 35 percent is for new housing. In the 1985 fiscal year, the total HIP budget was over $20 million—enough to repair 2,634 existing units and assist in providing closing costs and downpayments for 330 new homes for Indian home buyers.

Funding for HIP increased steadily between 1966 and 1979, but has subsequently declined slightly. In 1966, HIP consisted of twenty staff members responsible for administering a $996,000 budget. At its peak in 1979, the HIP's budget exceeded $24.4 million with a staff of 116. In later years, the program has been reduced to 80 staff members in charge of administering $20.8 million as of 1985. Moreover, given the rapid inflation in housing construction costs (of constant quality) and housing repairs, the volume of services provided by the program has fallen considerably during the first half of the 1980s. Still further, because of BIA's staff shortage at the field level, the agency has not been able to satisfactorily: (1) obtain accurate statistical data about housing needs at the reservation level, (2) inspect the construction work adequately, (3) provide adequate technical assistance to the tribes, (4) monitor the program's implementation to assure compliance with regulations and overall agency policies, and (5) perform a thorough ongoing evaluation of the program.

If funding for the program were increased, additional staff could be hired. Thus, a heavier emphasis could be placed on personnel knowledge in standard construction practices, including engineering assessments, construction management, cost accounting, architectural design, and housing program development. Not all of the criticisms of the BIA's Home Improvement Program should be directed at this agency. The tribes do not always select participating families on the basis of greatest housing need. In some cases, friends or relatives of tribal leaders receive program assistance even though their economic circumstances are so favorable that they are not eligible for assistance.

Since 1973, the Bureau of Indian Affairs has conducted a Resident Training and Counseling Program implemented by individual Indian housing authorities on various reservations. The overall goal of this training and counseling program is to enable Indian families to enjoy better living conditions through increasing their understanding of the benefits, requirements, and responsibilities of owning or living in a new home. In addition, this program also strives to acquaint home owners and tenants with home repair skills. It also provides housing authority personnel with a better understanding of the problems and anticipated housing needs of the occupants.

A few housing units per year are constructed on Indian lands through the use of more conventional financing resources such as those made available through the Farmer's Home Administration (FmHA), Veterans Administration (VA), and Federal Housing Administration (FHA). However, these sources have never been an important source of funding in regards to expanding the supply of Indian housing inventory.

Water and Sanitation

The water supplies and sanitation facilities provided to both the existing and new Indian homes are furnished by the Indian Health Service (IHS). The enabling legislation is the Indian Sanitation Facilities Act of 1959. From 1959 to 1982, the IHS has initiated more than 3,300 projects to provide Indian homes and communities with sanitation facilities. Once completed, 136,300 Indian residences will be furnished with running water and a means of safe waste disposal (HHS, 1983). One criticism of the IHS program is that it is not always well coordinated with HUD's or BIA's home building efforts. Thus, homes which are built by the latter agencies often cannot be immediately occupied because of delays in obtaining water and sewer hookups through the IHS program.

Summary and Discussion

Utilizing the 1970 and 1980 census data and other available statistics, this study has attempted to examine the trends/changes in the quality and the quantity of Indian housing in recent years. Based on the data presented here, Indian housing has improved since 1970. The American Indian–occupied units in 1980 were newer, less crowded, and better equipped than they were in 1970. These improvements are accompanied by higher rents and increased housing values. Indian home ownership also increased slightly during the 1970s, except on a number of large reservations where it declined dramatically.

In some respects, American Indians are sheltered better than blacks. American Indians are more likely than blacks to own a recently built, single family unit. This was also true in 1970. However, in contrast, the housing units occupied by Indians are likely to be smaller, more expensive, and more crowded than those occupied by blacks. Indians are also more likely to reside in temporary shelters such as mobile homes. In all comparisons, whites enjoy a much higher standard of housing than either American Indians or blacks.

Regarding housing by place of residence, the data yield few surprises. American Indians living on or near reservations, and or in nonmetropolitan locations endure much lower standards of housing than those in metropolitan, and nonreservation areas. However, American Indians residing in nonmetropolitan and/or reservation areas are more likely to own their homes than Indians in other areas.

The data for reservations are especially significant because they are the sites for virtually all special public housing programs for American Indians. Most of these programs are administered through HUD and the BIA, and emphasize assistance for low income renters, subsidies for renovation or construction, and developing public water and sewage facilities. The administration of these programs frequently suffers because of funding shortfalls, understaffing, and occasional mismanagement. Indian Housing Authorities are particularly troubled with delinquent tenants. Furthermore, as these programs solve one set of problems, they seem to create others. For example, tribal leaders complain that public housing programs discourage home ownership and indeed for many reservations, there is evidence of a precipitous decline in home ownership. It is important to point out that despite chronically poor housing conditions on many reservations, the Reagan administration has repeatedly urged reduction or elimination of existing programs.

The policy implications of this research stem from the conclusion that American Indians are still one of the most poorly housed segments of the American population. In our view, there is a definite need to upgrade American Indian housing, both in quantitative and qualitative terms. Yet, in the wake of skyrocketing housing costs and massive cut-backs in federal assistance, the outlook for sustaining the small gains of the 1970s is dismal. Therefore, a significant public policy commitment is imperative for realizing improvements in the future.

In view of the modest improvements and persistent problems that characterize Indian housing, reductions in current programs leave little room for optimism about the future. We believe, however, that program cuts underscore the need for extensive and detailed analysis of Indian housing conditions. We hope that this analysis has been a small step in this direction. There is a need to monitor and document the conditions of Indian housing inventory, and to identify potentially deteriorating conditions. Further analyses are also needed for developing innovative ways of solving housing problems, with or without federal assistance.

Notes

1. Although American Indians, Eskimos, and Aleuts are extremely diverse and have different culture, language, and historical backgrounds, all three are served by the Bureau of Indian Affairs. It is not always possible to obtain data separately for each group. For this reason, we are dealing with these groups as a whole. For the sake of *literary convenience*, when we write "American Indians," we actually mean "American Indians, Eskimos, and Aleuts," unless specified otherwise.
2. A Standard Metropolitan Statistical Area (SMSA) is a reporting unit used by the U.S. Bureau of the Census to identify large urban areas. For a more detailed and precise definition of an SMSA the reader is encouraged to refer to Census documentations. Since 1980, a new unit called SMA (Standard Metropolitan Area) has also come into existence.
3. A "householder" is defined as "the household member (or one of the members) in whose name the home is owned or rented."
4. The space available for this chapter necessarily limits the amount of statistical data that can be presented and discussed here. Comparisons with other groups are also per force brief.

Acknowledgments

Support for this research was provided by the Russel Sage Foundation and Social Science Research Council. The University of Maryland Computer Center also supported this work. Special credit is due to Dr. Jamshid A. Momeni for his helpful suggestions on an earlier draft of this chapter. The authors bear full responsibility for all opinions and any errors.

References

AIPRC (American Indian Policy Review Commission). 1977. *Final Report*. Washington, D.C.: GPO.
Brophy, William A., and Sophie D. Aberle. 1966. *The Indian: America's Unfinished Business*. Norman, Okla.: University of Oklahoma Press.
BIA (Bureau of Indian Affairs). 1979. Housing Program for Indians. Unpublished memo.
HHS (U.S. Department of Health and Human Services). 1983. The Indian Health Services: A Comprehensive Health Care Program for American Indians and Alaska Natives. Unpublished memo.

HUD (U.S. Department of Housing and Urban Development). 1983. *Indian and Alaska Native Housing and Community Development Programs, 1983 Annual Report to Congress.* Washington, D.C.: HUD.

———. 1985. Office of Indian Housing, unpublished tabulations, March 1985.

Levitan, Sar A., and Barbara Hetrick. 1971. *Big Brother's Indian Program With Reservations.* New York: McGraw Hill.

Meyers, John. 1985. Statement by John Meyers, Director-Designate, Office of Indian Housing, before the U.S. Senate Select Committee on Indian Affairs. Washington, D.C.: 27 February 1985. Unpublished memo.

Sorkin, Alan. 1971. *American Indians and Federal Aid.* Washington, D.C.: The Brookings Institution.

———. 1978. *The Urban American Indian.* Lexington, Mass.: D.C. Heath and Company.

Stea, David. 1982. Indian Reservation Housing: Progress Since the Stanton Report. *American Indian Culture and Research Journal* 6: 1–14.

Treuer, Margaret. 1982. *A Report on the Housing Conditions of American Indians and Alaska Natives in the United States. Part I: Indian Housing Conditions.* Native American Rights Fund.

U.S. Bureau of the Census. 1970. *Housing Characteristics for States, Cities, and Counties.* 1970 Census of Population and Housing. United States Summary. Washington, D.C.: GPO.

———. 1973. *American Indians.* Subject Report PC(2)–1F. Washington, D.C.: GPO.

———. *General Housing Characteristics.* 1983a. 1980 Census of Housing. United States Summary HC80–1–A1. Washington, D.C.: GPO.

———. 1983b. *Detailed Housing Characteristics.* 1980 Census of Housing. United States Summary HC80–1–B1. Washington, D.C.: GPO.

———. 1984a. *American Indian Areas and Alaska Native Villages.* 1980 Census of Population and Housing. Supplementary Report PC80–S1–13. Washington, D.C.: GPO.

———. 1984b. *Metropolitan Housing Characteristics.* 1980 Census of Housing. United States Summary HC80–2–1. Washington, D.C.: GPO.

Utley, Robert M. 1984. *The Indian Frontier of the American West 1846–1890.* Albuquerque, N.M.: University of New Mexico Press.

10

Housing Problems of Asian Americans

Julia L. Hansen

The objective of this study is to examine the conditions of housing units occupied by Asian Americans.[1] The first section describes trends in Asian American housing since 1950. The current housing status of Asian Americans is then analyzed with a focus on variability between Asian American ethnic subgroups, and differences between Asian Americans and whites. The variation in Asian American housing by ethnic subgroups is then analyzed with a focus on the variability between Asian American subgroups and their differences with whites. The interethnic variations are analyzed in view of the impacts of residential segregation and nativity on housing conditions. Differentials in Asian American–white housing conditions are examined with respect to the role of socioeconomic factors and locational differences.

Although housing units occupied by all of the major ethnic subgroups of Asian Americans appear to be improving, significant problems remain. Housing of Asian Americans is generally inferior to that of whites, in spite of Asian Americans' generally superior socioeconomic status. The problem of overcrowding is particularly severe. In addition to differences between whites and Asian Americans, large variations in housing conditions exist between different ethnic subgroups of Asian Americans. These variations appear to be related to differences in income and nativity, but not to differences in the degree of residential segregation from non–Asian Americans, which is low for all subgroups.

Trends in Housing of Asian Americans

Due to data limitations, trends in Asian American housing prior to 1970 are difficult to document. Therefore, specific trends are examined for the period 1970 to 1980 only. This is preceded, however, by a general look at Asian American housing prior to 1970.

Most studies of Asian American housing prior to 1970 focus on the Chinese and Japanese, the two largest ethnic subgroups during this time period. Kitano (1960), in a study of housing in the San Francisco Bay Area during the 1950s, documents housing conditions of Japanese Americans. Although the Japanese units were found to have adequate space, physical condition, and plumbing facilities, units tended to be old and many survey respondents were dissatisfied with their neighborhood.[2] Kitano (1960) attributes the problems of older housing and dissatisfaction with neighborhood to exclusion of Japanese Americans from Bay Area neighborhoods with new housing. Respondents in his survey expected to encounter discrimination in the housing market. According to Kitano (1960: 178), Japanese Americans during the 1950s found housing to be the "single most important area of discrimination."

Housing of the Chinese during the 1950s was identified by one author as the "next major problem, second only to immigration, that confronts all persons of Chinese ancestry. As a racial minority, they have a heart-rending time finding suitable housing" (Lee, 1960: 313). Lee (1960) describes housing of Chinese in Chinatown as overcrowded, lacking essential sanitary facilities, and physically deteriorated. Studies suggest that the housing choice of Chinese, as well as Japanese, was limited by discrimination at this time (Kung, 1962; Lee, 1960).

Although not possible to document, an overall trend of improvement in Asian American housing between 1950 and 1970 may be inferred by examining trends in housing occupied by whites, and trends in the socioeconomic status of Asians relative to whites. Data show that during the period 1950 to 1970, housing occupied by whites improved greatly. For example, the percentage of white housing defined as substandard—that is, dilapidated and/or lacking complete plumbing—fell from 18.2 percent in 1950 to 4.3 percent in 1970 in urban areas and from 59.1 to 13.7 percent in rural areas (Heilbrun, 1981: 350). At the same time, Asian Americans were making more rapid gains in socioeconomic status than were whites. "Multiple-item" indices of educational and occupational status calculated by Schmid and Nobbe (1965) show gains in the status of Japanese and Chinese Americans relative to whites from 1950 to 1960. Evidence points to an increase in the income status of Japanese and Chinese relative to whites during this time period as well. According to Schmid and Nobbe (1965) indices, Japanese and Chinese lagged behind whites in income status in 1960. By 1970, however, Census data show that both Japanese and Chinese had surpassed whites in income status, as measured by median family income.[3] If whites were able to improve housing conditions substantially during this period, it is reasonable to believe that Asian Americans were able to improve housing conditions as well.

Table 10.1
Selected Characteristics of Total and Asian American–Occupied Housing Units in
the United States, 1970 and 1980

Characteristics	Total	Asian American Ethnic Subgroups			
		Chinese	Filipino	Japanese	Korean
Owner–Occupied (%)					
1970	62.9	44.1	39.3	56.0	43.4
1980	64.4	54.5	55.9	59.0	44.5
Lack Plumbing (%)					
1970	6.9	6.3	8.0	2.7	22.6
1980	2.2	3.2	2.2	1.6	4.5
Overcrowded (%)					
1970	8.2	20.1	27.9	9.5	32.1
1980	4.5	17.2	26.2	5.5	29.8
30+ Years Old (%)					
1970	40.3	40.3	35.4	29.0	26.8
1980	36.9	36.9	26.2	25.5	20.5
Ratio of Percent Asian American–Occupied Units to All Units					
Owner–Occupied					
1970	1.00	0.70	0.62	0.89	0.69
1980	1.00	0.85	0.87	0.92	0.69
Lack Plumbing					
1970	1.00	0.91	1.16	0.39	3.28
1980	1.00	1.45	1.00	0.73	2.05
Overcrowded					
1970	1.00	2.45	3.40	1.16	3.91
1980	1.00	3.82	5.82	1.22	6.62
30+ Years Old					
1970	1.00	1.00	0.88	0.72	0.67
1980	1.00	1.00	0.71	0.62	0.56

Source: U.S. Bureau of the Census (1972, 1973b, 1983a, 1983b).

Census data indicate a clear trend of improvement in housing occupied
by Asian Americans since 1970. The data in Table 10.1 show improvement
in housing along all the dimensions shown and for all four Asian American
subgroups for which data are available. Particularly significant gains during
the seventies were made in home ownership by Chinese and Filipino Americans; in plumbing facilities by Korean Americans; and in obtaining newer
housing by the Filipino and Korean Americans.

The evidence on whether Asian American housing improved at a faster rate than did the housing stock in general is mixed. The indicators show improvement relative to national averages in terms of home ownership, housing age, and (in the case of Filipinos and Koreans) plumbing. It is seen, for example, that the ratio of the percentage of Chinese units which are owner-occupied to the percentage of all units which are owner-occupied rose from .70 in 1970 to .85 in 1980. However, overcrowding—as measured by the percent of units with 1.01 or more persons per room—in the Asian American units did not decline as rapidly as it did in the United States as a whole. As a matter of fact, while it fell in absolute terms, the relative incidence of overcrowding in Asian American units as compared to that in the United States as a whole, actually increased. The same phenomenon is observed with respect to the percentage of Japanese and Chinese units lacking plumbing.

Housing Status of Asian Americans in 1980

Housing data for the six largest ethnic subgroups of Asian Americans are available from the 1980 census. As seen in Table 10.2, the conditions of Asian American housing units vary tremendously according to ethnicity. As indicated by the data on home ownership, plumbing facilities, and overcrowding, housing occupied by Japanese is clearly superior to housing occupied by the other Asian American groups. Fifty-nine percent of Japanese units are owner-occupied, 1.6 percent lack complete plumbing, and 5.5 percent are overcrowded. Chinese, Filipino, and Asian Indians can be viewed collectively as occupying the second rung on the ladder of housing status behind Japanese. Korean housing occupies a third rung and is followed at the bottom by Vietnamese housing. Only 26.7 percent of Vietnamese units are owner-occupied, 5.1 percent lack complete plumbing, and almost half, 49.3 percent, are overcrowded. The extent of housing differences between the different groups can be illustrated by pointing out that Japanese housing resembles white housing much more closely than it resembles Vietnamese housing.

Housing of different Asian American subgroups is similar in one respect— it is generally not comparable to housing occupied by whites. With the exception of the plumbing indicator for Japanese units, all of the housing measures shown in Table 10.2 point to the inferiority of Asian American housing as compared to white housing. The area in which the greatest inequity is apparent is the area of overcrowding. The percentage of Asian American units which are overcrowded is substantially higher than the corresponding percentage of units occupied by whites. The incidence of overcrowding in Asian American units ranges from 1.9 to 17 times higher than the incidence in white units. An extreme example of this is the discovery by police in Santa Ana, California of a housing unit occupied by sixty-two Vietnamese refugees, who were apparently sleeping on the floor of the unit

Table 10.2
Selected Characteristics of White- and Asian American-Occupied Housing Units
in the United States, 1980

Characteristics	White	Asian American Ethnic Subgroups					
		Chinese	Filipino	Japanese	Asian Indian	Korean	Vietnamese
Occupied Units (in 1000s)	68,810	248	197	234	119	81	52
Owner-Occupied (%)	67.8	54.5	55.9	59.0	50.7	44.5	26.7
Lack Plumbing (%)	1.7	3.2	2.2	1.6	2.1	4.5	5.1
Overcrowded (%)	2.9	17.2	26.2	5.5	14.0	29.8	49.3
Ratio of Percent Asian American-Occupied Units to White Units							
Owner-Occupied	1.00	0.80	0.82	0.87	0.75	0.66	0.39
Lack Plumbing	1.00	1.88	1.30	0.94	1.24	2.65	3.00
Overcrowded	1.00	5.93	9.03	1.90	4.83	10.28	17.00

Source: U.S. Bureau of the Census (1983a).

in shifts (Hume, 1985). It is interesting to note that with respect to over-crowding, black housing is more comparable to that occupied by whites than is Asian American housing. The percentage of black units which are overcrowded, 11.2, is lower than that for all subgroups with the exception of Japanese. In addition to being considerably more likely to live in a housing unit which is overcrowded, Asian American households are more likely to live in units without complete plumbing for exclusive use and less likely to own their units. However, with respect to home ownership and plumbing, Asian American housing is generally more comparable to housing occupied by whites than is black housing.[4]

In addition to variation by ethnic subgroups, the Asian American housing varies considerably by region of the country. The data in Table 10.3 show that the problems of obtaining owner-occupied homes and units with com-plete plumbing are particularly great in the Northeast region of the country, and that the problem of overcrowding is particularly severe in the western region. On the other hand, the problem of overcrowding is least severe in the North Central region, and the incidence of units lacking plumbing is generally lowest in the southern region. The greatest regional variation is observed in the area of home ownership. For example, the percentage of Japanese units which are owner-occupied varies dramatically by region, ranging from 24.9 percent in the Northeast to 63.4 percent in the West.

In comparison, housing of whites does not vary greatly by region. There-fore, large variations in housing of Asian Americans by region translate into large variations in Asian American/White housing inequities by region. For example, as seen in Table 10.4, the Japanese/white home ownership ratio ranges from 0.39 in the Northeast to 1.01 in the West. Although the crowd-ing problem in Asian American units is most severe in the western region in absolute terms, inequality between Asian American and white housing in terms of overcrowding is greatest in the northeast. In general, Asian American housing is least comparable to white housing in the Northeast along the dimensions of home ownership and overcrowding, and in the West along the dimension of plumbing. In terms of plumbing and over-crowding, Asian American housing is *most* comparable to white housing in the south. In terms of home ownership, Asian American housing is most comparable to white housing in the west.

Analysis of Variations in Housing by Ethnic Subgroup

As alluded to earlier, Asian American housing varies greatly by ethnic subgroups. Several socioeconomic factors have been said to account for this variation. These include household income, household size, and character-istics of the primary householder such as education, occupational status, sex, and age (Kain and Quigley, 1972; Pascal, 1967). For example, work by Pascal (1967) shows that expenditures on housing are positively related

Table 10.3
Selected Characteristics of White- and Asian American—Occupied Housing Units
by Region and Asian American Ethnic Subgroups, 1980

Characteristics	White	Asian American Ethnic Subgroups					
		Chinese	Filipino	Japanese	Asian Indian	Korean	Viet-namese
Occupied Units as Percent of U.S. Total							
Northeast	22.2	26.2	10.4	6.6	32.5	19.5	9.6
North Central	27.3	8.9	10.2	23.9	15.1	13.9	27.3
South	31.4	11.0	10.4	4.9	23.6	17.3	31.1
West	19.1	53.8	69.0	82.5	20.0	48.1	45.3
Owner-Occupied (%)							
Northeast	63.3	38.2	46.1	24.9	40.6	34.1	21.1
North Central	71.6	53.4	57.6	46.1	54.4	49.9	28.0
South	70.7	59.6	57.6	46.1	56.7	49.3	33.4
West	62.9	61.4	56.9	63.4	55.8	45.4	22.9
Lack Plumbing (%)							
Northeast	1.8	4.9	2.4	3.9	2.6	5.2	6.1
North Central	1.6	3.4	1.9	2.3	2.1	4.8	5.0
South	2.0	1.5	1.1	1.8	1.5	2.7	3.8
West	1.1	2.7	2.4	1.4	2.0	4.8	5.8
Overcrowded (%)							
Northeast	2.4	20.4	16.6	8.5	15.8	27.1	37.2
North Central	2.3	12.7	16.2	3.3	10.7	19.7	39.8
South	3.4	14.8	19.1	4.2	12.5	27.0	45.8
West	3.8	16.9	30.2	5.5	16.6	35.0	57.3

Source: U.S. Bureau of the Census (1983a).

Table 10.4

Ratio of Percent of Asian American–Occupied Units to Percent White-Occupied Units by Selected Characteristics and Region, 1980

Characteris-tics/Region	Asian American Ethnic Subgroups					
	Chinese	Filipino	Japanese	Asian Indian	Korean	Viet-namese
Owner-Occupied						
Northeast	0.61	0.73	0.39	0.64	0.54	0.33
North Central	0.75	0.80	0.64	0.76	0.70	0.39
South	0.84	0.81	0.65	0.80	0.69	0.36
West	0.98	0.90	1.01	0.89	0.72	0.36
Lack Plumbing						
Northeast	2.75	1.37	2.23	1.45	2.92	3.45
North Central	2.16	1.17	1.42	1.33	3.03	3.15
South	0.73	0.57	0.91	0.73	0.73	1.91
West	2.50	2.24	1.28	1.85	4.37	5.31
Overcrowded						
Northeast	8.65	7.02	3.61	6.68	11.49	15.75
North Central	5.56	7.11	1.46	4.70	8.65	17.46
South	4.40	5.69	1.25	3.71	3.71	13.63
West	4.45	7.95	1.46	4.38	9.21	15.08

Source: U.S. Bureau of the Census (1983a).

to household income, household size, and education, occupational status, and age of the primary householder. Households headed by males have higher expenditures than similar households headed by females. Work by Kain and Quigley (1972) suggests that the probability of home ownership is positively related to household income, household size, and education and age of the householder. In addition, households headed by males are more likely to own homes than similar households headed by females.

The extent of socioeconomic differences between different subgroups of Asian Americans is illustrated in Table 10.5. Particularly pronounced are differences in income and poverty status. Median household income in 1980 ranges from a low of $12,500 for Vietnamese to a high of $22,500 for Japanese. Similarly, the proportion of families with income below the poverty line ranges from 4.2 percent for Japanese to 35.1 percent for Vietnamese. It is interesting to note that the difference in median household income between Vietnamese and Japanese is larger than the difference between the median household income of any group of Asian Americans and whites. In addition to ranking lowest in income status, Vietnamese also rank lowest in education and occupational status, where occupational status is indicated by the percent of employed persons in managerial and professional occupations. This percentage ranges from 13.4 for Vietnamese to 48.4 for Asian Indians. It is likely that the bottom ranking of Vietnamese in income, education, and occupational status contributes to their bottom ranking in housing status. Another contributing factor is that a relatively high proportion of Vietnamese households are headed by females.

Socioeconomic Differentials by Nativity

A possible source for the substantial differences in income, education, and occupational status between the subgroups is differences in nativity (i.e., percent foreign-born v. native-born), which is: Japanese, 28.4; Chinese, 63.3; Filipino, 64.7; Asian Indian, 70.4; Korean, 81.9; and, Vietnamese, 90.5 percent (U.S. Bureau of the Census 1983c).

Japanese, who have the highest median household income and who occupy the best housing, have the lowest proportion foreign-born, while Vietnamese, who have the lowest median household income and who occupy the worst housing, have the highest. In general, it is likely that foreign-born Asian American householders face significant economic constraints, due to their disadvantaged position in the labor market and its depressing effect on household income. Human capital disadvantages in the form of limited ability to speak English, little knowledge of the American social system, and little education and training relevant to employment in the United States are believed to contribute to relatively lower wages, a relatively lower rate of employment, and consequently to a relatively lower annual income. Incomes of foreign-born householders may be reduced even further by dis-

Table 10.5
Selected Socioeconomic Characteristics of Asian American and White Population
in the United States, 1980

| | Asian American Ethnic Subgroups | | | | | | |
Characteristics	Chi-nese	Fili-pino	Japa-nese	Asian Indian	Korean	Viet-namese	White
Median Income ($1000s)	19.6	21.9	22.5	20.6	18.1	12.5	17.7
HH* Below Poverty (%)	10.5	6.2	4.2	7.4	13.1	35.1	7.0
High School Grads. (%)	71.3	74.2	81.6	80.1	78.1	62.2	68.8
Median Yrs. of School							
Completed	13.4	14.1	12.9	16.1	13.0	12.4	12.5
In Manag./Prof Occup(%)	32.6	25.1	28.5	48.5	24.9	13.4	23.9
No. of Persons Per HH*	3.1	3.7	2.7	2.9	3.4	4.3	2.7
Female-headed HH* (%)	18.2	20.4	24.2	20.9	21.1	30.6	25.8

* Household(s).

Source: U.S. Bureau of the Census (1983c).

Table 10.6
Rank Correlation Coefficients between Selected Housing and Socioeconomic
Characteristics of Asian Americans

Characteristics	Percent Foreign-Born	Median Income	Percent Below Poverty
Owner-Occupied Units (%)	-.943*	+.943*	-.943*
Units with Complete Plumbing (%)	-.771**	+.943*	-.943*
1.00 or less Persons Per Room (%)	-.829*	+.829*	-.829*
Foreign-born Population (%)		-.829*	+.829*

* and ** significant at .05 and .0514 levels, respectively.

Source: Computed by the author.

crimination against immigrants in the labor market. Recent opinion polls showing that most Americans give loss of jobs as the main reason for opposing any influx of immigrants to the United States suggest a climate in which this type of discrimination may flourish (*Economist*, 1985). However, it should be noted that not all immigrants face disadvantages in the job market to the same degree. For example, those Vietnamese immigrants who arrived immediately following the Vietnam War were exceptional in terms of their familiarity with English and American social customs, and in terms of their educational and professional qualifications (*Economist*, 1985).

Table 10.6 presents coefficients measuring the degree of correlation between rankings of Asian American subgroups along the dimensions of 1) income status and housing status, 2) income status and percentage foreign-born, and 3) percentage foreign-born and housing status. Income is measured by median household income and the percentage of families with income below the poverty line. Housing status is measured by the percentage of units which are owner-occupied, the percentage with complete plumbing for exclusive use, and the percentage of housing units with 1.01 or fewer persons per room, based on the data from the 1980 Census of Population and Housing.

The rank correlation coefficients indicate a strong, positive correlation between income and housing status, a strong negative correlation between income and percentage foreign-born, and a strong negative correlation between percentage foreign-born and housing status. In all cases but one, the coefficients are statistically significant at the .05 level. These results suggest that foreign-born status may constrain income status, and hence housing status as well. One implication of this is that language and education programs for immigrants may be viewed as an indirect method of improving housing conditions for many Asian American households. It should be noted, however, that the housing choice of foreign-born householders may also be constrained by discrimination in the housing market arising from prejudice against immigrants, as well as from racial and ethnic prejudice.

Housing Conditions and Location

Another factor affecting Asian American housing differences is the location of different groups of Asian Americans within metropolitan areas. More specifically, the degree to which different groups of Asian Americans are segregated into so-called "ethnic enclaves." There is a tendency for recent immigrants, including Asian American immigrants, to locate in such enclaves. Early works on urban location (Park, 1923, 1926; Wirth, 1929; Burgess, 1928) emphasize this tendency. Such a tendency may arise as a result of discrimination against immigrants in the general housing market and/or as a result of certain disadvantages faced by immigrants. For example, language and related social and economic disadvantages faced by immigrant households may lead them to prefer living in an area with culturally similar households and possibly ethnic businesses. If the housing stock in such areas is inferior, then these households may face a trade-off between housing and the advantages of living in an ethnic area. That the housing stock in such areas may be inferior is suggested by some studies. Park (1923, 1926) and Wirth (1929) describe a competitive process of location selection which results in homogeneous neighborhoods, with groups that are more economically, politically, and socially advantaged locating in the more desirable areas. Warner and Strole (1945) argue that ethnic groups are initially segregated into the areas of a city with relatively low housing quality.

The existence of a trade-off between housing and the advantages of living in an ethnic neighborhood is suggested by the results of a study of desired residential mobility in San Francisco's Chinatown (Loo and Mar, 1982). The study concludes that, "Immigrants who have difficulties with American life and society can ease the extent of these difficulties by locating in Chinatown as the community offers a degree of social, economic and cultural security, albeit in a community with poor and inadequate housing" (Loo and Mar, 1982: 104). Studies suggest that the mechanism of housing improvement will generally take the form of residential mobility, i.e. movement out of the traditional ethnic area. It has been concluded, for example, that the permanence of San Francisco's Chinatown is attributable to the arrival of new immigrants to offset the "flow of more affluent, better educated residents out of the enclave" (Loo and Mar, 1982: 97). Lieberson (1963) identifies a positive relationship between residential desegregation of immigrant groups over time and increases in their socioeconomic status.

Existing studies thus suggest that there is reason to expect a relationship between housing and the degree to which different subgroups of Asian Americans are residentially segregated. This relationship is examined here using 1980 census tract data for the Los Angeles–Long Beach Standard Metropolitan Statistical Area (SMSA). The so-called *exposure rate* is used here to measure the absolute degree of segregation of a subgroup of Asian Americans from non–Asian Americans. In this case, the *exposure rate* measures the proportion of the population which is non–Asian American in the census tract in the particular subgroup of Asian Americans. According to Schnare (1980) *exposure rates* are calculated as follow:

$$AX = 1/A \ \Sigma_{i=1}^{n} \ A_i(M_i/T_i)$$

where
A_i = Number of Asian American subgroup in census tract i.
M_i = Number of non-Asian Americans in census tract i.
T_i = Total population in census tract i.
A = SMSA's total number of Asian ethnic subgroup.

That is, $A = \Sigma_{i=1}^{n} \ B_i$;

in this study n = 1,635 represents the number of census tracts.

All six subgroups of Asian Americans are found to have a very high level of residential exposure to, and hence a low level of segregation from, non–Asian Americans. Exposure rates in the Los Angeles–Long Beach SMSA for six Asian ethnic subgroups are calculated to be as follows:

Subgroup	Exposure Rate	Subgroup	Exposure Rate
Asian Indian	0.920	Vietnamese	0.860
Filipino	0.874	Japanese	0.835
Korean	0.861	Chinese	0.822

The above rates indicate that the proportion of non–Asian Americans in the census tract of the average Asian American ranges between a low of 82.2 and a high of 92.0 percent for Chinese and Asian Indians, respectively.[5] Variation in exposure rates between the ethnic subgroups is small. An examination of the rank correlation coefficients measuring the correlation between the exposure rate and three measures of housing characteristics indicates that the degree of variation in exposure which exists between the subgroups is not significantly correlated with the variation in housing characteristics.[6] This suggests that differences in the degree of residential segregation are not a major source of subgroup differences in housing. It should be noted, however, that the Los Angeles–Long Beach SMSA is unique in that it has a larger combined population of the six Asian American subgroups examined than any other SMSA in the nation. Therefore, the findings of this study may not be generalizable to other SMSAs.

Analysis of Asian American/White Housing Inequities

Two possible sources of housing differences between Asian Americans and whites are differences in socioeconomic characteristics, and housing market discrimination which limits the housing choices of Asian Americans. Differences in socioeconomic characteristics such as income can of course arise as a result of other forms of discrimination, such as that in the employment opportunities.

The data in Table 10.5 suggest that Asian/white differentials in housing cannot, in general, be attributed to socioeconomic differences. It is seen, for example, that with the exception of Vietnamese, median household income for each Asian American subgroup is higher than that for whites. Considering the importance of income as a determinant of housing status, such evidence might lead one to predict that Asian Americans would occupy *better* housing than do whites. Japanese in particular, rank considerably higher than whites in income status. Although all subgroups, except Vietnamese, have a higher median household income than do whites, three of these groups also have a higher family poverty rate, which could contribute to a higher incidence of housing problems. In the case of Japanese, however, who have a family poverty rate significantly lower than that for whites, the data suggest that it is difficult to explain housing differences on the basis of income differentials.

With the exception of Vietnamese, Asian Americans also appear to have higher educational and occupational status than do whites. In addition, with the exception of Vietnamese, the percent of households headed by females is lower for all Asian subgroups. Based on socioeconomic factors alone, then, one might expect that Asian Americans would have a higher rate of home ownership and a lower incidence of overcrowding than do whites.

One possible explanation for housing differences is that Asian Americans have different housing preferences as a result of cultural factors. It is difficult to believe, however, that this could account for the large inequities observed. A higher average household size for Asian Americans may contribute to the overcrowding problem, although household size is not larger for Japanese than it is for whites. Related to the issue of preferences, respondents in a recent survey of residents of San Francisco's Chinatown cited crowding as the most disliked quality of their neighborhood. Crowding was the most common reason given for wanting to move (Loo and Mar, 1982). Accordingly, it would not appear as if overcrowded conditions are sought out by Asian Americans.

There is a distinct dimension to Asian/white differences in housing. As discussed above, considerable regional variation in these differences exists. In other words, Asian American housing is much more comparable to white housing in some regions of the country than in others. The analysis in the preceding section indicates that one factor which may play a role is the

Table 10.7

Rank Correlation Coefficients between Percent of SMSA's Foreign-Born Asian American Population and Selected Housing Characteristics

Percent of SMSA's Foreign-Born Asian American Population

Percent SMSA Housing Units	Chinese	Filipino	Japanese	Asian Indian	Korean	Viet-namese
Owner-Occupied	-.814*	-.593*	-.729*	-.382	-.443	-.536*
Lack Plumbing	-.729*	+.050	-.514	+.050	+.357	-.275
No. of Persons/Room	-.582*	+.325	-.368	-.193	-.336	+.039

* Statistically significant at 0.05 level.

Source: Computed by the author.

variation in the geographic distribution of foreign-born Asian householders. Housing differences seem to be greatest in areas with a relatively high proportion of foreign-born Asian population.

The relationship between Asian/white housing differentials and the geographic distribution of the foreign-born is examined here using data for several metropolitan areas. Census of housing data for fifteen SMSAs with the largest concentration of each Asian ethnic subgroup are used to calculate rank correlation coefficients between selected SMSAs' Asian American housing characteristics and the SMSA's percent foreign-born.[7] The coefficient values, as shown in Table 10.7, indicate a large and statistically significant negative correlation between the ranking of SMSA's Asian/white home ownership rates and the SMSA's percent foreign-born in four of six cases.

However, a negative and significant correlation between the ranking of the SMSA's Asian/white plumbing facilities ratios and SMSA's percent foreign-born, and the ranking between SMSA's Asian/white overcrowding ratios and the SMSA's percent foreign-born is found in only one case. Since results differ according to the measure of housing used and by Asian ethnic subgroup, there is nothing to indicate the existence of a systematic SMSA differential in discrimination.

It is possible that Asian/white differentials across SMSAs in plumbing facilities and overcrowding are explained by the distribution of the races within SMSAs and the nature of the local housing stock.

Summary and Conclusions

An examination of the Asian American housing has revealed that although conditions are improving, this group continues to face significant problems.

Housing of Asians is generally inferior to that of whites, particularly in terms of overcrowding, but also in terms of home ownership and plumbing. The problem of overcrowding is most prevalent in the Western region of the country; the rate of home ownership is lowest and the incidence of units lacking complete plumbing is highest in the Northeast. Housing of Asian Americans is not comparable to that of whites in spite of the fact that all Asian ethnic subgroups, except Vietnamese, exceed whites in income, education, and occupational status. Japanese housing is inferior to that of whites despite the fact that median household income for Japanese is over 25 percent higher than median household income for whites. In terms of overcrowding, housing of Asians is less comparable to white housing than black housing is to that of whites. Resolution of the issue why Asian/white housing inequalities exist requires further research on the extent of current housing market discrimination faced by the Asian American subgroups.

Housing conditions of Asian Americans vary greatly within ethnic subgroups. The variations appear to be related to differences in income and nativity. Japanese, who have the lowest proportion foreign-born and the highest median household income, occupy the best housing, while Vietnamese who have the highest proportion foreign-born and the lowest median household income, have the worst housing. The degree of residential segregation of all subgroups from non–Asian Americans is very low. This is a positive finding.

From a policy point of view, while direct housing subsidies are probably needed for many Asian immigrant households in the short run, it is possible that language and educational programs would enhance their chances to improve both occupational and income status, and thus, housing in the long run.

Notes

1. U.S. Bureau of the Census does not provide separate data for Asians and Pacific Islanders. Thus, in this study, for the sake of literary convenience, whenever we write "Asian American," or simply "Asian," we mean Asian and Pacific Islanders.

2. Kitano's conclusion that units had adequate physical condition was based on the finding that 12 percent of units' exteriors and 6 percent of units' interiors were "shabby or neglected" according to survey respondents.

3. Median household income for Japanese, Chinese, and whites in 1970 were $12,847, $10,610, and $9,958, respectively (U.S. Bureau of the Census, 1973a, 1973c).

4. The percent of black units lacking complete plumbing for exclusive use in 1980 was 5.5, and the percent owner-occupied units was 44.4 (U.S. Bureau of the Census, 1983a).

5. Relative segregation values can be derived by comparing the exposure rates to the proportion of the SMSA population which is non–Asian American. A non-Asian

proportion of 94.4 in the Los Angeles–Long Beach SMSA indicates a very low level of relative segregation.

6. Rank correlation coefficients between the ranking of exposure rates and the percent of units which are owner-occupied, the percent with complete plumbing for exclusive use, and the percent overcrowded units are $+0.542$, -0.257, and $+0.143$, respectively.

7. Data used are those on nativity by country of birth. These data underestimate the percent foreign-born for Chinese and Asian Indians. This is not a problem as long as the bias does not vary by SMSA. The fifteen SMSAs used in this analysis differed for different Asian ethnic subgroups.

References

Burgess, E. 1928. Residential Segregation in American Cities. *The Annals of the American Academy of Political and Social Sciences* 40: 105–115.

Economist. 1985. From Saigon to San Diego. (27 April): 38–45.

Heilbrun, J. 1981. *Urban Economics and Public Policy.* New York: St. Martin's Press.

Hume, E. 1985. Vietnam's Legacy. *Wall Street Journal* (21 March): 1.

Kain, John F., and J. M. Quigley. 1972. Housing Market Discrimination, Home Ownership and Savings Behavior. *American Economic Review* 62: 263–77.

Kitano, H. 1960. Housing of Japanese Americans in the San Francisco Bay Area. In *Studies in Housing and Minority Groups,* edited by Nathan Glazer and D. McEntire. Berkeley, Calif.: University of California Press.

Kung, S. 1962. *Chinese in American Life.* Seattle: University of Washington Press.

Lee, R. 1960. *The Chinese in the United States of America.* London: Oxford University Press.

Lieberson, S. 1963. *Ethnic Patterns in American Cities.* Glencoe, Ill.: Free Press.

Loo, C., and D. Mar. 1982. Desired Residential Mobility in a Low-Income Ethnic Community: A Case Study of Chinatown. *Journal of Social Issues* 38: 95–106.

Park, R. 1923. A Race Relations Survey. *Journal of Applied Sociology* 8: 195–205.

———. 1926. Our Racial Frontier on the Pacific. *Survey Graphic* 9: 192–96.

Pascal, A. H. 1967. *The Economics of Housing Segregation.* Santa Monica: Rand Corporation

Schmid, C., and C. Nobbe. 1965. Socio-economic Differentials Among Nonwhite Races. *American Sociological Review* 30: 909–22.

Schnare, Ann B. 1980. Trends in Residential Segregation by Race. *Journal of Urban Economics* 7: 293–301.

U.S. Bureau of the Census. 1972. *Detailed Housing Characteristics. United States Summary* HC(1)-B1. 1970 Census of Housing. Washington, D.C.: GPO.

———. 1973a. *Characteristics of the Population: United States Summary,* Volume 1, Part 1, Section 2. 1970 Census of Population. Washington, D.C.: GPO.

———. 1973b. *Housing of Selected Racial Groups.* 1970 Census of Population. Subject Report HC(7)–9. Washington, D.C.: GPO.

———. 1973c. *Japanese, Chinese, and Filipinos in the United States.* 1970 Census of Population. Subject Reports PC(2)–1G. Washington, D.C.: GPO.

———. 1983a. *Characteristics of Housing Units: General Housing Characteristics-*

United States Summary, Volume 1, Chapter A, Part 1, 1980 Census of Housing HC80–1-A1. Washington, D.C.: GPO.

———. 1983b. *Characteristics of Housing Units: Detailed Housing Characteristics-United States Summary*, Volume 1, Chapter B, Part 1. 1980 Census of Housing HC80–1-B1. Washington, D.C.: GPO.

———. 1983c. *Characteristics of the Population: General Social and Economic Characteristics-United States Summary*, Volume 1, Chapter C, Part 1. 1980 Census of Population PC80–1-C1. Washington, D.C.: GPO. We have also used State Volumes: PC80-C6, PC80-C7, PC80-C10, PC80-C13, PC80-C15, PC80-C20, PC80-C22, PC80-C23, PC80-C24, PC80-C32, PC80-C34, PC80-C39, PC80-C40, PC80-C45, PC80-C48, and PC80-C49.

Warner, W. L., and L. Strole. 1945. *The Social Systems of American Ethnic Groups*. New Haven: Yale University Press.

Wirth, L. 1929. *The Ghetto*. Chicago: University of Chicago Press.

11

Minority Housing Needs and Civil Rights Enforcement

John M. Goering

Introduction

In May 1985, a police helicopter firebombed a building in Philadelphia encouraged in part because local residents in the "neat, middle-income neighborhood" complained of the dirt, rats, and noise coming from the building (Gruson, 1985: 1; Peterson, 1985: A1). The same day, the *New York Times* reported the results of a survey of New Yorkers which revealed that the majority lived in segregated neighborhoods, half were aware that their friends used racial slurs, and most felt there was a "harsher" mood in race relations. The survey reported that some blacks were expressing more conservative views towards race relations. One black teenager, reportedly shocked at finding books by Huey Newton and Eldridge Cleaver in his mother's bookcase, asked "how could you even be associated with that kind of revolutionary, radical philosophy?" (Dowd, 1985: B4).

The desire of black residents in Philadelphia to preserve the character of their neighborhood and homes, and the antipathy of some New Yorkers toward radical action, are snapshots of a shifting mosaic of minority attitudes, needs, and strategies for change. Is there a growing national mood of conservatism in the area of housing for minorities? Is there less to complain about and less to fight for in the area of housing and fair housing? What are the principle differences affecting the choices and options of minorities? What, in brief, are the obstacles to equity in minority housing opportunities in the 1980s?

The purpose of this chapter is to address these questions by examining three specific features of minority housing conditions and opportunities. The three areas are: 1) minority housing problems; 2) housing discrimination; and 3) civil rights enforcement in housing. These three areas will be explored using a number of data sources and evaluation reports in an effort to be clearer about the nature of the housing constraints affecting minorities in the 1980s.

Minority Housing and Segregation

The bulk of the housing stock in America is privately owned, with only roughly 3 percent subsidized by government agencies. As of 1983, there were nearly 92 million housing units available for occupancy of which slightly more than 7 million were vacant. Nearly 55 million of the 85 million occupied housing units were owner-occupied. Thus, roughly 35 percent of the American housing stock was for rent as of 1983. There were noticeable racial differences in homeownership of the stock with two-thirds of whites but only 45 percent of blacks and 43 percent of Hispanics owning their own homes.[1] Black households lived in 11 percent of all occupied units and Hispanics in 5 percent.

Recent research also documents important changes in the pattern of residential concentration or segregation of minorities. From 1970 to 1980, the level of segregation has declined throughout many metropolitan areas in the United States (Taeuber, 1983; Schnare, 1985). Although there are variations among regions and between cities, the index of dissimilarity as well as the exposure index reflect modest declines in the segregation of blacks and whites. The level of segregation for Hispanics declined between 1970 and 1980 in Denver and Phoenix but increased in Houston by 20 percent (James and Tynan, 1986). There has, then, been a slow, downward drift in the segregation of blacks and Hispanics in most, but by no means all, American cities. Such declines, if they were to continue at the same rate for the next 50 years, would still leave the average American city substantially segregated (Taeuber, 1983: 4). Measures of the extent of homeownership among minorities as well as indicators of residential segregation are only a small part of the picture of minority housing conditions. Information on housing need and costs constitute additional pieces in understanding the status of minority housing in the 1980s.

Minority Housing Needs: The Burden of Rising Costs

Housing need or deprivation is a term used to refer to a variety of conditions affecting the physical condition and affordability of housing. A family's housing need is most readily measured by three factors: the physical condition or inadequacy of their dwelling, the extent of crowding, and whether the family is paying too large a share of their income for housing.[2]

Measures of housing need or deprivation reveal that over the past several decades the physical adequacy of the American housing stock has improved enormously. Levels of structural inadequacy and crowding have declined dramatically. Physically inadequate housing conditions declined from 71 percent of all sources of housing need in 1960 to 53 percent in 1970 (Birch et al., 1973: 4–10). Overcrowded housing has also become much less important as a housing problem. The 1940s standard of adequacy was, for example, 1.5 or fewer persons per room. By that standard, overcrowding declined from 9 percent of occupied units in 1940 to 2 percent in 1970 and to less than one percent by 1980. Overcrowding, redefined as one or more persons per room, also diminished from 20 percent in 1970 to roughly 4 percent by 1980.

Several studies (Eribes and Karnig, 1980; Yezer, 1981; Bianchi, Farley, and Spain, 1982; James, McCummings, and Tynan, 1983) have examined how improvements in housing conditions have been distributed among whites, blacks, and Hispanics. The physical condition of the housing stock, for example, appeared to improve from 1940 to 1950 for blacks although the level of crowding remained unchanged. The proportion of crowding among nonwhite households in 1950 was three and one-half times greater than that of whites (Housing and Home Finance, 1952: 10). Nearly 27 percent of nonwhite homes but only 5 percent of white homes were classified as dilapidated in 1950 (McGraw, 1954: 57). Both structural inadequacy and crowding declined markedly from 1960 to 1977 with inadequacy declining from 13 percent to roughly 2 percent and crowding from 14 to 6 percent of all housing units (Bianchi, Farley, and Spain, 1982: 46). Cost burden was not a factor considered in these earlier studies.

Table 11.1 provides a description of the three indicators of housing problems including physical inadequacy, crowding, and cost burden, for white, black, and Hispanic households for 1975 and 1983. The data make a number of facts clear: (a) the amount of physically inadequate and overcrowded housing declined from 1975 to 1983, while cost burden increased as a problem for all racial groups; (b) renters generally have larger numbers of housing problems, with all renters regardless of race experiencing similar levels of cost burden. As of 1983, approximately one-third of white, black, and Hispanic households were paying more than 30 percent of their incomes for rent; (c) inadequate housing conditions still may be found in 20 to 25 percent of black homes and apartments and in 13 to 21 percent of Hispanic owned and rented units in 1983; and (c) white owners and renters have proportionally fewer problems than blacks or Hispanics.

Table 11.2 provides data on the percentage distribution of housing problems for white, black, and Hispanic occupied housing units for the years 1975 and 1983. For white owners and renters, cost burden is the most important housing need; one that sharply increased in importance for owners from 1975 to 1983 (an increase from 38 to 56 percent). At the same time, inadequate and overcrowded housing declined as a problem for all groups. White, black, and Hispanic renters had proportionally fewer prob-

Table 11.1
Housing Problems for White, Black, and Hispanic Households for Occupied
Units, 1975 and 1983 (in thousands)

No. of Units and Problems	White		Black		Hispanic	
	Owners	Renters	Owners	Renters	Owners	Renters
Occupied Units						
1975	42,280	19,615	3,295	4,249	1,345	1,769
1983	48,794	22,255	4,112	5,005	1,984	2,642
Inadequate						
1975	2,514	2,476	763	1,321	230	400
1983	2,369	2,325	786	1,267	265	549
1975 (%)	5.9	12.6	23.2	31.1	17.1	22.6
1983 (%)	4.8	10.4	19.1	25.3	13.4	20.8
Crowded						
1975	1,152	587	256	311	177	259
1983	673	558	187	276	174	362
1975 (%)	2.7	3.0	7.8	7.3	13.2	14.6
1983 (%)	1.4	2.5	4.5	5.5	8.8	13.7
Cost Burden						
1975	2,216	4,797	256	998	80	405
1983	3,878	7,321	520	1,675	183	848
1975 (%)	5.2	24.4	7.8	23.5	5.9	22.9
1983 (%)	7.9	32.9	12.6	33.5	9.2	32.1
Total with Housing Problems						
1975	5,882	7,860	1,275	2,630	487	1,064
1983	6,920	10,204	1,493	3,218	622	1,759
1975 (%)	13.9	40.1	38.7	61.9	36.2	60.1
1983 (%)	14.1	45.8	36.3	64.3	31.4	66.6

Source: Special tabulations of Annual Housing Survey. Bureau of the Census
and U.S. Department of Housing and Urban Development.

Table 11.2
Percent Distribution of Housing Problems for White, Black, and Hispanic
Households, 1975 and 1983 (in thousands)

Housing Problem	White		Black		Hispanic	
	Owners	Renters	Owners	Renters	Owners	Renters
Inadequate						
1975	42.7	31.5	59.8	50.2	47.2	37.6
1983	34.2	20.7	52.6	39.4	42.6	31.2
Crowded						
1975	19.6	7.5	20.1	11.8	36.3	24.3
1983	11.4	5.0	12.5	8.6	30.0	20.6
Cost Burden						
1975	37.7	61.0	20.1	37.9	16.4	38.1
1983	56.0	65.3	34.8	52.0	29.4	48.2
(N)						
1975	5,882	7,860	1,275	2,630	487	1,064
1983	6,920	11,204	1,493	3,218	622	1,759

Source: Special tabulations of Annual Housing Survey. Bureau of the Census
and U.S. Department of Housing and Urban Development.

lems with inadequate and overcrowded conditions than owners of the same racial groups. Black owners and renters had proportionally the highest levels of inadequate housing, with over half of all owners and 40 percent of renters reporting such problems as of 1983. Crowding remained a more serious problem for Hispanic owners and renters, although there were modest declines in overcrowding after 1975. However, Hispanics continued to experience ten to twenty percentage points higher levels of crowding than blacks or whites. As with whites, cost burden has sharply increased as a housing problem in the period between 1975 and 1983 for black and Hispanic renters. Black and Hispanic owners still experience less cost burden than white owners, with Hispanic owners reporting the lowest level of need in this area (30 percent).[3]

While the data in Tables 11.1 and 11.2 provide a general indication of the incidence of housing deprivation by race and ethnic origin, they do not identify the extent to which housing deprivation is influenced by the economic situation of the household. It may be that the lower rate of housing inadequacy or overcrowding among whites is simply the result of their higher average income or their smaller average family size. Because income, family size, and other relevant explanatory factors may vary by race and ethnic origin, it is necessary to control for these factors in order to assess whether there are important differences in housing conditions by race and ethnic origin that are not influenced by the economic position of minorities. One approach to this issue is to stratify households on the basis of the ratio of their income to the local median income adjusted for household size. It is important to note that the broad categorization of income in Table 11.3 does not fully control for the effect of variations within income categories. The median income for white households in 1983, for example, was $21,902; for blacks it was $12,429, and for Hispanics $15,906 (U.S. Bureau of the Census, 1985: 8). Thus there is a broader range of incomes for whites within the 80 percent and more of median income category which may conceal the influence of higher incomes on various housing problems.[4]

The data in Table 11.3 are, therefore, limited in their ability to control for all relevant influences on housing problems. Nevertheless they indicate the following:

a. There is a direct relationship between rising income and the decline in housing problems for all racial groups. Physically inadequate housing, crowding, and cost burden decline for whites, for example, from 60 percent for those earning 50 percent or less of the local median income to 8 percent for those having 80 percent or more of median incomes in 1983. For blacks the decline is from 76 to 26 percent and for Hispanics it is from 78 to 23 percent in 1983.[5]

b. For the poorest households (earning 50 percent or less than median income) whites have fewer problems than blacks or Hispanics. Also the poorest black

Table 11.3
Percent of Households Experiencing Housing Problems by Race, National Origin, and Income in 1978 and 1983 (in thousands)

0-50% of Median Income	White		Black		Hispanic	
	1978	1983	1978	1983	1978	1983
Physically Inadequate	15	12	36	29	27	23
Crowded	2	4	12	9	25	21
Physically Inadequate or Crowded	16	14	42	31	44	30
Cost Burden	31	52	28	61	27	63
Physically Inadequate, Crowded, or Cost Burden	44	60	60	76	62	78
Households (1000s)	14,139	18,938	3,734	4,636	1,440	2,005

51-80% of Median Income

	White		Black		Hispanic	
Physically Inadequate	9	7	24	23	17	14
Crowded	3	3	12	7	20	17
Physically Inadequate or Crowded	11	9	32	26	32	24
Cost Burden	9	17	5	14	5	20
Physically Inadequate, Crowded, or Cost Burden	19	26	36	41	35	44
Households (1000s)	12,360	13,723	1,688	1,770	968	1,010

81 or More of the Median Income

	White		Black		Hispanic	
Physically Inadequate	5	4	13	20	13	13
Crowded	2	*	8	5	11	9
Physically Inadequate or Crowded	7	5	19	13	21	17
Cost Burden	7	3	6	2	4	3
Physically Inadequate, Crowded, or Cost Burden	14	8	24	26	24	23
Households (1000s)	37,048	40,094	2,555	2,761	1,336	1,611

* Less than 1 percent (actually 0.1 percent).

Source: Special Tabulations, Annual Housing survey, 1978 and 1983. Housing and Demographic Analysis Division, PD&R, U.S. Department of HUD.

households are likely to experience more inadequate housing and less crowding than similarly situated Hispanics.

c. White households earning between 51 to 80 percent of the area's median income also have fewer housing problems than blacks or Hispanics earning similar incomes. The degree of crowding for households in this income bracket is virtually identical to poorer white, black, and Hispanic households. Cost burden, however, is a dramatically smaller problem for each group in the 51 to 80 percent bracket compared to poorer households, declining as a problem for whites from 52 to 17 percent, for blacks from 61 to 14 percent, and for Hispanics from 63 to 20 percent.

d. For households in the highest income bracket, cost burden declines in importance as a problem from 1978 to 1983. At the same time, physically inadequate housing increases as a problem for blacks and remains constant as a concern for Hispanics.

Physically inadequate and overcrowded housing has, therefore, become much less of a problem for whites, blacks, and Hispanics over the last several decades. In their place, the rising costs of renting or paying for a home has become the most salient problem at lower income levels. Most housing problems are powerfully influenced by the economic position of minorities with income and other housing market factors explaining from 30 to 70 percent of the differences between whites and blacks. There remains, however, a "net penalty" associated with being black and Hispanic which is independent of economic factors and which is associated with racial discrimination in housing markets (Farley and Colasanto, 1980; Bianchi, Farley, and Spain, 1982: 50).

Racial Discrimination in Housing

Discrimination in housing is a specific form of behavior by actors in the housing market that treats minorities differently solely because of their race, color, or other minority group attribute. The differential in treatment may result in minorities being rejected or excluded from certain housing opportunities or provided less favorable treatment than that provided to whites (Yinger, 1979: 430–31). Economists and sociologists have paid a modest amount of attention to addressing the empirical and statistical measures of different types and degrees of discrimination in the rental, sales, and credit markets (Pettigrew, 1975; Kain and Quigley, 1975; Schaffer, 1980; Lake, 1981; Goering, 1982). Far more effort at measuring discrimination has been made by public and private fair housing enforcement agencies.

These efforts have documented discrimination in the rental or sale of housing throughout all regions of the country, with higher levels of discrimination in rental markets. In some places minorities are told the apartment or home is unavailable while whites are offered the unit immediately. In other places there is a more subtle use of additional application and credit requirements for minorities. It appears that as of 1977, with just one visit to a single rental property manager, a minority is likely to experience discrimination nearly 30 percent of the time. In buying a home, a single visit to a real estate agent is likely to result in a 15 to 20 percent chance of discrimination (Newburger, 1984).

High levels of variability have, however, been found in the practice of discrimination among cities and metropolitan areas. In 1977, for example, discrimination in the rental market ranged from a high of 57 percent with a visit to one apartment building in Detroit, Michigan to a low of 7 percent in Harrisburg, Pennsylvania (Wienk et al., 1979: 180). More recent research confirms both higher levels of discrimination in the rental market as well as variations among cities. In Boston, Massachusetts in 1983 and in Sacramento, California in 1985, there was evidence of discrimination in nearly half the rental audits (Feins and Holshouser, 1984; Human Rights, 1985: 7). In Boston in 1983, for example, whites were shown 81 percent more units than nonwhites, and after four visits to rental properties the chances of discrimination were nearly 90 percent (Feins and Holshouser, 1984; Yinger, 1984). Also, minorities are often shown homes only in predominantly black or racially changing areas. In Evanston, Illinois in 1983, for example, 75 percent of whites were shown homes in a largely white area while only 12 percent of blacks were offered the same options (Lambert, 1984: 9).

Based on these measures of discrimination at both the national and local level, it has been estimated that there may be up to two million instances of discrimination against blacks in the rental and sales market of American cities. Although there are no accurate estimates of the level of discrimination experienced by Hispanic, Asian, and other minorities at the national level, there is no reason to assume that they are experiencing dramatically lower levels of discrimination in their search for housing. Indeed evidence on Hispanics suggests that they may encounter equal or higher levels of discrimination than blacks depending on their skin color (James and Tynan, 1986). Cumulatively, then, there may easily be up to four million acts of discrimination committed on an annual basis against all minorities in search of housing.

It is necessary to note, however, that housing discrimination may not be uniformly experienced within all urban areas and at all price levels of housing. In Denver, for example, discrimination was not found in all neighborhoods and Hispanics searching for rental units experienced discrimination in Hispanic neighborhoods (James, McCummings and Tynan, 1983). In Boston, no discrimination was found in units priced over $100,000 in 1981. This same audit also reported that real estate agents were not discriminating by either steering families to different neighborhoods or in quoting different terms or conditions for the sale.

Despite persuasive evidence that housing discrimination is a persistent

Table 11.4

Fair Housing Complaints Received by the U.S. Department of Housing and
Urban Development, by Race and National Origin, 1977–1983

	Race and Spanish Origin				
Year	White	Black	Hispanic	Asian	Total
1977–1978	158	2,157	159	39	2,513
1978–1979	170	1,850	187	50	2,257
1979–1980	117	2,021	165	34	2,337
1980–1981	116	2,612	228	32	2,988
1981–1982	151	3,296	287	161	3,895
1982–1983	135	2,937	312	49	3,433

Source: Fair Housing Complaints (Title VIII) recorded by HUD's
   Complaint and Compliance Review System, Office of Fair
   Housing and Equal Opportunity, HUD; for the fiscal year
   period October 1 to September 30.

feature of housing transactions, relatively few minorities file formal complaints of discrimination with either federal, state, or local fair housing
enforcement agencies. While there are roughly 80,000 complaints of employment discrimination annually, there are less than 5,000 complaints of
housing discrimination. The data in Table 11.4 indicate the number of fair
housing complaints filed by whites, blacks, Hispanics, and Asians during
the period 1977 to 1983. Only 17,000 complaints were filed with the Department of Housing and Urban Development (HUD) during this period,
with the bulk of complaints filed by blacks. Most of these complaints involved allegations of rental market discrimination. Hispanics appear to be
filing an increasing number of complaints, but still file only roughly 10
percent of all complaints. Asians clearly file only a handful of complaints
with no clear evidence of an increase since 1977.

What accounts for the remarkably low level of complaints of housing
discrimination by minorities covered by Federal, state, and local fair housing
laws? Is fair housing atrophying as part of the civil rights of minorities? It
seems clear that in the 1960s minorities were strongly supportive of fair
housing laws compared to whites (Wolfinger and Greenstein, 1968) and
were effective at political lobbying for new civil rights laws (Miroff, 1981;
Smith, 1981). There are a number of plausible, but untested, explanations
for the underutilization of fair housing complaint procedures.

One explanation is that there is increasing subtlety in the practice of
discrimination, and that minorities are unaware that they have been victims
of discriminatory treatment. A real estate agent or mortgage lender may
appear perfectly courteous and helpful to the minority and yet systematically

provide different or more information to similarly situated whites. Such differences in treatment are extremely hard to detect, especially if minorities are less aware of their fair housing rights. A survey in New Jersey reported only 20 percent of black homeseekers felt they had experienced discrimination; roughly 5 percent of whites also felt victimized mainly for reasons of age or sex (Lake, 1981: 129). No information was provided about whether the minorities who felt they had experienced discrimination knew that they had legal rights or that they made any use of them. Also, some households deliberately avoid looking for housing in certain neighborhoods because of the expectation that they might encounter hostility or discrimination (Weisbrod and Vidal, 1981: 472).

Another explanation is that minorities are less supportive of fair housing enforcement programs than they are of the general goal of equal opportunity in housing. That is, although they support the principle of equal opportunity, they are less supportive of specific programs designed to implement the goal. Support for this explanation can be found in a recent analysis of over thirty years of public opinion data on racial segregation and discrimination. Schuman, Steeh, and Bobo (1985) find that there is a substantial gap between the civil rights principles espoused by blacks and whites and the programs they are willing to support. There is, for example, a 25 percent gap between support of the principle of the right to freedom of choice in housing and support for fair housing laws by blacks—the gap for whites is 53 percent (Bobo, Schuman, and Steeh, 1986).

Third, minorities may be simply unaware that there are laws to protect them when they believe they have been victims of discrimination. In Detroit, for example, a survey of residents found that over half (53 percent) of blacks were unaware of any laws prohibiting discrimination in the sale or rental of housing; 37 percent of whites were also ignorant of the law's existence (Farley, Bianchi, and Colasanto, 1979: 112). Hispanics and Asians are likely to be even less aware of specific federal, state, and local fair housing provisions and procedures.

The Effectiveness of Fair Housing Enforcement

Yet another explanation for the minimal interest of minorities in complaining to government agencies about civil rights violations is their belief that such agencies are ineffective instruments for obtaining justice. Relatively little research has been conducted on the actual and perceived effectiveness or impact of fair housing law enforcement agencies in reducing discrimination (Parmley, 1977; Burstein, 1979; U.S. Commission on Civil Rights, 1979; Darden, 1982; U.S. Commission on Civil Rights, 1983).

Since the late 1940s, an increasing number of state and local fair housing enforcement agencies have been engaged in resolving complaints of housing discrimination and, in certain instances, of attempting to reduce the levels of discrimination throughout broad sections of the housing markets under their jurisdiction (Aquilar et al., 1980; Goering and Sacks, 1986). In 1968, the first federal fair housing law was passed banning discrimination in the rental, sale, financing, or advertising of housing on the basis of race, color, national origin, religion, or sex. With various exemptions, approximately 80 percent of the private housing market is covered by the federal fair housing law.

— The Fair Housing Law, or Title 8 of the Civil Rights Act of 1968, assigns to the U.S. Department of Housing and Urban Development the responsibility of receiving, investigating, and attempting to resolve complaints of discrimination using the methods of conference and conciliation. That is, following the receipt of convincing evidence of discrimination, HUD is only authorized to informally discuss possible resolution with the person complaining and the accused. HUD is also required to refer any complaints of discrimination to state or local fair housing enforcement agencies whose authority and powers are substantially the same as those of HUD. As of 1985, there were 100 state and local agencies receiving complaints of discrimination, as well as HUD funding, in their efforts to resolve fair housing complaints.

Table 11.5 provides a limited amount of evidence about the actual processing and resolution of fair housing complaints in the decade after 1975. The data indicate that an increasingly large proportion of cases have been referred to state and local agencies for processing; increasing from only seven cases in 1977 to over 2,000 in 1985. Since 1980, when HUD began to provide funding to state and local agencies to process fair housing cases, an increasing number of the cases have been closed by such agencies. Proportionally, the number of cases closed by state and local agencies has increased from 12 percent in 1980 to over 60 percent in 1985. The proportion of cases successfully resolved or conciliated by state and local fair housing agencies also rose from roughly 8 percent in 1980 to over 70 percent by 1985 (386 out of 530 cases in 1985).

Tables 11.6 through 11.8 provide a clearer description of the extent to which the *performance* of state and local agencies has improved since the inception of HUD's major fair housing enforcement funding program, the Fair Housing Assistance Program (FHAP). These data are drawn from an evaluation of the processing of 2,000 fair housing complaints handled by a sample of fifteen state and local agencies (Wallace et al., 1985). Table 11.6 indicates that fewer cases have been closed without any form of settlement since the beginning of FHAP; prior to FHAP twelve percent of cases were closed without settlement while after FHAP only 2.5 percent had no settlement. Table 11.7 indicates that there was a modest increase in the number of cases in which the complainant received a financial settlement (money only or money and a housing unit). There was a slight decline in the number of cases in which the defendant, or respondent, only agreed to

Table 11.5
Fair Housing Complaint Activity and Results, 1975–1985

Complaints/Results	FY 75	FY 76	FY 77	FY 78	FY 79	FY 80	FY 81	FY 82	FY 83	FY 84	FY 85
Complaints Received	3,167	4,121	3,391	3,126	2,833	3,036	4,209	5,112	4,551	4,533	3,310
Complaints Referred	NA	NA	7	219	210	434	1,661	2,670	2,736	3,062	2,106
Complaints Closed	2,525	4,801	2,982	3,872	2,918	2,848	3,746	4,479	4,665	4,642	2,386
By HUD	NA	NA	2,532	3,766	2,768	2,509	2,679	2,326	1,867	1,580	898
By State/Local	NA	NA	450	106	150	339	1,067	2,153	2,798	3,062	1,488
Conciliation											
Attempted	651	1,170	530	748	672	755	1,142	1,339	1,505	1,262	720
By HUD	NA	NA	514	731	643	703	884	697	576	378	260
By State Local	NA	NA	16	17	29	52	258	642	929	884	460
Successful											
Conciliation	355	670	277	354	373	535	828	946	1,102	827	530
By HUD	NA	NA	261	338	348	494	603	427	372	205	144
By State/Local	NA	NA	16	16	25	41	226	519	730	622	386
Monetary Relief											
($1000s)	NA	NA	370,838	147,968	376,013	448,550	676,271	698,508	478,043	940,314	671,332
By HUD	NA	NA	368,963	142,668	368,963	442,434	655,221	601,163	357,527	764,079	518,631
By State/Local	NA	NA	1,875	5,300	7,050	6,116	21,050	97,345	120,516	176,235	152,701
Units Obtained	NA	NA	68	85	202	481	535	1,078	520	359	181

NA: Data not available.

Source: HUD Complaints and Compliance Review System; 1985 data are up to 5-31-1985.

Table 11.6
Type of Settlement by Fair Housing Assistance Program (FHAP) Phase
(Percentages)

Type of Settlement	Pre-FHAP	Post-FHAP
	N = 712*	N = 372*
No Settlement	12.3	2.5
Pro-Respondent Settlement	46.6	54.5
Unsuccessful Conciliation	0.6	0.6
Pro-Complainant Settlement	40.6	42.4
Total (%)	100.0	100.0

* Data are weighted to account for Agency- and Case-level
  sampling. Base: Cases excluded if closed for lack of
  jurisdiction, failure to proceed on the part of the
  complainant or complaint withdrawal with no settlement.

Source: Fair Housing Assistance Program Evaluation,
   Case Record Abstract Forms.

Table 11.7
Type of Relief Granted for Pre- and Post-Fair Housing Assistance Program
(FHAP) (Percentages)

Type of Relief	Pre-FHAP	Post-FHAP
	N = 225*	N = 130*
Apology or Aff. Action	34.8	30.3
Next Unit	10.4	10.1
Money Only	24.7	27.1
Contested Unit	27.0	25.3
Money and Unit	3.2	7.1
Total (%)	100.0	100.0

* Data are weighted to account for Agency- and Case-level
  sampling. Base: All cases with some relief to complainant.

Source: Case Record Abstract Forms.

apologize to the complainant and to do some general form of affirmative
action at the firm or rental complex (a decrease from 35 to 30 percent of
relief). Finally, Table 11.8 indicates that there has been a marked increase
in the amount of money provided to complainants since HUD began assisting state and local agencies. The median amount of monetary relief, in

Table 11.8
Mean and Median Amounts of Monetary Relief: Pre- and Post-Fair Housing
Assistance Program (FHAP)

Program Phase	Weighted Mean*	Median*
Pre-FHAP (N = 58)	$530	$388
Post-FHAP (N = 41)	$982	$500

* Amounts are in 1983 constant dollars, adjusted by the
  Consumer Price Index.

Source: Case Record Abstract Forms.

constant dollars, rose from $388 to $500 dollars from the pre- to post-FHAP periods.

During this same time period, the performance of HUD fair housing enforcement offices also improved. In four out of ten HUD regional offices studied, the percent of cases resolved in favor of the person complaining increased from 25 percent before 1980 to 43 percent after 1980. Cases in which some monetary settlement or a housing unit were provided also increased over the same time period from 44 to 60 percent. The amount of monetary awards increased in constant dollars from roughly $400 to over $1,300 during the period before and after 1980.

There has, therefore, been a measurable increase in the effectiveness of fair housing enforcement agencies over the last five years. Critics may argue that the increases are not great enough or that the sample of agencies missed many more lackluster agencies whose procedures are less ineffective. Still others may feel that federal courts provide better relief in terms of both injunctions and monetary settlements. Despite such arguments, it is clear that the capacity of federal, state, and local agencies to enforce fair housing laws has measurably increased.

Conclusions

Minority households continue to experience substantial levels of housing deprivation, segregation, and discrimination. Their housing conditions, although gradually improving in physical condition and the extent of crowding, are increasingly affected by the higher costs of renting or purchasing a home. Minorities in search of decent housing will have to pay more, as well as risk experiencing either subtle or direct forms of discrimination, in order to find a home comparable to that of whites. All too often the act of discrimination will remain unfelt and undetected. Different or fewer apartments and homes are shown to minorities but not to whites.

There is nothing especially new in this account of housing deprivation and discrimination. Economic factors and discrimination have long been known to be fundamental determinants of segregated, and inadequate, or overpriced housing for minorities in most metropolitan housing markets. What is new is the divergence in opinions as to how to address inequities in housing affecting minority households.

There is a growing divergence in strategies for addressing minority social and civil rights issues. Some voices within the minority community, aware of the diminished popular support for civil rights issues, now argue for increased emphasis on internal or class-based strategies for reform. Loury (1985), for example, argues that federal or state programs are less relevant to the solution of minority problems and that new "constructive, internal institutions" need to be built to address the multifaceted problems confronting black Americans. This argument is complemented by those who argue that racial discrimination is less relevant in explaining the current position and opportunities of blacks and that antidiscrimination policies benefit very few, better-off blacks (Wilson, 1984: 99). Civil rights organizations, such as the National Urban League, indeed have "higher priority" issues to press for including jobs, welfare, and health benefits with discrimination and segregation perceived less critical (Leigh and McGhee, 1986). These priorities are also reflected in the recent choices of elected officials who, when asked to identify the most important barriers to decent housing, rank discrimination in last place (United States Conference of Mayors, 1984: 12).

At the same time, traditional civil rights organizations continue to press for more federal housing subsidies for minorities as well as stronger fair housing laws (Weaver, 1985). They view the federal government as both a prime cause as well as essential cure for the housing problems of minorities. Without any effective tools to address the myriad local housing market "imperfections," the federal government is the only efficient tool for policy improvements at a national level. Housing discrimination cuts across housing market and regions, and inadequate housing conditions are seldom effectively addressed without federal housing subsidies of one form or another.

Confusion and loss of enthusiasm for civil rights are compounded by a number of additional impediments which currently appear to affect the prospects for mobilizing support for a stronger fair housing agenda. Public opinion, as was suggested above, appears unsupportive of additional federally-imposed programs. Also, blacks and Hispanics do not appear to have coalesced around an agreed-upon civil rights agenda, further dissipating pressure for political mobilization (Ford Foundation, 1984: 42). Finally, the staggering growth of minority, female-headed households in cities has the potential to swamp policymakers' concerns for "technical" issues of fair housing law enforcement with broader issues of economic and racial equity.

It is not surprising, therefore, that the civil rights movement in the United States demonstrates neither great strength nor aggressiveness in the pursuit of a broad agenda of civil rights policy changes. National and local fair housing organizations have been impacted by changing popular "tastes" regarding racial equity as well as by reductions in funding for "discretionary" items such as civil rights enforcement. The National Committee Against Discrimination in Housing and National Neighbors, two of the major, national fair housing organizations, are both experiencing severe financial problems which limit their effectiveness in pressing for legislative or funding reforms.

To federalize or not the solution to minority housing problems is not an ideological contest likely to be won by any side. External events, outside the control of the leadership of the minority communities, appear likely to overwhelm most federal domestic policy options. Civil rights and the housing conditions of blacks and Hispanics are concerns which only influence the margins of current Congressional and Executive Branch planning. Only a substantial increase in organized support and lobbying for a broad range of civil rights protections is likely to achieve any credibility and impact. Such an agenda will, in the short run, probably only hold its own against forces aimed at reducing civil rights guarantees. It seems wiser, however, to pursue a more offensive rather than a defensive policy in order to secure as much leverage and credibility for future battles.

Notes

1. These data are drawn from the American Housing Survey (AHS) for which the most current data are for 1983. AHS data have been gathered by the Bureau of the Census since 1973 (Goering, 1980). Research using Census and AHS data for 1960 and 1977 reveals a larger increase in the rate of homeownership for blacks than for whites (Bianchi, Farley, and Spain, 1982: 47).

2. This measure of housing needs focuses on the conditions affecting existing housing and its occupants. It does not include consideration of the "need" for additional housing to accommodate the demographic increase in household formation. The latter issue has been considered elsewhere (Weicher, Yap, and Jones, 1981).

3. In 1980, the national median rent-to-income ratio was 27 percent. Families in the $15,000 to $20,000 range paid 20 percent of their income for rent. However, the average rent burden for households earning below $3,000 was 60 percent. The burden was 47 percent for poor households earning between $3,000 and $7,000 (Welfeld and Carmel, 1984: 298).

4. There is a progressive decline in inadequate housing with rising income (Bianchi, Farley, and Spain, 1982: 45; Apgar, 1985).

5. The inadequacy of housing conditions for Hispanics as a group masks considerable variation among the various subgroups which comprise "Hispanics." Cubans, for example, live in housing with fewer problems than Puerto Ricans (Office of Policy Development, 1980; Juarez, 1977).

Acknowledgments

A number of colleagues have offered suggestions, data, and advice in the preparation of this chapter. I am especially indebted to Iredia Irby, John Hakken, Yearn Hong Choi, and James Wallace. The views expressed in this article do not necessarily represent the views or policies of the U.S. Department of Housing and Urban Development or the U.S. Government.

References

Aguilar, Javier, et al. 1980. Developments in the Law-Section 1981. *Harvard Civil Rights-Civil Liberties Law Review* 15 (Spring): 29–277.

Apgar, William. 1985. Trends in Housing Quality and Affordability. Paper presented at conference on Housing Policies in the Eighties: Choices and Outcomes. Institute for Policy Studies. Alexandria, Va.

Bianchi, Suzanne, R. Farley, and D. Spain. 1982. Racial Inequalities in Housing: An Examination of Recent Trends. *Demography* 19 (February): 37–51.

Birch, David, et al. 1973. *America's Housing Needs: 1970 to 1980.* Cambridge, Mass.: Joint Center for Urban Studies.

Bobo, Lawrence, H. Schuman, and C. Steeh. 1986. Changing Racial Attitudes Toward Residential Integration. In *Housing Desegregation, Race, and Federal Policies,* edited by John M. Goering. Chapel Hill, N.C.: University of North Carolina Press.

Burstein, Paul. 1979. Equal Employment Opportunity Legislation and the Income of Women and Nonwhites. *American Sociological Review* 44 (June): 367–91.

Darden, Joe. 1982. Black Residential Segregation: Impact of State Licensing Laws. *Journal of Black Studies* 12 (June): 415–26.

Dowd, Maureen. 1985. Divisions Between Races Persist in New York City, Poll Indicates. *New York Times* (14 May): A1, B4.

Eribes, Richard, and A. Karnig. 1980. *Hispanic Housing.* Center for Public Affairs. Tempe, Ariz.: Arizona State University.

Farley, Reynolds, S. Bianchi, and D. Colasanto. 1979. Barriers to Racial Integration of Neighborhoods. The Detroit Case. *The Annals* 441 (January): 97–113.

Farley, Reynolds, and D. Colasanto. 1980. Racial Residential Segregation: Is It Caused By Misinformation About Housing Costs? *Social Science Quarterly* 61 (December): 623–37.

Feins, J., and W. Holshouser. 1984. The Multiple Uses of Audit-Based Research: Evidence from Boston. A paper submitted at the HUD Conference on Fair Housing Testing. (December). Washington, D.C.

Ford Foundation. 1984. *Hispanics: Challenges and Opportunities.* (June). New York: Ford Foundation.

Goering, John M. 1980. Housing in America: The Characteristics and Uses of the Annual Housing Survey. *Annual Housing Survey Studies No. 6.* Office of Policy Development and Research. HUD-PDR–470–2. (February). Washington, D.C.: U.S. Department of Housing and Urban Development.

————. 1982. Race, Housing, and Public Policies: A Strategy for Social Science Research. *Urban Affairs Quarterly* 17 (June): 463–90.

Goering, John M., and S. Sacks. 1985. Civil Rights Enforcement in a Federalist System: An Analysis of Policy Formation and Distribution. In *Public Policy Across States and Communities*, edited by Dennis Judd. Greenwich, Conn.: JAI Press.

Gruson, Lindsey. 1985. Police Firebomb House in Philadelphia Siege. *New York Times* (14 May): A1.

Housing and Home Finance Agency. 1952. *Housing of the Nonwhite Population: 1940 to 1950*. (July). Washington, D.C.: GPO.

Human Rights/Fair Housing Commission of the City and County of Sacramento. 1985. *Race Discrimination in the Sacramento Rental Market: Audit and Assessment*. Sacramento, Calif.: Human Rights Commission.

James, Franklin, B. McCummings, and E. Tynan. 1983. *Discrimination, Segregation, and Minority Housing Conditions in Sunbelt Cities*. Center for Public-Private Sector Cooperation. Denver: University of Colorado.

James, Franklin, and E. Tynan. 1986. Segregation and Discrimination of Hispanic Americans: An Exploratory Analysis. In *Housing Desegregation, Race, and Federal Policies*, edited by John M. Goering. Chapel Hill, N.C.: University of North Carolina Press.

Juarez, Assoc. 1977. Hispanics, Housing, and HUD: Final Report for the Development of Methodology for Involving the Spanish Speaking Community in HUD Programs. Unpublished Report submitted to Office of Policy Development and Research. Washington, D.C.: U.S. Department of Housing and Urban Development.

Kain, John, and J. Quigley. 1975. *Housing Markets and Racial Discrimination: A Microeconomic Analysis*. New York: Columbia University Press.

Lake, Robert. 1981. *The New Suburbanites: Race and Housing in the Suburbs*. New Brunswick, N.J.: Center for Urban Policy Research.

Lambert, Shirley. 1984. A Summary of a Sales/Rental Audit of Firms in Evanston. (November). Evanston, Ill.: The Evanston Human Relations Commission.

Leigh, Wilhelmina, and J. McGhee. 1986. A Minority Perspective on Residential Racial Integration. In *Housing Desegregation, Race, and Federal Policies*, edited by John M. Goering. Chapel Hill, N.C.: University of North Carolina.

Loury, Glenn. 1985. The Moral Quandary of the Black Community. *The Public Interest* 79 (Spring): 9–22.

McGraw, B. T. 1954. Desegregation and Open Occupancy Trends in Housing. *Journal of Human Relations* (Fall): 57–69.

Miroff, Bruce. 1981. Presidential Leverage Over Social Movements: The Johnson White House and Civil Rights. *Journal of Politics* 43 (February): 2–23.

Newburger, Harriet. 1984. Recent Evidence on Discrimination in Housing. HUD-PDR–786. Office of Policy Development and Research. Washington, D.C.: U.S. Department of Housing and Urban Development.

Office of Policy Development and Research. 1980. *How Well Are We Housed? 1. Hispanics*. (July) HUD-PDR–333. Washington, D.C.: GPO.

Parmley, Bruce. 1977. *State Agencies and Their Role in Federal Civil Rights Enforcement*. Washington, D.C.: Center for National Policy Review.

Peterson, Bill. 1985. Huge Fire Destroys House of Philadelphia Radicals. *Washington Post* (14 May): A1.

Pettigrew, Thomas. 1975. *Racial Discrimination in the United States*. New York: Harper and Row.

Schafer, Robert, and H. Ladd. 1980. *Equal Credit Opportunity: Accessibility to Mortgage Funds by Women and Minorities*. (May) HUD-PDR–551–2. Office of Policy Development and Research. Washington, D.C.: U.S. Department of Housing and Urban Development.

Schnare, Ann. 1985. Trends in Residential Segregation by Race in Illinois: 1960–1980. Unpublished working paper. Washington, D.C.: The Urban Institute.

Schuman, Howard, C. Steeh, and L. Bobo. 1985. *Racial Attitudes in America: Trends and Interpretations*. Cambridge, Mass.: Harvard University.

Smith, Robert. 1981. Black Power and the Transformation from Protest to Politics. *Political Science Quarterly* 96 (Fall): 431–43.

Taeuber, Karl. 1983. Racial Residential Segregation, 1980. In *A Decent Home*, edited by Citizens Commission on Civil Rights. Washington, D.C.: Center for National Policy Review.

U.S. Bureau of the Census. 1985. Current Population Reports, Series P–60, No. 146, *Money Income of Households, Families, and Persons in the United States: 1983*. Washington, D.C.: GPO.

U.S. Commission on Civil Rights. 1979. *The Federal Fair Housing Enforcement Effort*. Washington, D.C.: GPO.

U.S. Commission on Civil Rights. 1983. *Federal Civil Rights Commitments: An Assessment of Enforcement Resources and Performance*. (November). Washington, D.C.: Clearinghouse Publication 82.

United States Conference of Mayors. 1984. Housing Needs and Conditions in America's Cities: A Survey of the Nation's Principal Cities. (June). Washington, D.C.: U.S. Conference of Mayors.

Wallace, James, et al. 1985. Evaluation of the Fair Housing Assistance Program. (June). Cambridge, Mass.: Abt Associates.

Weaver, Robert. 1985. Fair Housing: The Federal Retreat. *Journal of Housing* 42 (May/June): 85–87.

Weicher, John, L. Yap, and M. Jones. 1981. National Housing Needs and Quality Changes During the 1980's. *Annual Housing Survey Studies No. 10*. Office of Policy Development and Research. (January) HUD-PDR–66. Washington, D.C.: U.S. Department of Housing and Urban Development.

Weisbrod, Glen, and A. Vidal. 1981. Housing Search Barriers for Low-Income Renters. *Urban Affairs Quarterly* 16 (June): 465–82.

Welfeld, Irving, and Joseph Carmel. 1984. A New Wave Housing Program: Respecting the Intelligence of the Poor. *Urban Law and Policy* 6: 293–302.

Wienk, Ron, et al. 1979. *Measuring Discrimination in American Housing Markets: The Housing Market Practices Survey*. HUD-PDR–444(2). Washington, D.C.: U.S. Department of Housing and Urban Development.

Wilson, William J. 1984. The Black Underclass. *The Wilson Quarterly* 8 (Spring): 88–99.

Wolfinger, Raymond, and F. Greenstein. 1968. The Repeal of Fair Housing in California: An Analysis of Referendum Voting. *The American Political Science Review* 62 (September): 753–69.

Yezer, Anthony. 1981. The Physical Adequacy and Affordability of Housing in America: Measurements Using the Annual Housing Survey for 1975 and 1977. Washington, D.C.: Department of Economics, George Washington University.

Yinger, John. 1979. Prejudice and Discrimination in the Urban Housing Market. In *Current Issues in Urban Economics*, edited by P. Mieszkowski and M. Strawszheim 430–68. Baltimore, Md.: Johns Hopkins University Press.

Yinger, John. 1984. Measuring Social and Ethnic Discrimination with Fair Housing Audits: A Review of Existing Evidence and Research Methodology. Paper presented at the HUD Conference on Fair Housing Testing. (December). Washington, D.C.

Selected Bibliography

Each chapter in this volume has its own rich source of references. But for those with further interest in minority housing problems and prospects, the following select bibliography may prove very useful. For a volume exclusively devoted to minority housing, the reader may see: *Housing and Racial/Ethnic Minority Status in the United States: An Annotated Bibliography with a Review Essay* by Jamshid A. Momeni (Greenwood Press, forthcoming in 1987).

Abrams, Charles. 1966. The Housing Problem and the Negro. *Daedalus* 95 (Winter): 64–76.

Bailey, Martin J. 1966. Effects of Race and of Other Demographic Factors on the Values of Single-Family Homes. *Land Economics* 42 (2): 215–20.

Baxter, Ellen, and Kim Hopper. 1982. The New Mendicancy: Homelessness in New York City. *American Journal of Orthopsychiatry* 52 (3): 393–408.

Berry, Brian J. L. 1976. Ghetto Expansion and Single-Family Housing Prices: Chicago, 1968–1972. *Journal of Urban Economics* 3: 397–423.

Birch, Eugenie Ladner. 1978. Woman-Made America: The Case of Early Public Housing Policy. *Journal of the American Institute of Planners* 44 (1): 130–44.

Birnbaum, Howard, and Rafael Weston. 1974. Home Ownership and the Wealth Position of Black and White Americans. *Review of Income and Wealth* 20 (March): 103–18.

Bullard, Robert D. 1983. Persistent Barriers in Housing Black Americans. *Journal of Applied Social Sciences* 7 (1): 19–31.

Courant, Paul N. 1978. Racial Prejudice in a Search Model of the Urban Housing Market. *Journal of Urban Economics* 5 (3): 329–45.

Daniels, Charles B. 1975. The Influence of Racial Segregation on Housing Prices. *Journal of Urban Economics* 2 (2): 105–22.

DeSalvo, Joseph S. 1976. Housing Subsidies: Do We Know What We Are Doing? *Policy Analysis* 2 (1): 39–60.

Farley, John E. 1983. Metropolitan Housing Segregation in 1980: The St. Louis Case. *Urban Affairs Quarterly* 18 (3): 347–59.

———. 1984. P* Segregation Indices: What Can They Tell Us About Housing Segregation in 1980s? *Urban Studies* 21: 331–36.

Ford, Larry, and Ernst Griffin. 1979. The Ghettoization of Paradise. *Geographical Review* 69 (2): 140–58.

Freidman, Lawrence M., and James E. Krier. 1968. A New Lease on Life: Section 23 Housing and the Poor. *University of Pennsylvania Law Review* 116 (4): 611–47.

Fried, Marc, and Peggy Gleicher. 1961. Some Sources of Residential Satisfaction in an Urban Slum. *Journal of the American Institute of Planners* 27 (4): 305–15.

Galster, George C. 1977. A Bid-Rent Analysis of Housing Market Discrimination. *American Economic Review* 67 (2): 144–55.

Glazer, Nathan, and Davis McEntire (eds.). 1960. *Studies in Housing and Minority Groups*. Berkeley and Los Angeles, California: University of California Press.

Goering, John M. 1978. Neighborhood Tipping and Racial Transition: A Review of Social Science Evidence. *Journal of the American Institute of Planners* 44 (1): 68–78.

Green, R. Jeffery, and George M. von Furstenberg. 1975. The Effects of Race and Age of Housing on Mortgage Delinquency Risk. *Urban Studies* 12: 85–89.

Hager, Don J. 1960. Housing Discrimination, Social Conflict, and the Law. *Social Problems* 8 (1): 80–87.

Hanna, Sherman, and Suzanne Lindamood. 1979. Housing Preferences of Blacks and Whites in Montgomery, Alabama. *Housing and Society* 6 (1): 39–47.

Hartman, Chester (ed.). 1983. *America's Housing Crisis: What is to Be Done?* Boston, MA: Routledge and Kegan Paul.

Henretta, John C. 1979. Race Differences in Middle Class Lifestyle: The Role of Home Ownership. *Social Science Research* 8 (1): 63–78.

Hirsch, Arnold R. 1983. *Making the Second Ghetto: Race and Housing in Chicago, 1940–1960*. Cambridge: Cambridge University Press.

Hirshen, Al, and Vivian N. Brown. 1972. Too Poor for Public Housing: Roger Starr's Poverty Preferences. *Social Policy* 3 (1): 28–32.

Horn, Frank S. 1958. Interracial Housing in the United States. *Phylon* 19 (1): 13–20.

Hunt, Chester L. 1959. Negro-White Perceptions of Interracial Housing. *Journal of Social Issues* 15 (4): 24–29.

Jackson, Hubert M. 1958. Public Housing and Minority Groups. *Phylon* 19 (1): 21–30.

Kain, John F., and John M. Quigley. 1975. *Housing Markets and Racial Discrimination*. New York: National Bureau of Economics Research, Columbia University.

Kantrowitz, Nathan. 1973. Ethnic and Racial Segregation in the New York Metropolis, 1960. *American Journal of Sociology* 74 (6): 685–95.

Kelley, Joseph B. 1964. Racial Integration Policies of the New York City Housing Authority, 1958–61. *Social Service Review* 38 (2): 153–62.

Kern, Clifford R. 1981. Racial Prejudice and Residential Segregation: The Yinger Model Revisited. *Journal of Urban Economics* 10 (2): 164–72.

King, A. Thomas, and Peter Mieszkowski. 1973. Racial Discrimination, Segregation, and the Price of Housing. *Journal of Political Economy* 81 (3): 590–606.

Ladenson, Mark L. 1978. Race and Sex Discrimination in Housing: The Evidence from Probabilities of Homeownership. *Southern Economic Journal* 45(2): 559–75.

Lake, Robert W. 1981. *The New Suburbanites: Race and Housing in the Suburbs.* New Brunswick, N.J.: Center for Urban Policy Research, Rutgers University.

Lieberson, Stanley. 1962. Suburbs and Ethnic Residential Patterns. *American Journal of Sociology* 67 (6): 673–81.

McGhee, Milton L., and Ann Fagan Ginger. 1961. The House I Live In: A Study of Housing for Minorities. *Cornell Law Quarterly* 46 (Winter): 194–257.

McKee, James B. 1963. Changing Patterns of Race and Housing: A Toledo Study. *Social Forces* 41 (3): 253–60.

Mandelker, Daniel R. 1977. Racial Discrimination and Exclusionary Zoning: A Perspective on Arlington Heights. *Texas Law Review* 55 (7): 1217–53.

Massey, Douglas S. 1979. Residential Segregation of Spanish Americans in United States Urbanized Areas. *Demography* 16 (4): 553–63.

———. 1981. Social and Ethnic Segregation: A Reconsideration of Methods and Conclusions. *American Sociological Review* 46 (October): 641–50.

Mayer, Albert J. 1957. Race and Private Housing: A Social Problem and a Challenge to Understanding Human Behavior. *Journal of Social Issues* 13 (4): 3–6.

Mayer, Neil S. 1985. The Impacts of Lending, Race, and Ownership on Rental Housing Rehabilitation. *Journal of Urban Economics* 17 (3): 349–74.

Miller, Alexander F. 1958. The Housing of Negroes in Oklahoma. *Phylon* 19 (1): 106–12.

Mitchell, Robert E., and Richard A. Smith. Race and Housing: A Review and Comments on the Content and Effects of Federal Policy. *The Annals of the American Academy of Political and Social Science* 441 (January): 168–85.

Newman, Sandra J., and Ann B. Schnare. 1986. HUD and HHS Shelter Assistance: America's Two Approaches to Housing the Poor. *Journal of Housing* 43 (1): 22–32.

Palmore, Erdman, and John Howe. 1962. Residential Integration and Property Values. *Social Problems* 10 (1): 52–55.

Peroff, Kathleen, et al. 1980. *Gutreaux Housing Demonstration: An Evaluation of its Impact on Participating Households.* Washington, D.C.: Government Printing Office.

Phares, Donald. 1971. Racial Change and Housing Values: Transition in an Inner Suburb. *Social Science Quarterly* 52 (3): 560–73.

Reid, Clifford E. 1977. Measuring Residential Decentralization of Blacks and Whites. *Urban Studies* 14 (3): 353–57.

Rich, Jonathan M. 1984. Municipal Boundaries in a Discriminatory Housing Market: An Example of Racial Leapfrogging. *Urban Studies* 21 (1): 31–40.

Roistacher, Elizabeth A., and John L. Goodman. 1976. Race and Home Ownership: Is Discrimination Disappearing? *Economic Inquiry* 14 (1): 59–70.

Saltman, Juliet. 1978. *Open Housing: The Dynamic of a Social Movement.* New York: Praeger.

Schafer, Robert. 1979. Racial Discrimination in the Boston Housing Market. *Journal of Urban Economics* 6 (2): 176–96.

Schnare, Ann B. 1976. Racial and Ethnic Price Differentials in an Urban Housing Market. *Urban Studies* 13 (2): 107–20.

———. 1980. Trends in Residential Segregation by Race: 1960–1970. *Journal of Urban Economics*. 7: 293–301.

Semer, Milton P., and Martin E. Sloane. 1964. Equal Housing Opportunity and Individual Property Rights. *The Federal Bar Journal* 24 (1): 47–75.

Stegman, Michael A. 1969. Kaiser, Douglas, and Kerner on Low-Income Housing Policy. *Journal of the American Institute of Planners* 35 (6): 422–27.

Struyk, Raymond J. 1975. Determinants of the Rate of Home Ownership of Black Relative to White Households. *Journal of Urban Economics* 2 (4): 291–306.

Struyk, Raymond J., and Marc Bendick, Jr. (eds.). 1981. *Housing Vouchers for the Poor: Lessons From a National Experiment*. Washington, D.C.: The Urban Institute Press.

Sussman, Marvin B. 1957. The Role of Neighborhood Associations in Private Housing for Racial Minorities. *Journal of Social Issues* 13 (4): 31–37.

Taeuber, Karl E. 1975. Racial Segregation: The Persisting Dilemma. *Annals of the American Academy of Political and Social Science* 422: 87–96.

Thomas, Robert H. 1984. Black Suburbanization and Housing Quality in Atlanta. *Journal of Urban Affairs* 6 (1): 17–38.

Thompson, Robert A. 1958. Social Dynamics in Demographic Trends and the Housing of Minority Groups. *Phylon* 19 (1): 31–43.

Wieand, Ken. 1975. Housing Price Determination in Urban Ghettos. *Urban Studies* 12: 193–204.

Yinger, John. 1978. The Black-White Price Differential in Housing: Some Further Evidence. *Land Economics* 54 (2): 187–206.

Zelder, Raymond E. 1972. Poverty, Housing, and Market Processes. *Urban Affairs Quarterly* 8 (1): 77–95.

Index

About the Contributors

All contributors have a significant number of scholarly publications. The following description is limited to the current position and one or two publications for each author.

SUZANNE M. BIANCHI is a demographer with the U.S. Bureau of the Census, Center for Demographic Studies. She is the author of *Household Composition and Racial Inequality*.

ROBERT D. BULLARD is an associate professor of Sociology at Texas Southern University in Houston. Dr. Bullard is a leading scholar in the area of black housing problems. He is the author of the forthcoming book: *Blacks in Boomtown USA: People and Neighborhoods in Transition*.

JOE T. DARDEN is the dean of Urban Affairs Programs and a professor of Geography and Urban Affairs at Michigan State University. Dr. Darden has served as an expert witness in court cases regarding school desegregation. He is the author of *Afro-Americans in Pittsburgh: The Residential Segregation of a People*. He was the recipient of Michigan State University's Distinguished Faculty Award in 1984.

REYNOLDS FARLEY is a professor in the Department of Sociology and a research scientist at the Center for Population Studies at the University of Michigan. He is the author of *Growth of the Black Population*, and the coauthor of the 1980 census monograph on the black population.

JOHN M. GOERING currently directs and conducts civil rights research and evaluation studies at the Office of Policy Development and Research, HUD. He is the editor of the forthcoming book: *Housing Desegregation, Race, and Federal Policies*.

JULIA L. HANSEN is an assistant professor in the Department of Economics at the University of Colorado at Denver.

MARY R. JACKMAN is an associate professor in the Department of Sociology at the University of Michigan. She is the coauthor of *Class Awareness in the United States*.

ROBERT W. JACKMAN is a professor of Political Science at Michigan State University. He is the author of *Politics and Social Equality*, and the coauthor of *Class Awareness in the United States*.

PETER KIVISTO is an assistant professor of Sociology at Augustana College in Rock Island, Illinois. He was formerly an administrator at a large Public Housing Authority and a research sociologist in the Office of Policy Development and Research, HUD. He is the author of the book, *Immigrant Socialists in the United States*.

MANUEL MARIANO LOPEZ is an associate professor of Sociology and director of Affiliate Area 8 of the Texas Data Management Program at Pan American University.

JAMSHID A. MOMENI is an associate professor of Sociology/Demography, and a senior research associate at the Institute for Urban Affairs and Research at Howard University. He is the author of *Demography of the Black Population in the United States* (Greenwood Press, 1983) and *Demography of Racial and Ethnic Minorities in the United States* (Greenwood Press, 1984).

CHRISTOPHER SILVER is an associate professor in the Department of Urban Studies and Planning at Virginia Commonwealth University. He is the editor of *Twentieth Century Richmond: Planning, Politics, and Race*.

C. MATTHEW SNIPP is an assistant professor of Sociology at the University of Maryland at College Park. He is the author of the 1980 census monograph on the American Indian population.

ALAN L. SORKIN is professor and chairman of the Department of Economics at the University of Maryland, Baltimore County. He is the author of several books including *American Indians and Federal Aid*.

DAPHNE SPAIN is an assistant professor in the Department of Sociology and Urban Planning at the University of Virginia. She is the coeditor of *Back to the City: Issues in Neighborhood Renovation*.